McGraw-Hill Guide to Effective Communications for MIS Professionals

Larry M. Singer

Ross Laboratories
Division of Abbott Laboratories

McGraw-Hill, Inc.

New York   St. Louis   San Francisco   Auckland   Bogotá
Caracas   Lisbon   London   Madrid   Mexico   Milan
Montreal   New Delhi   Paris   San Juan   São Paulo
Singapore   Sydney   Tokyo   Toronto

Library of Congress Cataloging-in-Publication Data

Singer, Larry M. (Larry Martin), date.
    McGraw-Hill guide to effective communications for MIS
professionals / by Larry M. Singer.
        p.   cm.
Rev. ed. of: Written communications for MIS/DP professionals.
© 1986.
    Includes bibliographical references and index.
    ISBN 0-07-057598-3—ISBN 0-07-057562-2 (pbk.)
    1. Management information systems.   2. Business communication.
I. Singer, Larry M. (Larry Martin), date.   Written communications
for MIS/DP professionals.   II. Title.   III. Series.
T58.6.S562   1991
658.4′038—dc20   91-33917
                                                                         CIP

Originally published as *Written Communications for MIS/DP
Professionals* by Macmillan in 1986.

2 3 4 5 6 7 8 9 0   DOC/DOC   9 6 5 4 3 2 1

ISBN 0-07-057598-3 {HC}
ISBN 0-07-057562-2 {PBK}

*The sponsoring editor for this book was Jerry Papke, the editing
supervisor was Fred Dahl, and the production supervisor was Pamela
A. Pelton. It was set in Century Schoolbook by Inkwell Publishing
Services.*

Printed and bound by R. R. Donnelley & Sons Company.

Contents

Preface   vii

Chapter 1. Human Communication in MIS: Beyond the Bits and Bytes   1

The Importance of Communication   3
Management Policy and Communication   4
How Does Technology Affect Technical Writing?   5
The Laws of MIS Documentation   5
Survival Depends on Person-to-Person Communication   6

Chapter 2. Effective Writing—A Short Course   7

Plan Before You Write: Logic, Audience, Terminology   8
The Natural Approach to Style   12
Reviewing Your Work for Conciseness and Clarity   16
Words to Avoid   17
Tenses   20
Summary of Key Points   21

Chapter 3. Project Development Documents   23

Project Life Cycle   24
Proposal or Concept Document   26
Feasibility Statement   29
Business Plan   33
Requirements Document   36
System Design Documents   39
Cost/Benefits Analysis   48
Programming Specifications   51
Chrono File   53
Summary of Key Points   54

Chapter 4. Internal MIS Forms   57

Service Requests   58
Project Reporting   64
Task Control   68
The Weekly Status Report   70
Experience Evaluation Forms   74
Monthly and Quarterly Reports   86
Memos   89
Unpleasant News   91
Summary of Key Points   92

Chapter 5. User Manuals—Preparation   93

Types of User Manuals   94
Techniques to Learn a Technical Subject   95
Understand the Audience   97
Getting Cooperation at the Start   100
Who Controls User Manuals?   102
Documentation Standards for User Manuals   103
Summary of Key Points   104

Chapter 6. User Manuals—The Mechanics   105

Overviews   106
Organization of the User Manual   107
Internals of the User Manual   109
Field Testing the Manual   112
Revisions   113
On-line User Manuals   113
Summary of Key Points   114

Chapter 7. Data Center Documentation   115

Run Sheets   116
Problem Reporting Logs   124
Special Procedure Documentation   129
Automated Operational Documentation   132
Master System Documentation   133
Data Center Statistics Report   134
Summary of Key Points   134

Chapter 8. Software Acquisition Documents   137

Vendor Evaluation Forms   138
Letter of Reference   143

Software Comparison Chart   145
Summary of Key Points   148

Chapter 9. Programming and Technical Documentation   151

Justifying Internal Documentation   154
The Data Dictionary   154
Documenting Programs for Maintenance Purposes   156
Documenting Programs to Explain Logic   157
Flow Charts   159
The Answer Book   160
The System Log   161
Summary of Key Points   162

Chapter 10. Strategic Documents   165

Evolution of Strategic Project Plans   167
Format of the Strategic Project Plan   168
Strategic Planning Documents   169
Summary of Key Points   175

Chapter 11. Agreements for Outside Services   177

Consultants   179
Application Software Maintenance Support   180
Application System Documentation   184
Summary of Key Points   186

Chapter 12. Word Processing, Graphics, and Spreadsheets   187

Word Processing and Electronic Mail   188
Word Processing Features   193
PC Graphics   195
Spreadsheets   203
Summary of Key Points   206

Chapter 13. MIS Presentations   207

Types of Presentations   208
Differences between Written and Verbal Communication   210
Preparation   211
Visual Aids   216
Practice   217
Delivery   220
Evaluation   223
Summary of Key Points   224

Chapter 14. Meetings   227

  Role of Meetings in MIS   229
  Myths and Realities of Decision Making   231
  Preparation   233
  Guidelines for Discussion Leaders   237
  Guidelines for Participants   241
  Summary of Key Points   241

Chapter 15. Desktop Publishing   245

  Applications for Desktop Publishing   246
  What is Desktop Publishing?   247
  Page Description Languages   249
  Typography   251
  Working with Printing Houses and Typographers   252
  Cautions and Concerns   258
  Summary of Key Points   260

Index   262

Preface

Computers are critical to the very existence of many companies, from the local hardware store to the largest multinational conglomerate. Yet many organizations with their own MIS departments—or those who work through service bureaus and other professional service companies via the outsourcing approach—are disappointed with general MIS performance. There are delays in developing new systems, misunderstandings between users and the technical staff, and embarrassing confusion among MIS employees themselves. Computers may be powerful machines capable of amazing feats of computation, but the people in charge of MIS cannot seem to put everything together in a timely manner. They point to new and expensive solutions, such as CASE and object-oriented programming. If senior management supports MIS with infusions of money, staff, and new technology, will the problems go away? Or is there an underlying problem in MIS?

One weakness is certainly poor communication. Many data processing managers and technicians simply cannot effectively share information through the written and spoken word, and the ultimate cost to the organization is staggering. Productivity suffers, morale declines, user confidence drops, and costs soar.

This book helps provide the solution. Each chapter is a self-contained unit that addresses a critical need in the MIS department. Many chapters have sample formats, from business plans that make sense to memos that actually communicate, which can be copied directly with minimal changes.

Even more importantly, this book presents working MIS documents that are a direct extension of a sound management philosophy. Every document in MIS should be carefully *engineered* to follow management direction! *Good technical writing encourages good management.* Poor technical communication reflects poor management.

This book is for everyone in MIS who deals with the written and the spoken word. Many of the answers are here!

Larry M. Singer

Human Communication in MIS: Beyond the Bits and Bytes

The MIS organization depends on written and verbal communication to share information with MIS staff, the user community, and corporate management. Unless ideas are shared effectively, things can come to a grinding halt. The weakest link in many MIS shops is not the computer applications, but the person-to-person communication that takes place—or, more correctly, does not take place. The format and nature of human communication is so important that it actually becomes management policy! All directors, managers, supervisors, systems analysts, technical writers, programmers, and users should understand the importance and role of communication in the MIS organization.

Written technical and business documentation includes any paper (or online text system) used to convey information about an MIS activity. This includes such widely varying documents as project proposals, memos, project plans, status reports, transcripts, business plans, budgets, system designs, programming specifications, feasibility studies, operating instructions, and user manuals. Virtually everyone in the MIS organization uses, writes, or updates technical documents. Further, many people in other departments rely heavily upon written communication produced by

MIS employees. The written information may be in a logical data model produced with a CASE tool or in a memo, but it is still written communication.

And virtually everyone in MIS communicates by mouth. The spoken word can either clarify or confuse.

This book is for anyone who creates or reads the following documents:

- Proposals
- Feasibility statements
- Business plans
- Requirements documents
- System designs
- Cost benefits analyses
- Programming specifications
- Chronological history files
- Service requests
- Project status reports
- Task control forms
- Weekly status reports
- Experience evaluation forms
- Monthly and quarterly reports
- Memos
- User manuals
- Operational run sheets
- Problem reporting logs
- Special procedures documentation
- Master system documentation
- Data center statistics reports
- Vendor evaluation forms
- Reference letters for software purchases
- Software comparison charts
- Program level documentation
- Flow charts
- System "answer books"
- System logs
- Graphs

This book is also for anyone who shares information or ideas through meetings, presentations, lectures, or discussions.

THE IMPORTANCE OF COMMUNICATION

Experience shows that many MIS professionals and managers do not appreciate the critical nature of the entire written communication process. MIS as a whole is often judged by the quality of various written documents and meetings, and the results are not encouraging. People tend to think that a confused, illogical, and hard-to-understand memo comes from a confused, illogical, and hard-to-understand person! Written material not only represents the author, but the entire department. Objectively, as MIS departments become larger and more involved with the day to day operation of their organizations, their written output becomes more important. Therefore, the value of all forms of communication is increasing. No longer are MIS employees dealing with small, easily controlled projects or application systems: many MIS projects involve millions of dollars and massive company commitments. Government regulatory agencies often review internal and external MIS documentation before certifying computerized systems. MIS is always a highly visible part of most organizations—witness the outcry when an online system crashes in the middle of the day! Visibility is not synonymous with basking in the limelight.

But things are not always perfect in the world of MIS. Company executives complain of consistently late projects, poor quality application systems, and a user-MIS relationship that resembles a war zone. The classic excuse is "We didn't know..." Users say they cannot understand MIS professionals. Programmers and analysts complain they cannot understand users. Programmers often say they cannot understand analysts. Computer operators have trouble understanding programmers. MIS directors are puzzled by their inability to control events instead of events controlling them. MIS employees as a group are frustrated by the "management by crisis" atmosphere that seems to pervade many data processing environments. And everyone is upset by the surprises, misunderstandings, mistakes, and confusion that surround many routine MIS activities like a hovering cloud. The solution is always the next technological wonder paraded before admiring throngs in the trade conferences. Technology, however, is not the answer.

What separates the smoothly running MIS departments from the ones who stumble from one crisis to the next? Why are some departments functioning like efficient information factories that produce exactly what they say when they say? Why do others resemble a collection of fragmented individuals who have trouble communicating with the person in the next office?

Obviously, there is no single answer that applies to all situations. But one basic, underlying factor that helps distinguish the efficient from the nonefficient (or, the "professional" from the "nonprofessional") is the quality of written and verbal technical communication. The difference is not necessarily quantity but rather the *quality*. Well managed departments tend to use clear, concise, and accurate means of communication: Their employees know when to pick up a phone and when to reach for a word processor. They know how much to write and how to communicate the essential ideas to the readers. They deliberately make the entire communication process easier for themselves and their users. They hold well controlled meetings and discussions that explain facts rather than emotions. Such employees understand how efficient communication improves productivity.

MANAGEMENT POLICY AND COMMUNICATION

Management direction is a combination of style, pattern, concerns, and attitude and differs from organization to organization. A department without management direction is in chaos! Managers often assume that documents, memos, and forms will automatically support their particular style. This assumption is often false: nothing of the sort "automatically" occurs! In theory, paperwork should always be consistent with official policy, but many managers do not realize that because of the *intrinsic power* of documents, written communications *become* management policy. The MIS director and his staff can order any series of policies they desire, but if the documents that run the department and its activities do not help implement that policy, their employees face an uncomfortable dichotomy.

For example, if an MIS manager demands improved project status information but the department continues to use an old form not suited to that directive, the request has been effectively ignored. If the MIS director wants to insure the feasibility of potential projects before authorizing development funds, his or her orders are worthless unless the systems analysts begin using effective feasibility statements. Employees need the tools to carry out their manager's orders. Every document in data processing should support management's general direction and specific policies: If they are incompatible with the general direction, over the long term the department will ultimately follow the direction perceived from the written documentation. Too many forms and documents have no obvious direction (since they were created in piecemeal fashion) and confusion wins by default! Written documents and their accompanying procedures often set the tone for the entire department. MIS directors can strive for better communication within their own group and with their user community, but unless they improve the forms, procedures, and reports used in daily activities their efforts may fail.

HOW DOES TECHNOLOGY AFFECT TECHNICAL WRITING?

The explosive growth of distributed data processing has increased the already dramatic need for good written communication. As computer power becomes readily available to departments logically and physically separated from MIS, users rely more on written documentation. Departmental computing is never an unimportant island in the corporate community: Critical decisions are often made on information provided by noncentralized MIS applications. Documentation and communication are literally the keys to mutual survival. While the "help desk" concept is important, users still require visual instructions to maintain their hardware and software environments.

The growth of PC networks has opened vast markets for good software that comes with clear, easy-to-follow documentation. Timesharing services require explicit online help functions that allow users to understand their services. Interfacing various application systems requires absolutely correct and understandable information. Some companies now screen potential software packages by evaluating their written documentation! The trend toward online processing has not diminished the value of documentation; instead, it has created a new set of requirements for "intelligent" documentation on a CRT.

THE LAWS OF MIS DOCUMENTATION

Unfortunately for the business world, only professional technical writers prepare themselves for the challenge of written communication. Everyone else seems to trust their skills to fate. Like a Greek tragedy, fate is not always kind, and by observing some MIS departments in action, one can often predict when and why things will go wrong!

The problems associated with poor written communication can be described in mathematical terms:

1. The number of problems in a new computer system is inversely proportional to the quality of the written specifications.

2. The older the documentation, the more likely it is to be wrong.

3. The more the documentation reads like a poorly written COBOL program, the higher the likelihood that only a poor COBOL programmer can understand it.

4. The greater the number of undocumented changes to a system, the higher the probability that those changes will be wrong, or that no one will understand the changes even if they are correct.

5. The more a company relies upon uncontrolled meetings and discussions to settle issues without documenting the results, the more misunderstandings will occur.

6. The greater the number of misunderstandings, the greater the probability that one of them will destroy the value of the entire project.

7. The number of serious design flaws in any computer system is directly proportional to the number of statements that say, "No, we don't need to write that down."

SURVIVAL DEPENDS ON PERSON TO PERSON COMMUNICATION

There are now few excuses for tolerating ambiguities, confusion, and potential misunderstandings in MIS person-to-person communication. Other professions learned long ago that precise written and verbal communication was essential to their survival. Architects, for example, generally design bridges with detailed blueprints before the building process begins, and the output tends to be correct—the two ends of a bridge meet exactly in the center. Tunnels blasted through mountains seem to always meet in the center. But the relatively young profession of data processing has not always learned that success is based partially on clearly written facts on paper and partially on precise information shared person to person.

Improving written communication is no longer a low priority issue. MIS directors have too many critical responsibilities to ignore the problem, and there is no longer any justification for trusting written and oral communication performance to the fates. Technical and business writing are merely skills that one can and should improve without feeling personal embarrassment. Now that management development books, seminars, and courses have been widely accepted, perhaps MIS professionals and managers can admit that most MIS employees also need to develop better communication skills.

This book is meant for those who are ready to learn.

Effective Writing—
A Short Course

Good writing skills are not a gift from heaven: They can be learned! Techniques such as the "objective" attitude, logical statements, audience analysis, and proper definition of terms will greatly improve any document. The "natural" approach to style makes written material easy to understand. This chapter describes specific ways to review your own work and locate the areas that need improvement. Finally, the chapter identifies words to avoid and ways to utilize tenses in a logical sequence. This is a short technical guide for those who would like to improve their own writing skills.

MIS professionals communicate with each other using system proposals, memos, user manuals, internal program documentation forms, customer request forms, operational instructions, and status reports of every conceivable description. The format and purpose of each document may differ, but the principles behind every piece of high quality writing remain the same. Effective written communication in any occupation or business follows several quite logical and relatively simple techniques.

Many people never try learning the skills of effective written communication, although some lucky individuals appear to have a natural ability. Those without this rare gift may not improve their written skills because they feel defensive or are actually ashamed of their writing performance. This attitude is common but counterproductive. Writing is merely another skill to be learned as one learns to analyze a system, debug a program error, manage a department, or even pluck a chicken. Indeed, the best analogy is to compare the task of writing to the practice of chicken plucking: Give anyone a chicken and they can eventually pluck most of the feathers. Give anyone a pen, a quill, a typewriter, or a word processor, and they will eventually write something. But in the real world there is a significant difference between a chicken well plucked in a cost effective manner and a chicken half plucked after three hours of frustrating effort. In the second instance the company with the costly but improperly plucked chicken may be on the road to bankruptcy. Unfortunately for most data processing installations, far too many documentation efforts resemble half plucked chickens.

Writing skills can be learned, even by those who were not born with a natural writing ability. It merely requires a little common sense, a few basic guidelines, and a willingness to practice. Most important, however, is the ability to constructively criticize your own work. Unless one is taking a writing course or has a very willing tutor, it is unreasonable to expect others to spend their valuable time analyzing your written communication in detail and making line by line or word by word suggestions. In most situations, MIS professionals or managers are on their own. The right attitude is, "I will be my own critic." The correct expectation is, "Criticizing my own work may be painful, but the results will be worth it."

PLAN BEFORE YOU WRITE: LOGIC, AUDIENCE, TERMINOLOGY

Before one starts keying into a terminal, the first task is to analyze the purpose of the document. If the author is not clear about the ultimate goal and the ideas to convey, the best writing techniques in the world will not save the document.

Planning before writing helps make the document *logical*. Every piece of writing is partially judged by its degree of logic: only those memos, reports, and proposals that demonstrate logical thinking will stand out in the mind of the reader. But what is logical communication?

Illogical writing is easier to explain, because it stands out like a payroll check $30,000 too high! People notice it immediately. But unlike the payroll error that is an object of laughter, the illogical document is ignored, rejected, or scorned. The author himself may be ignored, rejected, or scorned even if his idea is basically sound. It may not be fair, but people ascribe to the author the same characteristics they give to his written communication! *Many excellent ideas in MIS never get off the launching pad because the author did not present the written ideas logically.* Every phrase and sentence in the document must appear logical.

Consider the two bicycle repairmen from Dayton, Ohio who wrote a proposal in the early 1900s to their local bank for funds to develop a new device called an "aeroplane":

> Wilbur and I think that man can fly. If birds can, why can't people? This has been our dream since we were boys. Other inventors are now working on flying machines, and we can do it, too.

The second sentence that compares birds to men is illogical because the author provides no further support for his contention. Emotionally, the sentence could be appropriate, but it is totally unsuited for a business proposal. Logical writing often equates to appropriateness. The banker may stop at this point and reject all following arguments because he unconsciously assumes that if one statement is illogical, so is the entire idea. The third statement that other inventors are developing flying machines is indeed worthy of further discussion, for it suggests a reasonable business venture. But the previous sentence ruins any chance for approval. Birds are very light and have wings, while men are heavy and don't have wings. Any fool knows that. No wonder men cannot fly! Why don't those brothers stick to repairing bicycles and forget the whole silly idea?

If the ideas (and supporting reasons) are logical, the next step is to categorize the audience in terms that will help the author shape the document to his specific needs. For an individualized memo, the reader is obvious, but the typical piece of professional documentation has an audience of multiple readers with varying backgrounds and varying degrees of interest in the subject. The author should consider the "group" as the audience.

The following operations manual paragraph for data entry operators explains the procedures for requesting personal time away from the job:

> Operators must fill out a PRS-42 in duplicate with approval from an E-7 or above in that unit and give the required advance notice as specified in the current edition of Corporate Personnel Manual number 4 for non-exempt employees, as amended by Labor Policy II-14-1992 if the site is unionized.

Such wording is obviously inappropriate for data entry operators who have never reviewed Corporate Personnel Manual number 4, cannot differentiate an E-7 from a Z-2, and forgot to study Labor Policy II-14-1992 last night. A more effective description would be:

> If you need time off during the day, get a PRS-42 from the department secretary. Check the "personal" box, answer questions 1 through 4, and have either your supervisor or the unit manager sign the form. If your department is covered by union rules, ask the department shop steward if the contract has any special requirements for personal time off. Send the signed form to Personnel at least three working days before the scheduled absence.

Although the second version takes more words, any data entry operator reading the document would immediately understand the procedure. There is little opportunity for misunderstanding, because the author has considered the interests and experience level of his audience. Effective communication targets the specific reader.

Any writer must also remember readers' limitations. Will the Board of Directors understand the advantages of a data base approach to the new online order entry system? Should the proposal explain the critical differences between data base and conventional file designs? Do they care? Or would they be more concerned with the long term cost issues involved? Do they understand the exact meaning of "data base" in this project? Will computer operators automatically understand the business purpose behind the Credit Processing System and the legal implications involved in production delays? Do they really need to know? If the answer is "yes," the document written for computer operators must include those facts but avoid using terms that are more appropriate for the Legal Department.

The writer must also avoid insulting the maturity of the reader. After all, knowledge about a given subject (or the lack of knowledge) does not always equate with a person's innate level of intelligence. Albert Einstein may have known little about his car, but a mechanic would have made a serious mistake in telling the white haired old gentleman, "Don't worry, Al. It's very complicated. I don't think you could understand. Just trust me."

Consider the following set of instructions written for data entry operators:

> Take off your coat. Hang it in the closet. Sit down at your station. Lock your purse in the top right-hand drawer. Start work when the clock says 8:30. Look at the top left hand corner of the screen. If nothing appears, turn the intensity knob toward the right. If nothing still appears, raise your hand and ask for help."

Most experienced data entry operators would snicker at such childish and obviously insulting instructions. Laughing at a document may be a bad response, but it is preferable to another emotion caused by underestimating the vice president of sales. Consider the following proposal:

> Computers can only add, subtract, multiply, and divide, but they can help you track sales activity. Measuring the sales effort is hard. As a vice president, you want to know who has sold how much product, and who has sold the least. Isn't that important? You also want to know the relative gross margin of each sale. Isn't that also important?

Unless you are a senior vice president, president, chairman of the board, major stockholder, valued customer, or highly paid consultant, one seldom *tells* vice presidents anything. In fact, one seldom *tells* anyone anything.

Personal attitude will eventually surface in written communication, and even if the author has sized the audience correctly in terms of their sophistication and interest, he or she must always treat them with respect. After all, if readers are not worth a little respect, why bother writing to them at all?

Whatever the first ten commandments are, the eleventh commandment in technical writing should be "Define thy terms." Readers of MIS documents invariably complain that they do not understand the vocabulary or buzzwords. Is it the reader's responsibility to investigate any unfamiliar word? Definitely not! The responsibility lies with the author.

Names and terms in data processing can have opposite meanings to different people, depending upon experience, background, education, job responsibility, and personal mood when reading the document. If one asked ten different systems analysts to define the commonly heard phrase "acceptable online response time," one would get at least 15 answers. If one asked the same question a week later one might hear a new set of 16 opinions. The final definition selected by the MIS manager may change when he discovers the cost difference between providing one-second or two-second response times. Readers do not have to accept the definitions in a document, but they must understand the author's original definition. Communication is difficult unless the author and his reader have a common basis for understanding.

The confusion over technical terms is even more pronounced when communicating with other professions. Business terms such as *LIFO* and *FIFO* may sound like French poodles to a programmer/analyst, while a common MIS phrase such as *local area network* could mean the community public service television station to an accountant. Imagine the misunderstanding when the programmer/analyst and the accountant are trying to design an inventory valuation system on a proposed collection of personal computers linked together in both a local area network and a wide area network with a mainframe as file server. The MIS professional isn't any smarter than the accountant: Both have their areas of expertise, but both have a professional responsibility to provide clear, adequate, and useful definitions for any topic or word that could be misinterpreted.

Murphy's law applies to written communication: If any term can be misunderstood, it will.

If the audience is not in MIS, successful technical writers choose words that are meaningful to the reader rather than to themselves. Every author has a vast array of word choices when creating a document, and the ultimate choice should be partially influenced by the mind set of the reader. What words does he want to hear? Efficient written communication is concerned with the reader's expectation just as much as the writer's experience.

THE NATURAL APPROACH TO STYLE

Style is just as important to technical writing as it is in the rest of life. Data processing employees do not like to read a poorly written COBOL program any more than they like to read a poorly written memo, system proposal, or user manual. Nontechnical readers dislike confusing written material even more! Like beauty, however, style is truly in the eye of the beholder, and one can find many ways to achieve a good writing style. This section will present the "natural" approach, which is relatively easy but powerful method to achieve a positive writing style. (See Figure 2.1.)

Figure 2.1   The natural approach to style

> ✔ Use formal conversation as model.
> ✔ Be honest.
> ✔ Anticipate questions.
> ✔ Use examples.
> ✔ Vary sentence structure.

Writing with "style" often means the document seems "natural." Problems occur when writers attempt to become something they are not. As a general rule, the more complicated and formal authors try to become, the worse their documents. A natural piece of writing, on the other hand, has the correct blend of vocabulary, sentence structure, phrasing, and logical organization that helps readers feel comfortable. They may not agree with or even fully understand all the information, but the author has successfully communicated on a person-to-person level. Readers feel positive. New writers can develop this smooth blend of vocabulary, sentence structure, phrasing, and logical organization by consciously trying to become natural. There are five proven techniques that will help authors develop a natural style.

1. Use Formal Conversation as a Model

Often misunderstood, this admonition is often stated as "write like you talk." There are significant differences, however, between formal writing, formal conversation, and informal conversation. Consider the following memo from Peter Panic, Director of Operations, to Larry Ledger, Director of Accounting:

> Pursuant to the timing agreement reached on June 2, 1991, be aware that on at least four known occasions the Accounts Payable staff has requested an extension of the agreed upon deadline. Granting these requests to extend the standard APS hours for both inquiry and update has directly resulted in

delays in the critical path, including a two hour delay in starting the online Order Entry Function, which resulted in an estimated dollars loss of Type II orders of not less than $10,000, nor more than $20,000.

Peter's memo reads like a legal summons, and Larry Ledger may wonder if he should retain legal counsel before the matter reaches the Supreme Court! In reality, Peter is simply notifying Larry of a problem that needs resolution. The information in the document is accurate, but the style is totally unnatural. Formal writing is justified only in formal occasions which occur very rarely in MIS, and Peter could have communicated the same information orally with an *informal conversation*:

> Larry, we've been late in the critical path four times during the past two months. One instance caused a delay in Order Processing and Mark Muscle thinks we lost up to $20,000 in Type II orders! On those four occasions my people allowed APS to extend their operating hours. If you recall, back in June of 1991 we agreed to fairly strict AP hours. We want to help you guys out, but you see what can happen. I don't want that jerk Mark Muscle on my case again! You know how he can be. When can we talk about this problem?

The style of a phone call may be extremely natural (assuming Peter and Larry know each other well), but *informal conversation* is equally unsuited for written communication. If Peter insists upon a memo, he should use the style of *formal conversation*, which helps create a very natural blend of vocabulary and sentence phrasing:

> On four occasions during the past two months we have been late in the critical path. In fact, during one of those delays we could not bring up Order Entry for two hours and lost up to twenty thousand dollars in Type II orders. I have traced each of those occurrences to a request by APS to extend their online inquiry and update hours. Naturally, we try to accommodate AP because we know how your workload piles up. But if my Operations Manager violates the schedule we agreed to back in June of 1991, we risk delaying the critical path and losing more orders. Please call so we can discuss a resolution.

The preceding example of formal conversation transferred to paper (or electronic mail) carries all the important information, suggests a cooperative spirit, and uses a natural style that makes the reader feel comfortable. Larry feels that Peter is talking calmly and logically to him. *A natural writing style lets the reader concentrate on the material rather than the writing itself.*

2. Be Honest with Yourself and Your Readers

The old-fashioned virtue of honesty is critical to every form of human communication. The most effective writing tends to come from authors who use their natural tendencies to *write as they believe*. One should seldom if ever distort facts or misrepresent the truth, because the quality of work will usually decrease. Only professional or experienced writers are capable of presenting information they do not accept themselves. Lawyers, for example, require intensive practice before they can disregard personal feelings and create legal briefs for an opinion they do not share. It can be done, but it requires special training. If at all possible, professionals in MIS should write what they consider the truth. Only on rare occasions should they ignore that important rule.

3. Anticipate Questions

Readers who are interested in the subject may formulate important questions as they read the document, and good technical writing anticipates the questions and provides the answers. The most common question is, "What happens if..." Unsophisticated users especially may wonder about matters that would surprise the typical MIS professional. Other readers may silently ask themselves questions but dismiss their own concerns as stupid. What happens if the customer on the phone suddenly cancels the order? Must order takers call data processing for help? Should they call the supervisor? Have they ruined a five million dollar computer? The answer to the question may be given in the appendix or on page 49, but the reader starts to worry on page 2!

Consumers of technical documents must understand their responsibilities when something goes *wrong*. Customers on the phone do cancel orders after saying, "Forget it. I'll call back. My 3-year-old just got a headlock on the German Shepherd." Data entry operators accidentally call up the weekly update screen instead of the online inquiry. Users get strange codes on their CRTs. The warehouse manager reading a proposal for a new location system wonders what will happen when the computer goes down. The author has a special responsibility to anticipate obvious questions and problems, and incorporate the answers directly in the text. People often care more about what happens when things go *wrong* rather than when things go *right*.

4. Use Examples

Even the most thorough explanations of a proposed idea, concept, or procedure can be confusing because people rarely think in a formal, descriptive manner. Nontechnical readers reject documents that have the slightest hint of complexity, and many MIS professionals themselves dislike long verbal explanations. The best way to explain complicated matters is to provide examples and verbal illustrations. The examples can be serious, humorous, or somewhere in between, but readers have a better chance of understanding when the document provides specific examples.

New technical writers and systems analysts occasionally forget there are situations where humorous examples are inappropriate. When writing to a senior MIS manager about the need for training, one would not create a funny story about a clumsy MIS director who could not even turn on a PC. Humor is justified only when the story or example will not attack others who may either read the document or hear about the humorous piece. Humor does help communication, but consideration for others is always more important.

The more complicated the information, the more one needs examples. Also, when the material is extremely dry, the author should consider an occasional example merely to liven up the document. Murphy discovered another observation relating to technical writing: If the reader can fall asleep, he will.

5. Vary the Sentence Structure

Any document with a consistent, repetitive sentence structure is unbelievably depressing to both mind and body, and always seems unnatural. Consider the following subtle example:

> The purpose of the Inventory Control System (ICS) is to control inventory and reduce investment. ICS tells the buyers how much they have and how much it costs. It also helps track purchase orders and discovers overstock situations. The buyers need ICS and ICS needs the buyers. They must pay close attention to the reports, and they must correct errors as soon as they appear. ICS interfaces with the Sales System and it also interfaces with the Accounting System. Management uses the summary ICS reports and the buyers use the detail ICS reports.

After several more paragraphs the reader would fall into a sing-song mental pattern because each sentence contains two thoughts with the conjunction *and*. Most readers will anticipate the next sentence! By simply rearranging the sentence structure, the paragraph will convey the same information but not cause terminal boredom for anyone doomed to study the ICS system documentation.

> The purpose of the Inventory Control System (ICS) is to control inventory and to reduce the inventory investment. Because it tracks purchase orders and discovers overstock situations, ICS tells the buyers how much they have and its relative cost. ICS also interfaces with both the Accounting System and the Sales System, which requires ICS errors to be corrected immediately. In general, management looks at the summary ICS reports and the buyers use the detail ICS output. ICS is an important tool for many departments here at Wonderful Widgets.

Varying sentence structure should not be carried to extremes, because the document will look as if it has been generated by a computer rather than a human. Using a varied assortment of phrases, conjunctions, and clauses will make the document appear natural.

REVIEWING YOUR WORK FOR
CONCISENESS AND CLARITY

Writing is an art as well as a skill, and one can perfect an art form only by practice. But technical writers (including programmers, analysts, and managers) seldom get the feedback that artists need to polish their craft. Rather, MIS authors must be their own critics and review their own work. After the words are typed or printed from the word processor, authors must change their orientation from creator to critic. They must now play the role of an interested reader who is not afraid to suggest improvements. Once technical writers accept the belief that their creations are not perfect, they can begin the laborious process of improving their work.

Technical writing is often criticized for its wordiness, and the solution is to make every sentence concise. A concise sentence or phrase comes directly to the point, without going around the proverbial mulberry bush, through the proverbial mulberry bush, or on top of the proverbial mulberry bush. Consider the following example:

> The Accounting Department will consider all important variables and work in conjunction with Data Entry to develop a mutually agreed upon schedule in terms of month end cutoffs as they affect both the Accounting Department and Data Entry.

The statement should be more direct:

> The Accounting Department will work with Data Entry to develop a mutually satisfactory month end cutoff schedule.

Both examples convey essentially the same message, but the second version uses less than half the words. While word counts are not always a valid measure of conciseness, the first example is so long the reader may get lost in the mulberry bush somewhere between the first word and the last word.

Making sentences, phrases, and paragraphs concise requires a slightly masochistic tendency to deflate one's own ego. The author can use a nasty red pen (or the equally nasty delete key on the word processor keyboard) to eliminate extra words and phrases but still retain basic information. The goal is to write simply. Words are only a tool to communicate, and there is nothing mystical about them. If a thought can be expressed in ten words, why use 20? From a purely business standpoint, it is more efficient to write and have someone read ten words than 20. Cutting unnecessary words is an easy way to improve writing that is wordy or overly confusing.

Clarity deals with the choice of words: an otherwise routine piece of writing can become a dynamic communication device when the author replaces dull words with more exciting ones. No, an MIS document is not designed to elicit passion or incite people to revolution, but it should never be boring.

Words are like people—some are positive, definite, and exciting, while others are negative, unclear, or boring. Consider this summary of a new online order entry system which cost a company over $500,000 and a massive overtime effort by programmers, analysts, and users:

> The new online system should reduce the processing time from customer to shipping, decrease the number of errors, and lower our inventory.

The information may be correct, but the board of directors may question the results of their $500,000 investment. The programmers, analysts, and users who sacrificed countless nights and weekends would share that feeling of concern. Just a few additional words (and specific rather than general facts) will make the system seem worth the time, money, and extra effort:

> The new online order entry system will slash the total processing time from the phone call to shipping by 500 percent, virtually eliminate out-of-stock situations in the warehouse, and reduce our $25,000,000 inventory investment by at least 3 percent.

The difference between the two examples is striking. The second illustration uses *both positive adjectives and measurable facts*. These two simple techniques in combination can increase the clarity of any piece of writing. Be positive. Be measurable.

Clarity suffers when the author uses buzzwords that are never defined. Any long document that contains numerous technical or business terms should have either a glossary or adequate definitions spread through the document. Assuming that the reader will know the current buzzwords, abbreviations, or obscure business terms is often a dangerous assumption. Even communicating within the MIS organization is difficult, as system software professionals seem to use an entirely different language than business systems analysts, and neither group may understand the terminology of process controller programmers on the factory floor. And MIS employees may not understand the data collection terminology in the laboratory, or the complex budgeting manipulations necessary during the year end closing. If a memo or proposal is to be clear, the terminology must be explained.

WORDS TO AVOID

Some words function like a diamond drill, while others have all the impact of a dull screwdriver. An author's ultimate choice of words is influenced by his style of writing, depth of vocabulary, and perceived audience. The systems analyst who feels comfortable with a more formal approach to writing will generally avoid informal, casual terminology. The manager with a degree in English literature may have a wider range of vocabulary than one with a high school education. The operating software manager writing a data base proposal to the vice president will use terms he or she perceives a vice president will prefer. Yet in each case, the author has two challenges. First, within inherent personal limitations of vocabulary, select the appropriate word that conveys the exact meaning. Second, avoid words that hinder effective communication.

How can words interfere with communication?

Excessive abbreviations make any document choppy and difficult to read. When determining if abbreviations are justified, the author should consider not only the primary reader but all recipients of the document. A final proposal, for example, may be directed toward the user project manager, but will also be reviewed by the accounting manager, MIS director, manufacturing supervisor, and senior vice president as well as five members of the project team. The user project manager who has been intimately involved in the design process, will understand the abbreviations, but the other readers may not. The accounting manager may not translate *PDL* into *page description language*, which could be obvious to anyone on the project team familiar with desk top publishing. Even if abbreviations are used, the author should explain each abbreviation the first time it is used in the document. This simple practice reduces the chance for misunderstanding. However, a few commonly accepted abbreviations are always acceptable and do not need definition. The term *MIS*, for example, stands for *management information systems*, but virtually every reader of MIS related documents would be familiar with that meaning.

Fad words are terms that are popular but lose their original meaning due to overuse or misuse. MIS is particularly susceptible to buzzwords, slogans, or labels that appeal to the current management team or a popular idea in information systems. For example, in some companies the term *opportunity* replaces every *problem*. A true *opportunity* becomes impossible to identify, since the term has been used for situations that do not fit the standard dictionary definition. In organizations with highly centralized management structures, the term *approval* is frequently overused to the point where every paragraph in every memo contains a variation of the word *approval*. Another fad term is the noun *issue*. Every problem is not an issue. The phrase *strategic project* is a buzzword that enthusiastic professionals attach to every idea, from the critically important to the mundane. Fad or popular words can be used, but only with caution. The best writers consciously avoid fad words and look for precise, dictionary driven terminology.

Redundant words and phrases are a common error in technical writing and business writing. Some authors deliberately use redundancy in the belief that extra words help emphasize essential ideas. Highly skilled authors such as novelists occasionally use redundancy but only in specific situations. Successful novelists are experts at using words and know when to break the rules. The average technical or business writer should look for other ways to strengthen his writing skills. Other writers accidentally create redundant sentences because they do not edit their work to identify and eliminate unnecessary words.

Redundancy is generally caused by a desire to over-explain. For example:

> The report I am writing to you is my current evaluation of the project.

The phrase "I am writing to you" is redundant. Obviously, the author is writing a report to the recipient. The sentence could be shortened and still retain the same meaning:

> The report is my current evaluation of the project.

Adjectives can be redundant when they repeat the same description:

> The perfect, error-free, mistake-free, daily sales analysis was accepted by the user.

The MIS staff may be justifiably proud of their complex daily sales analysis, but the sentence is still redundant and will confuse rather than impress. If an analysis is perfect, it is also error free. If an analysis is mistake free, one would expect it to be error free. A mistake-free and error-free analysis also implies perfection. Any of the three terms would suffice:

> The perfect daily sales analysis was accepted by the user.
> The mistake free daily sales analysis was accepted by the user.
> The error free daily sales analysis was accepted by the user.

Trying to sound overly formal may cause redundancy.

> My answer is in response to your question regarding online response time.

By definition, an answer is a response to a question. If the writer is about to provide an answer, one can assume he has been asked a question, or a problem has been stated. A more efficient statement is:

> My answer regarding online response time is...

Simple wordiness will lead to redundant phrases.

> The user manual will assist the user in operating the software.

The purpose of any user manual is to assist the user. Therefore, the author could rephrase the sentence by eliminating the extra words:

> The user manual will assist in operating the software.

The incidence of redundancy increases when writers try to add precision: They believe extra words offer greater accuracy or impact. False!

Readers willingly ignore an occasional redundancy, but a document filled with redundant words and phrases is hard to understand. Redundancy is a natural tendency, even among experienced technical writers.

TENSES

MIS professionals often describe actions or events. When translating the sequence of activities into words, they may use present, past, and future tense in the same document. Many writing assignments *require* the same paragraph to have mixed tenses, but the manner in which the sentences are presented determines if the reader will be confused. Although it is easier for the author to construct all paragraphs with the same tense, many situations require mixed tenses. Consider the following example:

> The design phase of the accounts receivable project is in progress. We defined the ten major requirements but will review them again next week, although the systems analyst did evaluate the disk space implications. A formal status report will be written next week, since the hardware consultant approved the transaction count estimates.

The information may be accurate, but the reader will wonder, "Who did what, when was it done, and what will be scheduled next week?" A second or even third pass may be needed. The sentences reflected the time sequence of each event, but presented the story in a way that confused the reader. Tenses were mixed indiscriminately. By organizing the facts in a logical manner, the author can still mix tenses but communicate more effectively:

> The design phase of the Accounts Receivable project is in process, and a formal status report will be issued next week. Ten major requirements were defined. The systems analyst evaluated the disk space implications, and the hardware analyst approved the transaction counts. The major requirements will be reviewed before the status report is written.

The facts are identical, but the second paragraph presents an orderly sequence of events. The first sentence is a topic or summary sentence that defines the most important point. The next two sentences provide detail. The last sentence defines a task that must be done before the formal status report can be issued. The reader *understands* the sequence of events. Tenses can be mixed but only in an orderly progression of events.

When criticized for their lack of effective writing skills, MIS professionals complain that they are not experts in language. Even many full-time business writers do not remember the difference between present perfect and past perfect tense. Few writers can recite the correct use of the subjunctive mood from memory. Such information is handy, but hardly necessary to the systems analysts, programmers, and managers who routinely compose working documents. Common sense, a careful review of every draft, and a willingness to correct one's own work is the best way to avoid confusion caused by incorrect tenses.

SUMMARY OF KEY POINTS

- Effective writing is a learned skill.
- The most important requirement is the ability to constructively criticize your own work.
- Plan before you write:
  Make your ideas logical.
  Analyze the needs and characteristics of your audience.
  Define all terms clearly.
- Style is important in technical writing. Achieve a positive style by using natural words, phrases, and sentences.
- Five rules for natural writing are:
  Use formal conversation as a model.
  Be honest with yourself and your readers.
  Anticipate questions and provide answers in the text.
  Use examples that your audience will understand.
  Vary the sentence structure to avoid boring the reader (and yourself).
- The first draft is only a start. Review your work carefully and pretend you are the audience. Examine each sentence and paragraph for clarity. Look for ways to say the same thought in fewer words. Try for tight, concise writing. Use positive, active words, and include measurable facts as often as possible.
- Avoid excessive abbreviations. Define an abbreviation the first time it is used.
- Do not use fad words because they are popular.
- Redundancy may be a natural tendency of many people, but it is easy to remove by editing the first draft.
- If a paragraph requires the use of past, present, and future tenses, arrange the sentences so that the information is presented in a logical sequence.

3

Project Development Documents

*Developing a new system or modifying an existing one is
always a challenging opportunity, but many projects are not
successful. They may be late, over-budget, incomplete, or
ultimately cause more problems then they solve. One solution
is to improve the quality of every document produced during
the development cycle. Poorly designed documents cause
errors, mistakes, and misunderstandings. This chapter
presents eight important documents that can be used in
virtually any development methodology. Systems analysts,
technical writers, and users will find this chapter a
"one-source" guide for high quality, efficient, and accurate
documents. Managers responsible for development projects
will find answers to their project management problems!*

An unfortunate joke in data processing circles is that professionals who have
the least to do with a large, important project get promotions, while the rest
find new jobs! Is project management always that complicated? Is MIS
management doomed to suffer with late projects, angry users, and frustrated professionals? Of course not. The ultimate solution may involve more
user participation, online prototyping, CASE, code generators, and faster
development techniques, but one basic prerequisite is *high-quality project
development documentation that follows a logical, management-oriented
policy*. The best methodology in the world will not succeed with poor written

documentation. The best development technology will not succeed unless the supporting documents are clear.

THE PROJECT LIFE CYCLE

Volumes have been written, consultants have gotten rich, and wars have been fought over the "best" project development methodology. In the late 1970s and early 1980s such arguments peaked, and many experienced project managers now follow one of two paths. They select the one they are most familiar with or they develop their own variation based upon the current situation. Perhaps all methodologies are correct: The difference is not *which* one is used, but *how* it is implemented. Methodologies have a common link: many of them are implemented via the written word. Even structured analysis with data flow diagrams or entity relationship models still requires written documents to support the graphics. If the supporting written material is implemented well, the project has a chance for success.

This chapter describes eight documents appropriate for several popular approaches to project development (see Figure 3.1):

1. Proposal or concept document
2. Feasibility statement
3. Business plan
4. Functional specifications
5. System design
6. Cost benefits analysis
7. Programming specifications
8. Project history or "chrono" file

Large or complex projects may need all eight documents, but other projects may skip one or more steps in the development cycle. These documents are *recommendations* rather than absolute necessities. The project manager must decide on a case-by-case basis which steps (and corresponding documents) are justified based on his knowledge, experience, understanding, and perception of the project complexity. Another key factor is degree of risk. The more steps a manager skips in the formal development cycle, the greater his risk of failure.

For example, a written cost benefits analysis would show that computerizing Shipping Manager Terry Transit's daily schedule will cost $20,000. But if Department Clerk Annie Axle does the same job with her 3×5 card file in seven minutes every day, one would immediately question the value of the project: Twenty thousand dollars in analyst and programmer time will pay for many seven-minute efforts by Annie. Unless there are other benefits—such as greater accuracy or future integra-

Figure 3.1   Documents in project life cycle

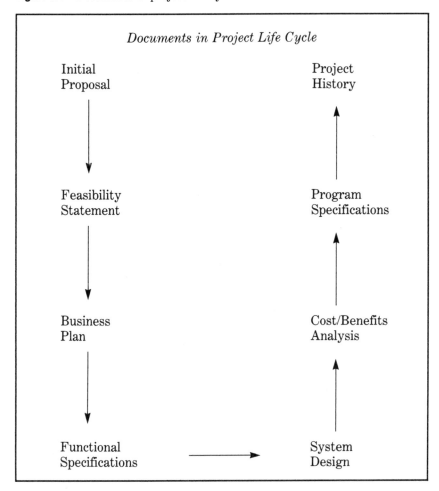

Documents in Project Life Cycle

Initial
Proposal

Project
History

Feasibility
Statement

Program
Specifications

Business
Plan

Cost/Benefits
Analysis

Functional
Specifications   →   System
Design

tion into other systems—the project may not be justified. Without a formal cost benefits document, management could easily make the wrong decision. *Good documentation practices lead directly to good management decisions.*

One can go beyond the realm of practicality by insisting that every request follow the complete series of steps. If Accounting Manager Larry Ledger wants three more lines printed on each page of the Trial Balance report, the MIS director could require a concept document, feasibility statement, business plan, functional specifications, cost benefits analysis, system design, programming specifications, and project history file. Or, he could simply call Charley Cobol and ask him to increase the linecount by three. If the MIS director has any sense, he will follow the second approach. *Too much documentation is just as bad as not enough.*

PROPOSAL OR CONCEPT DOCUMENT

A proposal triggers the project development cycle. A simple user request—even if scribbled on a napkin from the company cafeteria—is simply a preliminary version of the formal proposal. The purpose of a proposal is to explain the need, estimated scope, and possible design for a new project or a major enhancement to the current application systems.

Who should write the proposal? The user, an independent business systems analyst, or an MIS professional? The best results occur when users, independent analysts, and MIS staff jointly create the document. It is irrelevant which department claims official ownership. In the era of the 1990s, as user participation becomes an absolute necessity rather than simply a "nice-to-have" idea, intensive MIS-user cooperation at the start of a project is vital. Even the most sophisticated users typically have only one fourth the information necessary for a good proposal—MIS employees have another one fourth. The interaction between the two groups will provide the missing 50 percent.

Proposals should include any cautionary information as well as the more obvious good news. If Shipping Manager Terry Transit wants his freight payments computerized, but knows that in two years the company will be considering an accounting package that could include freight control, he should mention that possibility. Any fact or future event that makes the concept less justified or more complicated should be mentioned, since bad news will eventually surface. A proposal should be a complete picture of the concept rather than a one-sided sales gimmick.

Creating a successful proposal requires that users have access to an MIS manager, programmer, or analyst during the "blue sky" stage of the project life cycle. Allowing such access for "dreaming" is more cost effective than keeping users away from the MIS staff because it will help reduce the wasted effort when users propose unjustified or even impossible ideas. It is less expensive to catch errors before they go into the MIS pipeline and demand precious management and technical resources. Users working in a vacuum may create empty ideas in the same way that the MIS staff working in a vacuum may create equally empty ideas. Conversely, either group can miss simple alternatives that will solve their immediate needs. When Marty Markdown in Merchandising has a brilliant idea but cannot share his thoughts with a technical analyst, he may come up with the following suggestion:

> Buyers and their assistants spend a lot of time looking for negative stock balances and negative costs. We spend most of Monday morning just scanning each report to catch minus numbers, to which we give priority. I suggest that inventory reports be changed so that any negative number prints in red rather than in black ink. This will save the merchandise staff many hours of tedious work. When can you have it ready?

Since most high-speed impact and laser printers today use only black ink, the concept is not feasible. Had Marty worked with System Analyst Frank Flowchart, the two would have proposed the more obvious solution of a separate report for negative numbers. Marty did not use his time efficiently because he did not have access to an MIS professional for blue sky thinking.

Even if the user has a good idea, without MIS counsel he or she may fail to communicate essential facts. Consider this proposal for a purchases reconciliation system written by a very frustrated accounts payable supervisor:

> When invoices come in to the accounts payable system, I have a hard time deciding whether to pay them immediately or verify them first. How do I know if International Screws really sent 40 cases of number six steel screws? If I call Fred Fastener in purchasing, he will say, "That was two months ago. I can't remember. I can't recall every shipment. Do I look like an elephant?" If I call Peter Pallet in the warehouse he will say, "We marked the receipt two months ago. I don't remember if there were really 40 cases. I can't remember those details. Do I look like an elephant?"
>
> It's true I get copies of the receipts, but they come in randomly, some are illegible, and I miss almost half of them. I would need four more clerks just to manually match receipts against invoices.

The problem is real but the proposal is incomplete. The reader thinks, "But tell me more!" This paper should be interpreted as a call for help rather than a formal proposal! With a little help from an MIS analyst, the request could be rewritten.

> When many invoices come in to Accounts Payable, we have no way to verify the warehouse actually received all of the merchandise being billed. For example, if we get a bill for 40 cases, we don't know if the warehouse actually received 40 cases. We manually match only those invoices and receipts over $7,000, so the majority never get checked.
>
> Since the computer has captured receipts in the inventory system, can you enter invoices and match them against receipts? We will then pay every matching invoice and investigate any discrepancy beyond a variable dollar amount. We need that amount variable by vendor because we suspect some manufacturers routinely overbill us.

The preceding document touches both sides of an idea, but one vital ingredient is missing: Why do the project? Where is the justification? A more experienced systems analyst could rewrite the document and force any cost conscious executive to stand up and cheer:

> The majority of invoices that come to Accounts Payable are paid without question–only invoices with a total dollar value over $7,000 are routinely matched with warehouse receipts. Last year Wonderful Widgets paid over $3.2 million in invoices that were never verified. Since most vendors know our lack of payment control, we are open for widespread cheating. Assuming an overcharge rate of only 1 percent, we overpaid $32,000 last year.

The inventory control system already captures receipts and adjustments. If we create a perpetual file of invoices sorted by invoice number and date, we could match all receipts against invoices on a weekly basis. This new system should catch all deliberate overcharges and errors.

This last version has the spark of *justification*, which will even excite the company president! A proposal should tell the reader *why* the idea is important. In fact, the author has deliberately understated his case: A 1 percent overcharge rate assumes that 99 percent of the vendors are honest. What if the rate is really 3 percent? Then Wonderful Widgets lost $96,000 instead of $32,000! And the problem continues every year. Think about the impact on the bottom line! A good proposal requires some degree of salesmanship, but the author should stay on the side of conservatism.

Along with the proposal itself, the complete package should contain a cover memo and an appendix, and should answer the following questions:

1. What is the business or scientific problem?

2. Is the problem important enough to be solved by computer?

3. Why can't it be handled by the current procedures or systems?

4. What should the computer solution include?

5. Who has been involved in the proposal preparation?

6. When does it have to be done?

The following cover memo helps answer those questions:

FROM: Joyce Journal–AP Supervisor
TO: Mark Muscle–Vice President
SUBJECT: Accounts Reconciliation Problem

Attached is the proposal for computerizing the matching of our invoices and receipts. As we know, Wonderful Widgets may be overpaying a tremendous amount on invoices less that $7,000, but we have absolutely no way of knowing. The proposal has been prepared by Larry Ledger, myself, and Frank Flowchart from MIS.

Our heavy purchasing period comes in May. If we have the computerized matching in place by April, it could have a potentially large effect upon next year's bottom line.

I will set up a meeting later this month to discuss the proposal and any questions you may have.

Thank you.

The appendix attached to a proposal may seem out of place, especially when it includes technical notes in mysterious data processing jargon. But the very act of contemplating an idea or suggestion with a user often generates details about justification, cost, design problems, advantages, and disadvantages that will be useful in the future. Unless such potentially valuable tidbits are preserved on paper, they may be forgotten, and the company will lose its investment in people time. Raw, hastily edited notes are not impressive, but adding them to the proposal keeps them alive for the next set of players. *One basic purpose of technical writing is to preserve knowledge gained on company time.*

FEASIBILITY STATEMENT

The first task faced by MIS management is to evaluate the practicality of the proposal. The outcome of this analysis is expressed in a short but vital document called the feasibility statement. The purpose is to either recommend some form of continued action or suggest rejecting the idea. Good project management requires that MIS take a stand early! *Creating the feasibility statement may be the most ignored step in the entire systems development life cycle.*

A common complaint from senior managers is that MIS spends considerable time on ideas or proposals that eventually prove too costly, too undefined, or simply impractical. Even worse is the classic explanation given by the frustrated MIS professional who casually mentions, "Well, we knew it wasn't feasible three months ago when we first talked about it." Then why did the company spend three months investigating that idea? Perhaps because MIS management did not routinely insist upon a feasibility statement for every proposal!

People resources today are simply too valuable to waste on ideas or concepts that will obviously never see the light of day. Even internal corporate political considerations no longer justify working on suggestions that are not valid.

The characteristics of a feasibility statement depend on the complexity of the concept and the outcome of the analysis. If no research is needed, or the concept is both practical and worthwhile, the statement will be simple. But to examine the feasibility of a purchases reconciliation system, the analyst may study the current inventory system (receipt information), discuss a new master file (to capture invoices), and work with the users (to scope reporting requirements). The final answer may be, "Yes, it seems feasible in our environment with current hardware." If, however, the idea is good but hardware resource limitations make it impractical without a major hardware investment, the recommendation may be negative. The feasibility statement needs enough supporting evidence to convince an objective third party that the recommendation is fair.

A good feasibility statement for the purchases reconciliation system might be:

> The proposal for an automated purchases reconciliation system appears reasonable. Since the Inventory Control system captures all receipts, we now have half the required data. By a rough estimate (based on last years invoices), the current data entry staff could absorb the load of entering all APS invoices if

done on a daily, non-critical basis. However, we should be prepared to add at least one full time operator to handle priority AP batches. Alternately, the new online General Ledger package could be used to capture invoices with slight modifications. Since we have never worked with purchases reconciliation reports, we must spend large amounts of time designing the reports, and be prepared for major changes once the system is in production.

Operationally, we should have no trouble running several new weekend jobs after the final Inventory Control update and reporting jobstreams.

We briefly considered buying the module available from the General Ledger vendor, but our specialized receiving procedures would require costly modifications to any purchased package. Therefore, we should write the system in house.

In our opinion, the proposed purchases reconciliation system is both useful and feasible from a business standpoint. While it is impossible to estimate the cost, based on previous experience I predict that developing a reconciliation system will be roughly comparable to the Expense Tracking system created in 1992.

Most readers would agree with the conclusions and suggest continuing the project (which actually means adding it to the MIS priority list). Yet the feasibility statement does not paint a completely happy picture. It mentions the need to add additional data entry staff to handle other critical work that will be displaced. It warns about major changes to the reporting structure once the system is complete. A good feasibility statement must have both sides of the question.

Systems analysts dislike the common management request to provide project development estimates before the team has started the design phase! In the preceding example, the author has cleverly avoided giving a number but has given his management a reference point almost as good: He compares this new proposal to a completed project. The feasibility statement is not the place for cost estimates, but the author should provide some indication for management. Such comparisons are often the best way to communicate scope, effort, and probable cost.

What happens when the systems analysts find themselves with more questions than answers? The purpose of the feasibility statement must then change. Rather than serving as a definite recommendation, the feasibility statement should become a "road map" for the next decision point. This is not to avoid an immediate decision; rather, it provides management with a plan to make the best possible choice. *As technology increases in complexity, feasibility statements themselves will become more difficult.* If the analyst team cannot make a recommendation, they must suggest ways to eventually make a recommendation.

A common dilemma in today's complex technical environment is that the evaluating team needs more research before they can provide any recommendation. They are confident they can suggest the correct path, but they need additional resources or analysis time. Companies who are considering a decision support system (DSS), for example, may find it difficult to judge the feasibility unless they have in-house expertise with DSS packages and their use. The initial feasibility statement should honestly admit this lack of knowledge, but not quite in the blunt manner chosen by the new systems analyst Tina Template:

> After examining the proposal for a decision support system submitted by Vice President of Sales "Honest John" Jones, I am stumped! I've never worked with a decision support system. After reading the brochures I am even more confused about their value. The cost is astronomical! We could hire three more full-time programmers for what the package costs. Is it feasible? I wish I knew!

Following a stern talk with her boss, Tina rewrote the document in a more professional manner:

> After studying the proposal for a decision support system submitted by Vice President of Sales "Honest John" Jones, I recommend that a team of MIS and sales department staff examine the brochures and some additional material I will provide. A good DSS package is very expensive and many complex factors help decide if the purchase is feasible. Since no one in the company has worked with a true DSS, we are all in a new area.
>
> I suggest the MIS managers select a financial systems analyst and a programming supervisor to meet with "Honest John" or his designates. After an estimated six one-hour sessions, the team should give one of three recommendations:
>
> 1. The probable benefits are not worth the cost, at least at this time.
> 2. The idea is interesting, but needs a long-range research plan.
> 3. The benefits appear justified, and we need an action plan to select the best package.

Tina's second version implies exactly what her first document stated— she is baffled! But it provides a logical plan, or "road map," to reach the next logical milestone. It is perfectly acceptable for the feasibility statement to say, "I don't know." It is not acceptable for the feasibility statement to stop at that point. The author must suggest the next move.

Deciding between feasible and nonfeasible involves many variables. For example, consider a buyer who is thoroughly pleased with her interactive file maintenance system, and now wants an interactive purchase order system. The feasibility statement is:

> Freda Fashion's proposed interactive purchase order system would be a great help to the entire buying staff. There is no doubt about the technical feasibility. Yet before committing additional resources to a design effort, we need to understand the implications of this proposal.
>
> Our Systems Software department is already investigating a new relational data base to integrate all merchandising applications. The interactive file maintenance system was a "quicky" CICS system and uses a special minifile that actually passes transactions to the nightly batch update. To generate

online purchase orders, we must create three additional minifiles and then duplicate the processing during the overnight runs. We already have serious control problems with the first minifile, and several more could cause additional production errors.

Technically, we can bring up a CICS mini purchase order system within a few months, but this means allocating our limited online expertise to specific applications rather than the already approved Unified Merchandise Control System.

While slanting the statement toward a rejection, the writer did not formally express an opinion. The MIS director is free to consider the economic and political benefits without worrying about the technical issues. The author has stressed business concerns that may make the project not justified. The feasibility statement can include virtually anything that has a significant bearing on the practicality and value of the proposal. Analysts should open their minds to the business and political worlds around them as well as the more familiar technical arena. Even the factor of "lost opportunities" is valid for consideration, if the author remembers the primary assignment is to concentrate on evaluating one specific idea at a time.

Writing style and content are critical when delivering negative recommendations. Consider a feasibility statement written by the same new systems analyst Tina Template:

The proposed automatic freight payment system does sound promising, but other factors make the idea impossible. First, the freight clerk, Wilma Wheel, cannot even turn on her typewriter without help, let alone operate a microcomputer. Terry Transit smokes those big smelly cigars that will foul up any electronic device. Also, he has a nasty habit of kicking both people and equipment when they do not function according to his standards. Finally, those truck drivers I met could never stop long enough to enter their own rate codes. Unless the people in the Shipping Department are fired, I do not feel that a computerized freight payment system is practical at Wonderful Widgets.

Tina will never win friends and influence people with her statement. Yet she may have discovered considerations that make the proposal impractical. The staff may not be able to handle a microcomputer, and the truck drivers may find it troublesome or time consuming to enter their own rate codes when they are rushing to meet tight schedules. But this same information can be communicated in a less insulting manner.

The proposed automatic freight payment system on a microcomputer does sound useful, but we have found other concerns. The office staff has never worked with CRTs. The office itself is not air conditioned or humidity controlled, and smoke from cigarettes and pipes can damage sensitive electronic equipment. The truck drivers may find it difficult to enter codes since they are typically on very tight schedules with less than 10 minutes per changeover. If we are willing to address those problems in detail, we should consider the project at some later date.

While the first version is more colorful, and accurately describes the Shipping Department environment, the second effort conveys the same information in a more professional manner. If the MIS director wishes to visit the Shipping Office, he can personally observe Terry Transit smoking a big, smelly cigar and kicking the file cabinet when a drawer sticks. He can casually notice Wilma Wheel spending five minutes looking for the power switch on her electric typewriter. He can be pushed out of the way by large, burly truck drivers madly rushing to their new assignments. But this tactful feasibility statement allows all parties to blame the rejection on the cost of air conditioning and lack of CRT experience. No one is insulted, and Tina Template does not have to face a large, angry shipping manager smoking a big, smelly cigar. If an idea must be rejected for personnel reasons, in the public document the author should provide a reasonable excuse that will satisfy the human ego. Truth in technical writing is important, but not at the cost of bruised egos and damaged relationships. Even large, angry shipping managers have feelings.

BUSINESS PLAN

Business plans are not only for multimillion dollar projects. Even relatively small efforts that seem complex, require capital expenditures above a certain amount, or appear "high risk," deserve a separate document *that analyzes both the development effort and the project from a business standpoint.* So-called business plans that describe only the project or only the development situation will leave many unaddressed questions. Good business plans are difficult to write, but they are a key document that can separate the failures from the successes. The business plan—sometimes known as a "sanity check"—is management's "control knob" on MIS activities.

A complete business plan has seven sections (see Figure 3.2):

1. Executive summary

2. Scope

3. Assumptions and open issues

4. Objectives

5. Interfaces

6. Resources and plan for next stage

7. Estimated timetable

Even the most comprehensive business plan is usually less than ten double-spaced pages, not including graphs or charts. Considering human nature, documents over that length tend to be ignored, returned to the in

Figure 3.2   Complete business plan

✔ Executive summary
✔ Scope
✔ Assumptions/open issues
✔ Objectives
✔ Interfaces
✔ Resources and plan
✔ Timetable

basket, or simply put aside. By keeping the paper relatively short and using a businesslike approach to the material, the author will communicate successfully to a greater number of readers. Except in the assumptions and open issues section, the document should stay with generalities rather than specifics. *A business plan is the "road map" that tells MIS where to go and how to get there.* It is more of a procedural document than an informational one.

Mechanical preparation is also important. Since senior level managers are accustomed to professionally prepared documents such as sales brochures, the author should use the best printing, cover, and folder possible. Even the title page should be impressive. Salesmanship is an important factor in most technical writing assignments, but the business plan requires extra effort.

A complete business plan has several sections. The *executive summary* describes the project, estimated resources, development approach, potential benefits, and possible problems. It is two pages or less, and is written as a standalone document. The summary should be the most polished section in the business plan.

The *scope* sets the official boundaries and limitations for the project team. It answers the twin questions, "How far will the project go?" and "What will the project encompass?" This section defines the responsibilities of the project team as perceived by the author. Merely stating these perceptions will often generate fascinating discussions, and should help prevent future misunderstandings.

The *assumptions and open issues* section lists the major assumptions that have been identified in previous meetings and significant open issues that must be resolved at some point during the life cycle. Critical open questions may later impact the scope, cost, and benefits of the entire project. The business plan does not settle those issues, but simply identifies them for management attention. The business plan for a development project is a perfect opportunity to place important matters before senior management in a nonthreatening manner.

The *objectives* section describes the purpose and goals of the project. Like the assumptions and open issues portion, this page will encourage all parties to understand the perceived purpose of the project. As organizations become more complex, the search for a common set of goals—even in seemingly obvious projects—becomes equally complicated.

The *interface* section lists the application systems, departments, and operating units which will directly or indirectly interface to the project. The purpose of this information is to alert other areas that their assistance may be required in the future. As many MIS managers have discovered, one of the most dangerous aspects of the systems development cycle is the interface that was forgotten! The interface section may be complemented with one or two data flow diagrams if the team is using structured analysis tools.

The *project plan* lists the people and computer resources needed for subsequent phases of the project. Although the business plan is too early in the development cycle for definite commitments, the author should attempt to quantify needed support. Management wants some indication of analyst, programmer, and user effort, as well as some opinion concerning machine utilization.

The *calendar* identifies the major developmental milestones that will occur during the design, development, and installation process.

A business plan should never be submitted as a surprise to MIS or company management! At least one draft must be circulated to selected individuals before the first official version is published, and their comments or suggestions should be carefully considered. Not only will those changes help clarify the document, but incorporating even minor suggestions is an excellent way to make those readers feel ownership toward the business plan. People will instinctively search for their comments or their ideas. Human nature can be used to the author's advantage. The writer is not being dishonest or sneaky—it is good sense to incorporate reasonable suggestions from people who must eventually approve the document.

The information in the business plan will seldom remain etched in stone. As the requirements and system design phases discover new facts or possibilities, the author will revise his business plan. *An out-of-date business plan is worse than no business plan at all.* Even organizations change, and the longer the term of the project, the more opportunity for changes that affect every ongoing development project. Those new directions and policies cannot be ignored, because the business plan is probably the most publicized MIS-produced project document outside MIS. The business plan must be updated as the situation changes.

Updating the business plan on a word processor is relatively simple, but each change should be flagged, either by an indicator in the margin, a change page that tells the reader which sections and paragraphs have been modified, or both.

The decision to include costs in a business plan depends upon the organization. Many senior managers insist that any paper with the title "business plan" address the cost issue, at least for budgeting purposes. Although the business plan is formulated early in the development cycle, the author should estimate both development and ongoing costs. Of course, when the project changes, or as more details are filled in, the cost data must be revised.

REQUIREMENTS DOCUMENT

A requirements document may be called *functional specifications, user requirements, deliverables,* or *user definition.* Whatever the name, the purpose of the requirements document is to define the perceived needs from the viewpoint of both the user and MIS. Requirements documents that only consider user needs and ignore technical considerations are often confusing and incomplete: Requirements documents that concentrate only on the MIS aspects are even worse.

The format and length of the document varies according to the complexity or scope of the project, but most requirements documents include the following topics (see Figure 3.3):

1. Overview and purpose
2. Input
3. Processing
4. Output
5. Integration considerations (including data base relationships)
6. Timing and operational factors
7. Hardware requirements
8. Appendix

The *overview* states the purpose of the proposed application or system, the scope of the project (taken from the business plan), and briefly describes the major functions.

Acceptable requirements documents can vary from five-page summaries to 500-page volumes. Therefore, the overview should contain a statement that explains the level of detail and how the team selected that particular level. If there is no explicit statement, the reader will naturally assume the requirements are complete. This may lead to a serious misunderstanding! Yet specifying the level of detail is simple. The overview may state: "The user requirements in this document are complete as we currently see them."

Figure 3.3 Requirements document

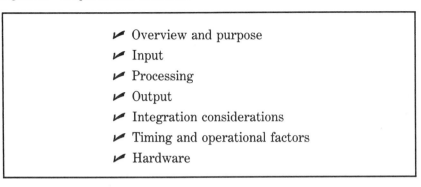

> ✔ Overview and purpose
> ✔ Input
> ✔ Processing
> ✔ Output
> ✔ Integration considerations
> ✔ Timing and operational factors
> ✔ Hardware

Or, another version could be, "The information in this paper presents only general user requirements, and the design phase will further define additional requirements." Either approach lets the reader know exactly what to expect.

If the project deals with a typical business application, the *input* section describes the batch, online, or machine collected transactions. If the proposal concerns a new computer, the input section would discuss such factors as operating control parameters or electronic components that regulate the system. Even many exotic MIS projects have input requirements, even if they are not immediately apparent. For most business type applications, this section answers the question, "What will the user give the system?"

Processing summarizes the computer manipulations of data and the relationships between data elements. In an inventory control system, for example, the processing section would contain formulas in user understandable terms to calculate the final cost of items received at the warehouse.

The *output* section describes reports or CRT screen formats that reflect the combination of input data and processing. A summary of hard copy reports should include such aspects as availability (daily, weekly, monthly, yearly, or on request), headings, columns, and important data fields. If the system includes a user-oriented report writer, the analyst should help create at least one sample report format with the code required to generate the sample. Even the ad hoc inquiry feature needs at least one or two examples. CRT screens should be described so the users can appreciate the very critical human engineering considerations of an online system.

Missing from many requirements documents is the purpose behind output reports or screens. Asking a user to define each purpose often initiates a dialogue that helps both the user and MIS analyst. For example, after MIS has spent ten weeks creating the new overstock report, exactly *how* will it be used by the buyers and warehouse staff? Has the user defined the procedures necessary to derive maximum benefit from this new report?

Is it usable? If not, what other information is needed? *The output section of the requirements document will be the starting point for the user manual!*

When considering changes to an existing system, the *integration* section is often the most important. Many errors in development projects are caused by a failure to define interface points and the snowball effect resulting from last minute changes. Even data base-oriented shops may still have integration problems. The author must not rely only on the MIS technical wizards—sophisticated users may have special insight that will help the analyst team locate and target those integration points. Again, structured techniques such as data flow diagrams can replace some of the textual integration information.

Timing and operational factors are important if they are not specifically described in the input or processing sections. Some user requirements lose their value the longer the input is separated from the output. In other situations, the timing is dictated by external demands such as accounting calendars or machine availability. Some analysts label this section as the "limitations" of the project.

The document needs a section on *hardware* requirements if the proposed idea demands specialized hardware or software. Today most business application system generally develop their hardware requirements as part of the system design phase.

The *appendix* is a vital section that includes supporting material of every kind. Random notes concerning user needs, design requirements, or potential implementation problems, are perfect candidates for the appendix. Sometimes an author discovers other papers or detailed explanations that are inappropriate in the body of the document, but will be needed in subsequent development stages. The appendix is simply a mechanism to store valuable knowledge gained during the requirements phase, and pass that information to other workers.

Requirements should be categorized in three relative levels: absolute, recommended, and optional. A requirements document that simply lists requirements and does not differentiate between them fails in its mission. *All requirements are not alike: Some are vital, some are important, and others are merely wishful dreams.* The author can separate the important from the less important by classifying every requirement in the following manner:

Absolute: Those requirements that make the project virtually useless if MIS cannot deliver them

Recommended: Those requirements wanted by the user (or MIS) but the project is still useful without them

Optional: Those requirements that are "nice to have," but are not critical to the project design

Both recommended and optional requirements are subject to later negotiation. If, for example, an optional requirement is found to cost half as much as the rest of the design, the project team can legitimately suggest dropping that requirement. However, experienced systems analysts seldom use the word *negotiable* when explaining the three-layer approach to requirements definition.

Users who have never seen this format may stubbornly insist that everything they ask for is absolutely essential to the project, the corporation, and the entire planet earth. Their attitude is exaggerated but understandable, if they have suffered through previously incomplete or late projects. Users may worry that MIS will immediately forget every requirement not classified as absolute. The MIS management team should carefully point out that by defining the degree of need in the requirements document, MIS hopes to avoid such battles. Also, asking a user to make those judgments on a case-by-case basis during the more time critical detailed design or programming process is both unfair and inaccurate. The best time for making difficult value judgments is during the requirements phase, when the user is conceptualizing the entire system at one time.

SYSTEM DESIGN DOCUMENTS

If the functional specifications answer the question "what," the business plan tells the reader "why," the system design answers the final question "how."

The purpose of a system design is to take information from the requirements document, feasibility statement, and business plan, and create the best solution for the organization. A thorough design team will consider these critical factors:

User needs

MIS environment

Cost considerations

Technical requirements

Company policies

Other projects planned or in progress

Customs

Estimated life cycle of the system

Risk value

Availability of resources

Degree of user participation

Political importance

Implementation schedule or timing requirements

The technical writer must understand three significant differences between other MIS documents and a true system design. First, the system design must be *easy to change*. Second, the design should be written with almost *standalone sections*. Third, the text must contain numerous *references to other sections* to help the reader locate additional information.

A business plan and requirements document are relatively stable. They may be issued several times as major changes are made to the scope or purpose of the project, but those documents are generally fixed. The systems design, however, is a working document that is meant to change. The first version may be literally torn apart by users, MIS technicians, and managers. The second version may suffer even worse treatment. There is nothing wrong with critical comments—in fact, they prove that readers are taking the design seriously!

The second difference is that other project documents are written as an integrated whole, but a systems design must serve as a reference document, and should contain virtually standalone sections. For example, the programmer needs one place to search for relevant facts and will dislike spending hours searching through a 100-page document looking for needed information about a specific topic. While the business plan or requirements document may be studied once or twice, the systems design will be used continually during the project by a wide variety of readers. It never goes away. It may be cursed or praised, but it lives forever.

Creating sections or chapters that are almost "standalone" is a frustrating challenge for many authors: Writers normally create papers that do not repeat information or facts. They want their document to become a cohesive whole. But a system design document is never a candidate for a creative writing award. A business plan should be compared to a beautiful work of art that communicates in smooth, flowing language, while the systems design document is a very dull but necessary set of blueprints. There are techniques to liven up a design document, but material as dull as blueprints will never make exciting bedtime reading. To create standalone sections, the author must include enough material in each logical unit so the reader will have all necessary information in that section. The writer must occasionally repeat detail already found in other units, and provide complete explanations throughout the text. Larry Ledger may not enjoy reading about the LIFO inventory posting process he designed three years ago, but a programmer/analyst reading a design for inventory valuation needs complete information. *A systems design with standalone sections will dramatically help the programming, systems, and user staff who work with the design document.*

Even when the author has done a truly outstanding job of creating standalone sections, some readers will invariably need more information. It is impossible to repeat everything any reader may eventually need. Therefore, the system design document should contain specific references to other chapters or units. For example, if the design for an integrated manufacturing system mentions the effects of government regulations in several places, each instance should point directly (by title and section number) to the chapter devoted entirely to government regulation. It is more efficient for the knowledgeable author to provide the pointers to related material than to have the readers search the document themselves. The goal of an effective system design document is to communicate easily by saving the reader time and effort.

Two very good design documents may have different levels of detail. One can be a large, massive volume that contains every known fact about the project, while the other equally successful document presents only enough information for the next stage of the project. The latter approach assumes that some of the design effort can be left to the programmers or programmer/analysts. There is no absolute guideline, but the level of detail must be determined logically for that particular project. The authors or department managers cannot simply ignore the question and hope for the best. The analyst team should never choose the level of detail by a toss of the coin, the degree of management pressure, or the next impending deadline. Rather, the decision can be made by answering several important questions:

Will the project team use traditional programming techniques, or are they implementing any fourth generation development tools?

Will the project be developed inhouse? Or will the development be given to an outside group?

Are the developers familiar with the application or business concepts? Are they senior or junior level people?

How much effort can the users realistically donate to the programming phase?

Will the original systems analyst be heavily involved in the programming?

Does the design contain any new technical concepts?

What degree of risk does the project have?

Are the users cooperative?

Is management flexible enough to leave some unanswered issues for the detailed programming stages?

When the analyst team has answered those questions, they can intelligently plan the level of detail required in their specific project.

The best design documents use both text and graphics, because each appeals to different types of readers. Flow charts, diagrams, and graphic symbols are an excellent method to portray relationships, while text seems to be better for communicating specific information. Human nature also plays a part. Some people simply prefer graphics while others ignore pictures and go straight to the written word. A document that has both techniques has a better chance of communicating effectively to more readers. Although graphics are becoming more popular (due to the excellent graphics capability in some word processing systems), text will always be important. A document that relies only on symbols will lose many readers. Likewise, another document that ignores the value of graphics will lose an opportunity to communicate, because text alone does not always do the job.

One common graphic tool is the classic *HIPO* method developed by IBM. Some authors have developed variations such as input-process-output (IPO). HIPO, which stands for hierarchical-input-process-output, analyzes a system from the standpoint of specific user input, computer processing, and resultant output. Although various MIS departments differ in their implementation of HIPO charts, most MIS professionals use a format with three horizontal or vertical areas labeled "Input," "Process," and "Output." HIPO charts work well when the author can portray the system logic in hierarchical terms, since the initial (or level 1) HIPO chart can summarize each function as it relates to the general system flow. Each succeeding HIPO diagram analyzes a function or process in more detail.

Standard flow chart symbols will also work, if the audience is familiar with their purpose. In practice, each systems analyst typically chooses the graphics tool he or she has personally worked with, or the method chosen as the MIS standard.

If they decide to use any form of graphics, they should be consistent. That is, if the first of five major topics have data flow diagrams, the other four topics should also have similar charts. Any inconsistency will leave the reader puzzled, and will ultimately hurt the communication process.

There is no perfect format for a system design document. Rather, the team should start with a complete list of topics or sections and create an individualized structure for each document. The differing needs of each project invariably require a customized organization. Complex system designs may use all the recommended sections (and perhaps additional topics), while another project may need only a few items. *It is unrealistic to force all design documents to follow a rigid, unchangeable standard format: They should follow similar guidelines, but the author needs some degree of freedom.* The following list is only a guide to help analysts quickly determine *what* topics should be covered and the proper sequence.

A complete design document for a complex MIS business application may contain the following sections:

1. Informational pages

2. Summary

3. Assumptions and guidelines

4. Overall system flow

5. Inputs

6. Processing logic

7. Outputs

8. Error conditions

9. Hardware, software, and personnel requirements

10. Interfaces with existing systems

11. Appendix
   a. User responsibilities
   b. Timing Considerations
   c. Technical notes
   d. Potential problems and drawbacks
   e. Summary of rejected alternatives
   f. Cost estimates
   g. Development timetable
   h. Definitions
   i. Miscellaneous

Design documents that propose a new software product use a different format:

1. Product summary and features

2. Market survey and current competition

3. Sales and marketing strategy

4. Product life cycle analysis

5. Appendix
   a. Potential risks
   b. Cost analysis
   c. Technical notes

Formal design documents have three informational pages.

1. The *title page* displays:

The formal name of the project.

An informal subtitle that explains the formal title (official titles are notoriously uncommunicative)

Original issue date, revision number and date, geographical location if important

Names of the authors, organization, or department.

Any document intended for outside use must have a complete mailing address. The version number and its corresponding revision date tells the reader immediately if he is using the current document. Imagine the frustration when a busy professional discovers he or she has spent six hours reading an obsolete design!

2. The second page contains *signoffs* by the appropriate managers, users, technical experts, or customers. Many potentially embarrassing misunderstandings are avoided when the system design document itself has spaces for approval signatures, which leaves the responsibility squarely in specific hands. The analyst team will also find increased cooperation from various individuals and departments when their names are on the approval page. In some situations, the approval list will have the most senior person first. In other cases, the first person listed will be the user or manager who is ultimately responsible for the system operation. Sensitive analysts will consult their own manager to understand the political environment before creating the approval list, which will help avoid ego problems. The approval page format is another example where logical documentation techniques force good management procedures.

3. The *change control* page lists all important changes that have taken place since the last release of the document. For example, the accounting manager who has studied the initial design and found seven unacceptable recommendations, can review the change control page to determine if the objections have been resolved. The analyst must never force a busy reader to search through a 75 page document merely to discover what items have changed—the author can save readers valuable time by using the change control approach.

One note of caution: Analysts under extreme pressure from management to finalize a design project may be tempted to sneak in changes they know should be highlighted through the change control page technique. The basic concept of change control assumes trust between the author and the reading audience, and a single violation will destroy the author's credibility. Other members of the project team could then see a carefully nurtured attitude of positive cooperation replaced by a wary and distrustful user base. The penalty for dishonesty in technical writing is both immediate and severe.

The following example illustrates the first three pages of a business oriented systems design document.

Title Page:

Worm Farm Management System

A new online interactive application system to manage the accounting and inventory control functions of Dirt Enterprises, a subsidiary of Wonderful Widgets, Inc.

by Karen Keystroke
Systems Analyst
Dirt Enterprises
Muddy Flats, Iowa
July 1, 1992
This document is: Version 3
Issue date: September 4, 1992

Second Page:
Changes since version 2. All changes in the text have been flagged with an "x" in the left hand margin.
1. Discarded plan to band all worms with an ID tag. We will band only adult worms (online volume cut in half).
2. Added three extra month end reports.
3. A worm accidentally sliced in pieces will be tracked by separate data base records linked to the original worm as the parent. Only the most three recent choppings will be tracked.
4. Created separate worm history data base for outstanding reproducers.

Third Page:
This design must be approved by the following people:

	Signature	Date
Herman Dirt	_____	_____
President, Dirt Enterprises		
Gary Grimy	_____	_____
Production Manager		
Carl Crawly	_____	_____
MIS Manager		
Terrance Tightwad, III	_____	_____
Controller		

The *summary* highlights the most important features and provides the reader with a good overview. As with the business plan, many casual readers will study only the summary, and the author should write the summary very carefully. Many times the analyst can copy the summary from the requirements document or business plan, with just a few minor changes. In technical writing, borrowing from one document to feed another is perfectly acceptable—in fact, such copying is an excellent idea!

During any design process, the analyst team creates a set of *assumptions and guidelines* in their conversations. These assumptions may dictate the system design choices. Unless the author understands that virtually all departments have unwritten policies that drive the direction of various projects and activities, he will find it awkward to specify them on paper. Some experienced analysts claim it is more difficult to define these assumptions than to create the design itself! Entire organizations themselves usually function through a set of policies, guidelines, helpful hints, customs, and the personal preferences of senior mangers. This is often described as the company's "style," and it definitely affects the entire design process.

Even a moderately complex system design requires a separate section that presents the *system flow* from a user and technical viewpoint. The reader must understand the mechanics of the application in terms of his input, the computer processing, and the output. Although graphs or charts are ideal methods to communicate, a *User/Computer Timing Chart* is an easy to use textual method. This simply describes the logical sequence of events. This approach uses a page split down the middle. The column on the left is labeled "User" (or given a more specific title), and the right column is labeled "Computer." Normally, action 1 is under the User column, and action 2 is the corresponding Computer processing. Action 3 may then be another user response. In complex environments the user may perform several actions before the computer performs any actions. A side-by-side timing chart is an excellent way to visualize human-machine interfaces.

These User/Computer Timing Charts are essential when the system design requires specific human responses or activities as a prelude to computer processing. To understand an online receiving system in a warehouse, for example, readers of the document should review several important manual activities that must be performed before, during, and after the computer actions. Unless the development team and the user representatives share a common understanding of the timing involved with man/machine interactions, the company risks serious problems during implementation. *A business system usually involves people as well as computers*. A design document that concentrates only on the MIS aspects of a new system or major modification is confusing, frustrating, and incomplete at best. At worst, it could destroy the project.

The following is a simple example of a User/Computer Timing Chart.

Receiving department	Worm farm management system
1. Truck pulls up to dock with shipment of worms. Clerk enters PO number from driver's bill of lading.	
	2. System verifies open PO number, and displays vendor, expected number of cases, and due in date.
3. Clerk counts number of cases and compares to Bill of Lading. If any problem he notifies Purchasing. If a match, he enters receipt transaction.	
	4. System marks PO as "received," adds to overnight AP batch log, and sends online notification to Worm Quality Control (WQC).
5. Clerk removes 5 worms at random, verifies color, length, and weight. If within standards, he enters level 1 QA acceptance.	
	6. System prints an inspection report on receiving dock with vendor quality history information.
7. Clerk sends inspection report and bill of lading to Worm Inventory Control (WIC).	

The formats of the *input, processing,* and *output* sections of the systems design document depend upon the needs of the project and the experience of the analyst team. Some technical writers copy the style of related design documents, while others choose the format that has served them successfully in the past. Structured techniques such as data flow diagrams are excellent tools to explain information processing.

The *input* section will describe such functions as transactions, completed forms, data collection, and information from other application systems. A comprehensive input section describes every user, computer, and machine interface into the system. Since users will probably study the input section more than any other portion of the document, the analyst should carefully present the input side of the design in user terminology as well as in technical jargon.

Processing links information from the input side of the system with the actual computer manipulations. Processing logic will not function in a complete vacuum. Very rarely will any system design propose a completely standalone system that has no relationship to a current data base or information file. In many cases, a proposed system uses some current information, facts, processing, logic, or data from existing files. The author should define the processing enough so that a programmer/analyst can immediately understand the basic logic requirements. He or she may not comprehend enough details to create a program flow chart, but the processing section in any design document should provide a firm starting point. When unclear about the technical requirements, the author must ask for assistance. The ultimate readers of the processing section will be glad to help: After all, they depend upon the system design document and especially the processing section for their success.

The *output* section is easier to write. Analysts describe such visual output as CRT screens or hard copy reports. Systems with a report generator will require a list of data elements available to the user along with sample reports. If a query or ad hoc language is used, the author should give several examples. A project that contains user-oriented fourth generation languages still requires an output section, although the analyst team may provide examples and procedures rather than detailed output formats.

Error conditions are often neglected, because the author generally includes them randomly throughout the document. While various errors and their resolutions should indeed be mentioned in each section or chapter, complex application systems need a separate error condition section that discusses only problem resolution. Things do go wrong! Readers often take a devil's advocate position and consider the effects of incorrect transactions, computer unavailability, and other assorted disasters. What happens if a general ledger chart of accounts error happens on an accounts payable transaction? What is the correction procedure? How does the system respond? When must it be corrected? The answers may be scattered throughout the document, but concerned users (and equally concerned MIS professionals) feel more comfortable when they discover all the answers to these disconcerting questions in one place.

The *hardware, software, and personnel requirements* section contains the resources necessary for development and continued operation of the system. Most installations have standard formats used in budget planning documents that can be successfully copied to the systems design paper. If not, the author can simply state the requirements in a line-by-line arrangement.

If the proposed system will *interface* with any existing application, data base, process, or machine, the systems design document should identify and discuss each interface. Some analysts mention each interface point briefly and allow the staff in the development phase to investigate the details. Others spend considerable time researching the problems caused by an interface. Either approach is valid, as long as the authors and their managers understand the decision.

The *appendix* is a collection of valuable information that does not fit into any mainline section. Such facts tend to be specific to one group or person, and are not applicable to a wider audience. If material applies to several people or a group, the author should use it in the main sections. If, however, the information appeals to one person or is so technical that most readers would immediately turn the page, it belongs in the appendix. The author of a system design document without an appendix may be in trouble! Either everything is crammed in to the main body, or some facts that are important to selected individuals are not included. Whatever the reason, the MIS director should prepare for future problems. An appendix may not look impressive, but it serves a useful purpose.

COST/BENEFIT ANALYSIS

After the system design has been accepted, one important step remains. Management must now answer the ultimate question: Is it worth the effort and cost? The vehicle to solve the puzzle is a *cost/benefits analysis* that compares development and operating cost to the tangible and intangible benefits. If the comparison is favorable, the project should continue. If not, reason dictates that the proposal be modified or even scrapped. While some analysts attempt a cost/benefits analysis for large, complex projects before the system has been designed, the value of such an exercise is limited. Only the system design will tell management the true cost of the project, and only after the analysis and design effort will the project team and users understand the true benefits of a new application.

The term *intangible benefits* frightens not only many technical writers, but the most fearless management team. Some organizations ignore the cost/benefits analysis and make the ultimate decision by default. Tangible benefits, of course, are easy to calculate and senior managers expect some justification. But most organizations fail to make the cost/benefits analysis part of the traditional project review procedure. Should a specific project be implemented? In some situations, if no one objects, the project is put on the pending list, and if the senior vice president thinks the concept is an excellent idea, the project will be given top priority. The lack of a cost/benefits analysis for major projects is a form of management by crisis, management by default, or even management by squeaky wheel. Good management policy requires that all major projects include a cost/benefits analysis after the system design phase. Managers who claim they can make logical business decisions without a cost/benefits analysis usually make second-rate decisions.

The format of a cost/benefits analysis is simple: Section A contains the estimated development and ongoing costs; section B describes the benefits and the final recommendation. The entire document is rarely over two or three pages. Experienced analysts add a final paragraph that gives a level of confidence concerning all the costs and benefits in the document. A high level of confidence suggests that management can trust the analysis and its conclusion, while a low level of confidence (with appropriate reasons) raises a caution flag. It is a fact of life in the world of information systems that some estimates are better than others, and the organization who understands this reality can make more accurate business decisions.

Developmental costs are estimated separately for detailed design, programming design, programming, testing, documentation, and implementation. While there are many accepted ways to report such estimates, a simple method that can be easily explained is the concept of *calendar weeks*. That is, if a task is estimated at six calendar weeks, an experienced programmer would complete that assignment in six weeks if assigned to that job full time. This estimate takes into account normal administrative time (usually 15 percent), but it does not consider multiple assignments, vacations, or illnesses. It also assumes an experienced programmer or analyst, not one who needs specialized training. The calendar week concept is still a useful tool for roughly estimating development projects and can later be converted to precise workday estimates when the programming specifications are complete. For planning purposes, MIS managers can then factor in the degree of experience of likely candidates, the probability of multiple assignments, and the other risks.

Ongoing costs are difficult to estimate because companies have various ways of computing chargeback costs ranging from the very accurate to the very ridiculous. One may argue that an inhouse computer with excess capacity is actually free for additional batch applications, other than for incidental materials such as tapes and disk packs. The operations manager, struggling to justify the budget, would naturally disagree, while the company president might agree in principle since it will not increase the expense line on the profit and loss statement. Even if the requesting department is charged on some proven resource unit type accounting method, how much does the new system actually cost to run? Which cost should be used in a cost/benefits analysis?

Systems analysts, user managers, and MIS directors have spent many frustrating days pondering that problem, but the obvious solution is to use *both* costs. Or, if there are three reasonable ways to view the operating costs of a new system or application, the technical writer should list all *three!* For example, a valid ongoing cost estimate charged to the requesting department could be listed as $5,000 a month for computer time or as a much lower $100 a month for increased material expenses. Both are "correct," and management should see both sides of the costing issue.

Hardware purchases can be more complicated when tax laws allow purchases to be charged in various ways that can affect the cost/benefits analysis. Can these ten additional CRTs be amortized over five years if they are purchased? What about leasing them and using the capital for another purpose? An accountant familiar with the business side of data processing can make suggestions as to the accounting, depreciation, and tax liability considerations. Authors of cost/benefits analyses should never simply report raw numbers when it comes to hardware. Instead, they should work with an accountant and present several scenarios that will have different financial effects.

On a more basic level, many MIS directors complain that systems analysts not familiar with computer hardware consistently underestimate the final cost of new hardware and its supporting equipment. A classic example is the case of an expensive minicomputer, disk drive, and printer sitting idle because the systems analyst forgot to check the power requirements, and the units cannot be plugged in until the electricians install new wiring even more expensive than the hardware! Slight omissions can be disastrous when trying to estimate costs.

The benefits section includes both the tangible and intangible benefits. It will answer the question, "Why should we spend x number of dollars doing this project?" Tangible benefits are those which can be measured in terms of dollars saved or time gained, while intangible benefits are those hard to quantify advantages that will increase productivity, improve quality, or provide better information for management decisions. Given a choice, the author should concentrate on the measurable benefits such as manpower savings (reduction in staff or possible reassignment of people), lower operating expenses, or a better opportunity for using financial resources. But as data processing automates more and more of the routine production jobs, it becomes more difficult to show direct cost benefits. Systems analysts must use their creative ingenuity to explain those intangible but important benefits. Just how much better is online journal entry editing than batch editing? Will productivity increase significantly? How much is online processing worth to the organization and its bottom line?

There are no easy answers to such complex questions and experienced analysts have not found the "perfect" way to explain intangible benefits. One obvious method is to carefully paraphrase those in the company who have a strong opinion as to the value of the project. While possibly prejudiced in favor of his/her own idea, the originator of the concept he may still have the best mental picture of how to sell the intangible benefits to others. The systems analyst should work with the user in documenting these improvements or advantages, although some human perceptions tend to be more emotional than factual. Accounting Manager Larry Ledger may laugh and say, "Of course we need online editing. Any fool can see that." With a little encouragement and the right probing questions from the analyst, Larry may be able to provide a few subjective but nonetheless impressive reasons that make online editing a valid company objective.

Even if the cost and benefits sections are accurate, the conclusion section may still be relatively complicated. The systems analyst who writes the cost/benefits analysis may be emotionally involved with the concept (since he has spent much of his time on the project) and may be unaware of the current MIS situation. But the authors must provide some recommendation, even if they do not understand all the commitments and pending projects that will enter into the final decision. Systems analysts may not have input into the final decision making process, but their responsibility is to weigh the cost against the tangible and intangible benefits and make the best value judgment.

PROGRAMMING SPECIFICATIONS

After the project is approved, the technical staff must prepare the detailed program specifications. Even prototyping languages require a few notes before designing the screens and reports! While some new fourth generation languages are indeed moving away from this classic stage of application development by generating their own "source code," the third generation language of COBOL will be around for a long time. Program specifications are the communication vehicle between the designer and the programmer.

Some managers are tempted to slight the program specification stage, especially when the staff who created the system design will do the detailed programming. This is risky because third generation languages are too primitive. The logic and detailed coding are often too complicated for even a good programmer to take a system design and create the individual program modules. Although a few rare design documents do have enough specific detail so they can be used as programming documentation, most experts feel that systems built with any third generation language still need specifically tailored documentation that can be easily transferred into source code.

The degree of detail in programming specifications depends upon the complexity of the modules, the skills of the technical staff, and their familiarity with the application. If the project involves extensive changes to an existing system, and the programmer will make complex logic changes, the programming specifications should describe not only the changes but any critical existing processing as well. Even if the new requirements are spelled out in great detail, programmers may stumble if they do not understand the relationship of the changes to the existing logic.

The nature of programming specifications depends upon the management policy concerning technical documentation in general. Does the organization have any program level documentation in place? If so, can the programmer/analyst use that same format in creating new programming specifications? Professionals should try for consistency even if the existing formats are not totally acceptable, since *the programming specifications of today should become the maintenance documentation of tomorrow.* Therefore, programmer/analysts should keep one eye on their own needs, and the other eye on the needs of the programmer who will maintain the application next year. They may get a splitting headache, but such thinking encourages the efficient use of company resources. Documentation is a company resource just as much as a building, a computer, or a stamping machine.

Program level documentation may be changed more frequently than design documents. As new programmers learn about a module or make extensive changes, they may be willing to update the program level documentation if:

The supervisor encourages the practice.

They are given adequate time.

The process is relatively easy.

The ideal medium for program level documentation is an online system that interfaces with a word processing package and allows the computer to handle the mechanical problems of formatting the output.

There are many styles of program level specifications (under several names), but two of the more common "generic" approaches are the IPO (input-processing-output) and the MTM (module to module). Some programmers use a combination of these two classical approaches. They are known by many names, are described by numerous authors, and exist in multiple variations, but these two approaches are the basic foundation of many existing documentation schemes. Advocates of certain programming practices will insist that program design specifications follow their own brand of documentation. The structured programming adherents, for example, have definite ideas about detailed programming documentation which have proved successful in a number of situations. But it is unwise to assume that all environments, organizations, and projects should always follow one specific format unless management has made a conscious decision to follow one particular design methodology. The purpose of mentioning the

IPO and MTM approaches is simply to present useful examples that may or may not fit a particular project.

The input-processing-output technique is an older method that analyzes a program in terms of data and files coming in, the processing that must be applied, and the output such as reports, record streams, CRT screens, messages, or data files. This style can apply equally well to both online and batch programs and can be adapted to data base or telecommunications environments.

The MTM method is appropriate when a program or system will consist of many separately compiled modules, each of which has its own particular function such as input, processing, or output. Each module has a specific purpose with one entry and exit point, and the true complexity—from a programming viewpoint—is relating each module to the main calling routine. The module-to-module approach is useful when the programmer anticipates major logic changes in the system once it is in production. The MTM approach is similar to structure charts described by the structured programming advocates.

CHRONO FILE

History is fascinating. When the inevitable questions arise after a project is complete, analysts and managers scratch their collective heads and ask, "What exactly happened?" and "When did it happen?" Hopefully, the purpose is not so much to fix the blame, but to answer valid questions and help the organization learn from the past. Project management systems generally do not supply the answer, although they do track detailed project schedules.

The chrono file should be kept by the project leader or section manager and should begin at the feasibility stage. If a project leader has not been assigned during the feasibility stage, the systems analyst should start the file himself by logging in any facts relating to the timing and individual accomplishments, even if they are only one line notations.

Useful information in a chrono file might be:

- When did the design phase start?
- Who did the initial write up?
- How much time did he spend on it?
- How much user involvement did it require?
- Who approved the design, and who provided internal communication?
- How long did the approval process take?
- Who requested changes to the design, and how long did each change take?
- Did the change require a full reevaluation of the project?
- Who gave the first cost estimates and when? How far off were they?

If the project leader keeps his chrono file continually updated, he will have an extremely valuable history document that will trace the key events and dates. While other formal reporting procedures can be helpful, a manager who wants to analyze project history should utilize the chrono file as a document designed specifically for that purpose.

SUMMARY OF KEY POINTS

- Good documentation practices can solve many project management problems; conversely, many problems in project development are caused by poor documents.

- The proposal should be written by both users and MIS.

- The proposal document should include justification—why is the idea important?

- The proposal package needs a cover letter and an appendix.

- The feasibility study may be the most forgotten document in MIS, yet it forces MIS management to take an early position. Is the project feasible? This document will often save wasted, unproductive effort.

- Both business and technical factors are important in the feasibility study.

- If the MIS analyst cannot recommend a course of action, the feasibility study must include suggestions on the next step in the evaluation process.

- Business plans are important for large projects, and small ones that are complex or have a high risk factor. The business plan is a road-map that tells MIS where to go and how to get there. It is a procedural, management-oriented document.

- In every requirements document, explicitly state the level of detail and why it was chosen. The readers must understand if the requirements are complete or only a starting point.

- Each requirement should be labeled as either absolute, recommended, or optional. A document that merely lists requirements without comparing their relative importance may cause problems in the development cycle.

- System design documents are a reference tool. They must be easy to change, and written in standalone mode.

- For system designs, use both graphics and text to communicate effectively.

- There is no single format best for all system design documents. The analyst or technical writer should customize his work to fit the situation.

- System designs should always list the assumptions and guidelines used by the analyst team.

- The writer should emphasize error handling and error recovery procedures—people want to know what happens when things go wrong.

- The cost/benefits analysis tells management if the project is worth doing, after the system design and before any programming. This is a final check on feasibility that prevents major disasters.

- The programming specifications for a new project should eventually become maintenance documentation.

Internal MIS Forms

*This chapter provides models for service requests, project
status reports, task control forms, weekly, monthly, and
quarterly status reports, experience evaluation forms, and
memos. Without efficient and effective internal forms and
reports, the MIS department can flounder in a sea of
miscommunication. Well designed forms are an extension of a
sound management program: Every aspect of each form serves
a specific purpose. MIS managers and senior professional
staff can use these ready-to-copy examples to revitalize their
internal communication.*

MIS paperwork should be viewed as an *opportunity*, because various forms
and reports both determine and help implement management direction. In
effect, they become management policy, and the difference between a well
run organization and one that merely stumbles along is often the quality of
its internal paperwork. If the paperwork situation is a nightmare, the rest of
the department may be equally as frightening.

Reports and forms must be standardized for the same reasons that
companies standardize programming languages. A shop that allowed
programmers to choose their own language would be a disaster, and in a
slightly less dramatic way a department that allowed staff members to
choose their own reporting or documentation format will be equally unorganized. Standards will pay off in terms of more efficient communication

and greater productivity. Reasonable standards help communication rather than hinder it.

While it is not possible to cover the complex subject of forms design in this text, managers who implement standardized forms should always consider human psychology. For example, if a particular form provides a relatively large amount of space for a particular question, the respondent will be encouraged to fill the space. A very large section labeled "problems" suggests that the respondent conjure up a significant amount of written explanation. A smaller space for the category of "Any other matters to report?" will discourage a response. People unconsciously complete a questionnaire or form in a manner that will please the originator. The forms designer or manager should always test forms and report formats on perceptive volunteers who can point out such subtle but important factors.

SERVICE REQUESTS

A good service request form must be complete enough to identify the request and its disposition, but easy for all to understand. The form is a working document that enables MIS management to track the request, its eventual completion, and its effect upon other systems, applications, or departments. The service request form becomes a permanent document available to auditors. It may even have legal retention requirements, as with industries that deal with the Food and Drug Administration, Environmental Protection Agency, or the Department of Defense.

The basis of every service request is the identification scheme to track and log requests. Obviously, each request must have some identification number or tag, but a simple sequential numbering scheme is inefficient. Request number 765 tells nothing significant about the request, except that it is after 764 and before 766. Since each request must be identified anyway, it is logical to develop a scheme that conveys some information about the nature of the request. There are many ways to create meaningful identification systems, and it is possible to develop horrendously complicated schemes that look great on paper but fail miserably when put into practice.

A simple but effective method uses the following format:

YY-SS-0001-T

Where YY is the last two digits of the year, SS is the two digit or two character mnemonic for the application system involved, 0001 is the sequential number, and T is the type of request.

With the year as the first segment, requests can be logged in chronological sequence and retrieved according to date, although date of submission varies in importance from installation to installation.

The two-position system identification breaks down requests according to the nature of the application or production system. Many shops are organized by support teams, or have individual programmers assigned to a group of specific applications. A request that has a PY for Payroll or an AP for Accounts Payable immediately identifies the responsible area or department.

Once assigned to a request, the identification number will not change, except for the type. In many business data processing organizations, a request to investigate a problem or condition may cause the originator to ask for a programming change. The original form can be used by simply changing the type code to indicate a system change rather than a research investigation.

The basic type codes are:

I = investigation

P = reported problem that needs research

A = serious problem that needs immediate research

D = data modification

F = file or data base error

C = application system change

H = assistance needed from programming

J = special job needed

R = rerun needed

M = miscellaneous request

A few of the countless variations on this identification format are:

- Using the calendar month instead of the year, if chronological order is extremely important.

- Using the year and calendar month (YYMM).

- Replacing the two position application mnemonic with the two or three position name of the requesting unit, such as ACC for accounting, FIN for finance, and MER for merchandising.

- Replacing the two-position application mnenomic with a code for the name of the analyst or manager taking the request.

- Adding a priority code as the first digit of the sequential number, where a 1 could indicate the lowest and a 5 the highest priority. However, since priority in some companies can change as often as the phases of the moon, this approach can be confusing.

Each installation needs an identification scheme that will allow a staff member to quickly categorize any request. The format should not be cumbersome or people will hesitate to use it. The identification method should answer the basic questions of who, where, and when.

A standard format for a service request form is shown in Figure 4.1.

Figure 4.1   Service request form

Form: DP-1

Wonderful Widgets, Inc.
Management Information Systems Division
SERVICE REQUEST

Please fill out section A, except for the two entries labeled "For MIS Use Only."
If you have any questions, please see Procedure Manual Three, Form DP-1.
Thank you.

Section A

Date_____   For MIS use only
Submitted by_____   *************************************
Department_____   * Log number_____-_____-_____
Phone_____   * Received by_____
Office number_____   *************************************
Requested priority

                              Emergency_____
                              Immediate_____
                              Normal_____
                              As time permits_____
                              Time critical_____

When do you need it done?_____
Application system:_____
Do you want to be notified by phone when this request is done?
yes _____
Do you want to talk about this request in person?_____
Description of request_____
_____
_____
_____
_____

Thank you. This ends section A.

Section B: For MIS Use Only

Evaluated by_____
Date received_____ Time received_____
Type: (If the type changes, cross out the old classification)
Serious problem that needs immediate attention   A_____
Problem that needs research   P_____
Application system change   C_____
Data modification   D_____
Assistance needed from programming   H_____
Investigation   I_____
Special job needed   J_____
Miscellaneous request   M_____
Rerun needed   R_____
Initial priority: 1 2 3 4 5   Date_____
Second priority: 1 2 3 4 5   Date_____
Third priority: 1 2 3 4 5   Date_____
Disposition:_____
Applications involved:_____

Route to other groups?_____

Figure 4.1   *(Continued)*

Date routed:_____ Routed to:_____

_____

Estimated completion date_____
Followup requirements_____

_____

Comments_____

_____

_____

Most forms need accompanying instructions. Certain employees have trouble completing forms and reports even when the author believes his or her masterpiece can be filled out by any intelligent second grader. It is the responsibility of the author and the management to verify that most forms are designed not only to follow management policy but to consider "human engineering." Instructions can be embedded in the form or in a separate document.

The following set of instructions applies to the MIS service request shown in Figure 4.1.

The purpose of this form is to help MIS serve you better. The more accurate the information, the better we can serve your needs. DP-1 is easy to use–just follow the instructions for each line.

Date.. Use today's date in month, day, year format.

Log number .... Do not fill in!

Submitted by............................. Your first and last name

Received by .... Do not fill in!

Requesting department .... Use the formal department name followed by your section or group name.

Submitter's phone
   and office number.................... Use your extension and office number. If you are located in the Office Annex, put an A after your office number.

Priority requested .... How critical is this request?
Use "emergency" only if it is a serious production problem or if the request must be completed ASAP.
Use "immediate" only if the request has a deadline within 72 hours.
Use "normal" most of the time.
If the request has a low priority, check "as time permits."
If you check "normal" but the request must be done by a certain time, check "time critical."

When do you need it done?...........   If there is a time requirement, list it here. Use the line only if the requirement is important.

Application system(s) ....   If you know the specific applications involved, list them on this line. If you are not sure, leave it blank.

Do you want to be notified by phone when request is done? .....   Check "yes" if you want to be called. (We always send you a copy of the completed request form.)

Do you want to talk about this request in person? ....   Check "yes" if you need a meeting to discuss the request or the timing. We will then contact you.

Description of request ....   Please describe what you need. Use extra pages if necessary. Attach any other paperwork that provides information. Try to be complete, but don't worry about MIS jargon.

If you are not sure which MIS department needs to review your request, send this form to MIS Control (office 407-B). However, if you are reasonably certain which MIS group will handle your request, send the form to that group in care of the production services coordinator. Be sure to keep a copy for yourself.

The MIS control clerk, production services coordinator, or unit manager will send you a copy with a tentative completion date in the upper right hand corner. Next to the estimated completion date will be the MIS priority code, with 5 the highest and 1 the lowest. If you do not agree with either the date or the priority, please call the unit manager.

We may contact you for additional information. We always try to be as accurate as possible, and sometimes we have questions that must be answered before we can give you an estimated completion date.

When your request has been completed, MIS will send you another copy of the completed request. If you checked "Do you want to be notified by phone when it is done?" the MIS control clerk will call or leave a message with your department secretary.

If you have any questions about the form, your request, or its current status, please contact MIS Control at extension 4598, or the unit production services coordinator.

Thank you.

The back of most MIS service request forms is the ideal location to track the status, condition, and disposition of the request. Figure 4.2 illustrates a format that can track requests over the entire maintenance or development cycle.

The back of the form should hold at least two repetitions of this information, because many requests are moved from person to person as the assignment becomes more difficult or the priorities change. The coordinator

Figure 4.2 Back of the service request form

                  For MIS use only   Log: ____-____-____

Date assigned_____ Assigned to_____
Instructions_____
_____

Estimated completion date_____
Time critical?_____ For more information see_____
Completion date_____ Filed by_____
User notified on_____ Notified by_____

Date assigned_____ Assigned to_____
Instructions_____
_____

Estimated completion date_____
Time critical_____ For more information see_____
Completion date_____ Filed by_____
User notified on_____ Notified by_____

can easily attach additional request forms and use only the back to track the request as it is moved to a third or even a fourth person. Requests often move from department to department, such as from Programming to Data Control to Operations.

While forms are traditionally oriented toward hard copy, request forms can be put online—if the majority of users have access to a CRT. However, if most requests come with attached paperwork such as flow charts, memos, report samples, or formulas, it is more efficient to use hard copy request forms. Paper may seem old-fashioned to those accustomed to online, interactive processing, but it still can be an effective medium for communication.

The proper management of service requests is a complex topic with its own rules and procedures, most of which vary from organization to organization. The most effective rules for controlling request forms are:

1. Process all requests within four business days. The user should receive a copy with the MIS portion filled out, or an explanation for any delay. Even if it will take six months or six years to complete a request, the user should know that MIS did review his idea. This four-business-day requirement is an excellent way to demonstrate a businesslike attitude.

2. Keep only one copy of the request in MIS. Duplicate copies of the same request may cause the same problems as duplicate data: It is difficult to keep them current. Even at the embarrassing risk of losing an occasional request, the analyst or programmer handling the assignment should keep the MIS copy. Of course, if the request is entered into an online tracking system, that material will never be lost unless the system crashes and erases the data.

3. Request forms must always have current status information. Some analysts and programmers dislike record keeping and forget to update the form as work progresses. Such employees rely only on their memory. This is a poor business practice that encourages misunderstanding and confusion.

4. When the task is complete, notify the user. Never assume requestors will magically know that their problem or special computer run has been completed. Few users have taken advanced training in mind reading and ESP. Notifying all users (both internal and external to MIS) is another simple but professional business practice.

The internal tracking device for service requests is the request log, which lists all pending requests and their current status. Without an accurate request log, it is virtually impossible to properly manage large numbers of work requests. More than three requests is usually considered large.

A sample format is shown in Figure 4.3, but hard copy logs are both cumbersome and inefficient. Logs work best when stored on online.

PROJECT REPORTING

Project management is a fascinating subject. The trade press is filled with advertisements and discussions of various project management systems and related software. MIS executives quietly exchange horror stories at professional meetings. The comparative evaluation of one particular method is beyond the scope of a text on technical communication. Howev-

Figure 4.3 Service request control log

Form: DP-2

Wonderful Widgets, Inc.
Management Information Systems
SERVICE REQUEST CONTROL LOG

Status Codes: I (in evaluation) H (hold) W (in progress)
C (complete) A (assigned but not started)
X (complete and user notified)

Log	Description	Received	Prty	Assigned to	Assigned date	Type	Status

er, virtually all project management methodologies depend upon a written document to communicate their status. Yet even diverse project management approaches may have similar reporting requirements. In general, the readers of any project management report need answers to five basic questions:

- How is the budget?
- How much progress has been made since the last report?
- What major checkpoints have been reached?
- What is the next major checkpoint?
- Are there any outstanding problems we should know about?
- Are you on schedule? If not, why?

The difference between useful and useless project control forms is not the volume of information, but the efficiency of communication. How well does the form convey information? Good project control forms are not only easier to use, but *help professionals accurately evaluate their positions.* After completing the form, employees should understand where they stand in relation to their project responsibilities.

Standardized project control forms and procedures help the staff become familiar with a consistent set of requirements. Project managers should seldom be allowed to experiment with reporting formats if the shop has workable standards. Experimentation is often justified in some aspects of data processing, but project management is too important to be left to a manager's whim. Rather, management as a team should select one format that satisfies the requirements and not change unless someone clearly demonstrates a better tool.

Of course, every form will eventually change, as managers and employees gain experience with its positive and negative aspects. Changes, however, should be approached cautiously, but the organization should never be afraid to strive for improvement.

Any flexible and practical project control form meets seven basic requirements:

1. The form should be easy and quick.

2. It should allow the staff member to provide information simply by circling a description or making a checkmark, rather than writing words or phrases. Most project management answers can be anticipated by the designer of the form, so the author can create a format that reduces unnecessary writing.

3. The document should not use complicated project management jargon. If a form contains vocabulary that can only be understood by staff members who have read the latest ten books on project management theory, the form will handicap employees rather than help them.

4. The form should have free form space to allow the employees to enter additional information.

5. It should be positive rather than negative. Project control forms which stress the problem aspect of data processing are depressing. Problems, complaints, and frustrations are intrinsic to data processing, but a form which has the heading "List Problems Here" in overwhelming large red letters, encourages people to focus on the negative aspects. Rather, the titles and sections should emphasize the progress made instead of the problems that hindered the employee. The author should even avoid using the word problems if at all possible, since other words such as difficulties or roadblocks convey the same meaning without the frustrating connotation.

6. The project control form should be professionally printed, either by a printer or through desk top publishing. The form should not simply be typed by the secretary and then photocopied. A sloppy or primitive looking form encourages sloppy or primitive reporting habits.

7. The format should help employees visualize their progress as it relates to the *total project development schedule*. It should allow them to arrange their deliverables so that they can see their status in relationship to the critical project milestones. Such checkpoints should not be limited to the conventional categories of code, compile, and test, but should use events in time that are meaningful for that particular project and the people who will be using that form.

Figure 4.4 lists a sample project control form which can be used by programmers, programmer/analysts, systems analysts, and technicians.

Evaluating project control forms is more of an art than a science. Since professionals differ in their quantity and quality of written expression, a manager may find one employee willing to write ten pages every week and another employee who provides "yes-or-no" answers to complex questions. A set of instructions along with feedback from the supervisor will help staff members judge the amount of effort needed to communicate essential information.

The sample project reporting form in Figure 4.4 may seem self-explanatory, but some employees will be confused by certain questions, especially those that allow free form answers. Only instructions can prevent this frustrating situation!

Figure 4.5 illustrates sample instructions that can be used for the project reporting form in Figure 4.4.

The sample project reporting form is obviously an instrument of a sound management philosophy. Employees are asked to anticipate problems, which places the burden of prediction where it belongs. They must categorically state if they are on schedule. The question on critical path needs will make them aware of timing restrictions. The form asks if they have enough

Figure 4.4 Project reporting form

Form: DP-3

Wonderful Widgets, Inc.
Management Information Systems Division
PROJECT REPORTING FORM

Name_____ Dept._____ Number_____ Date_____
Project name_____ Project code_____
Period covered from:_____ TO:_____
Circle the activities in progress:

design	program specs	code	testing	interface
unit testing	user education			documentation
implementation	follow up			internal documentation

1. List tasks/deliverables completed during this reporting period.

Task/deliverable	Start Date	End Date	Planned Date

2. List any tasks or jobs in progress:

Task	Status	Estimated End Date

3. List any holdups or stumbling blocks encountered during this reporting period.

4. Do you have any goals for the next reporting period that are not mentioned in Question 2?

5. Do you anticipate any difficulties during this next reporting period?

6. Are you on schedule with your assignments?

7. List the assignments of other project team members or users which could have a critical path impact on your progress during the next two reporting periods.

Figure 4.4 *(Continued)*

8. Do you have enough project work to keep busy during the next reporting period?

_____

9. List any significant nonproject work you have performed during this reporting period. Estimate the time spent and the degree of difficulty.

_____

_____

10. Is there anything else your manager should know about your work or the project itself?

_____

_____

_____

11. Would you like a conference with your manager?
    Yes_____   No_____

---

productive work to keep busy—if not, the supervisor will find them some. The questions place responsibility directly on the staff member. There is no doubt on a week by week basis if the professional is on schedule, faces critical path delays, or has enough work to do. This form will help implement a management policy of no surprises.

TASK CONTROL

First level managers often notice that a few programmers, programmer/ analysts, and systems analysts accomplish several times more than others in the department. They are commonly described as "good workers" or "highly motivated." Perhaps one reason for the startling difference in performance is that the professionals know how to manage their time, while the amateurs let their time manage them. Self-motivation is also an important factor, but even highly dedicated employees cannot function at full productivity unless they are in control of their tasks, assignments, and daily schedules.

The human mind is notoriously poor at monitoring multiple tasks and schedules at the same time. While a few lucky people can correctly juggle many assignments simultaneously, most of us need a written tool that tells us what we are working on, how long it should take, its relative priority, and its relationship to other tasks. Those tools are commonly called "project plans" or "task control forms," and they help the professional arrange his time to accomplish the most.

Task control forms vary with the nature of the position and the type of person involved. Some jobs in MIS—such as systems analysts doing research on wide area networks—require very little specific task control. They may have general weekly or monthly goals, but their day-to-day performance is directed by what they find in their reading or contacts with other organizations using local area networks. Other positions—such as a

Figure 4.5   Instructions for project control form

Form DP-4
Wonderful Widgets, Inc.
Management Information System Division
Instructions for Completing Project Control Form

Identifying Information:

—Fill out your name, department, employee number, and the date (normally a Monday).
—Write the formal project name and code as listed in your MIS Procedures Manual.
—For a weekly reporting period, enter the "from" date as last Monday, and the "to" date as last Friday. For a monthly report, use the "from" date as the first Monday of the calendar month and the "to" date as the last Friday of the calendar month.
—Your project manager may give you special dates for monthly reporting.
—Circle the activities that best describe your status. If you are just finishing one and starting another, circle them both. If these terms do not describe your situation, write your own descriptive name.

Status

1. List completed tasks during this reporting period. Use the task name from your project plan. Enter the date completed and the estimated date from the project plan. For "date complete," use the date when all follow-up work was finished.
2. Enter all project related tasks in progress, but do not include production support or other assignments. The "percent complete" should describe where you stand today. Use a percent figure in "tens," such as 40 or 50 percent complete. Enter the date you started the task, and the date you expect to finish. The estimated end date does not have to match the project plan end date, but should reflect your current estimate.
3. List any holdups or roadblocks you have faced during the past week (or month if you are on monthly reporting). These can be unexpected design problems, changes in specifications, test time limitations, etc.
4. Define your goals for this week (or month) for the project. Do not repeat any listed under Question 2.
5. List any anticipated difficulties during this next week (or month).
6. Are you on schedule according to the current Project Plan? If not, list any reasons that help explain the situation. You may refer to Questions 3 and 5, but do not repeat information unless absolutely necessary.
7. List the assignments of other project team members that could hold you up if those tasks are not complete. Use your copy of the Master Project Plan and look at Critical Path junctions for the next two reporting periods. Write the task number and name.
8. Do you have enough productive work to keep busy? This refers only to project work. If the answer is "no," your manager will contact you.
9. List all nonproject work (but not administrative or reporting duties) that have affected your performance. Mention only assignments that were not budgeted in your Project Plan. For example, include production support tasks only if they went beyond the time originally allocated.
10. Is there anything else your project manager should know about this past week (or month), or about your general progress?
11. Do you wish to meet with your project manager to discuss either this report or the project itself?

programmer/analyst doing production support or a manager supervising a project team—will have specific duties. Those individuals can benefit most from some type of task control form.

A simple manual approach for employees who have rapidly changing assignments is a set of plain 3 × 5 filing cards (one card per task) with the following information:

Work request number

Task name

System

Source of request

Date due

Estimated hours

Actual hours

Completion date

Follow-up needed?

These headings can be arranged in a logical order that fits the needs of the organization. If management decides to use a manual card approach, the format should be standardized across all departments in MIS. This information can also be stored in an online system which will give other people the ability to see assignments and progress. An online method is preferable to a card system if the system is designed for simplicity. A common mistake is that managers designing an online system put in so many bells and whistles that the application becomes cumbersome for the employees, which inevitably means it will slowly fade into oblivion, much to everyone's relief. Simplicity is more than a virtue when implementing task control procedures!

Once the system is installed and the staff becomes familiar with its operation and benefits, management can slowly add features to provide additional reporting capabilities.

WEEKLY STATUS REPORTS

The weekly status report is an MIS tradition as much as empty pizza cartons scattered about the offices of programmers facing a deadline. Most staff level employees fill out a report weekly (or at least monthly), and they usually dislike it just as much as their managers dislike reading them. The problem is not the concept of weekly reporting, but rather that many weekly status reports are virtually worthless. Everyone involved learns the truth very quickly. The staff members know that the status reports do not truly reflect their week, and the manager discovers that weekly reports are seldom useful for either people or task management. Some first line supervisors tend to treat the weekly status report as another paperwork nuisance that must be completed before the real work begins.

How unfortunate for everyone in MIS! The weekly status report is a perfect opportunity for employees to show what they have accomplished and where they now stand, and an equally promising opportunity for management to capture the activities of each staff member for the previous week. The weekly status report should become one of the most important management tools available to junior, middle, and even senior managers. This is possible only if MIS managers consciously decide to create a good, workable format.

Even the best format is useless unless the procedures associated with weekly reporting are just as logical. Some excellent guidelines are:

1. *Several forms of weekly status reports are needed.* One weekly status report format will never apply to all employees. Staff members have different roles and responsibilities at different times, and it is difficult to create one generalized status report that will handle everything from production support assignments to feasibility studies. If job responsibilities are significantly different, management should provide significantly different weekly report formats.

2. *Managers and supervisors should also submit written status reports.* Many MIS organizations do not require employees at the supervisory level or managerial level to fill out their own weekly reports. In those cases, staff members who have made it to a management position feel they no longer must account for their time. This is an incorrect assumption if management is truly concerned with the productivity of everyone in the department. MIS executives should insist that first- and second-level managers also complete weekly reports (their report formats will be designed specifically for management activities). A manager's time is just as valuable as the time spent by a programmer/analyst installing the new payroll system. In fact, one could argue that since managers are typically paid more than line employees, their time should be tracked more carefully!

3. *A good form will encourage two-way communication by allowing employees to initiate* informal dialogues or formal meetings with their manager. Every form should have a statement such as, "Do you need to discuss anything with your manager?" Even if the manager has a strong open door policy, certain employees are reluctant to make the first move, and the paperwork can be their icebreaker.

4. *Each weekly status report should be used as an evaluation tool.* When the inevitable question arises during the annual performance appraisal of, "What exactly did he do?" the manager should review the stack of weekly reports in chronological order. One criterion for judging a form is its usefulness in employee evaluations. *If the manager cannot use the weekly report for performance evaluations, the form needs improvement.*

5. *Warn employees that their weekly report will be used in their performance appraisal.* While other factors will certainly enter into the final evaluation picture, the weekly report will be a major tool for grading their progress toward previously assigned goals.

6. *Provide weekly feedback for a weekly report.* All employees need feedback concerning their weekly report, even if the manager simply says, "I can't read this line." If their manager even appears to ignore weekly reports, employees will become careless and lose interest in tracking their accomplishments. If the manager does not care about weekly reporting, neither will their employees.

7. *If staff members spend virtually all their time on a project, allow them to use the project control form as their weekly report.* If another reporting method gives the manager a fair indication of the entire weeks effort, the manager should never insist upon duplicate reports. Common sense is a good yardstick for applying standards.

8. *Require goals, but understand the complexities of goal setting.* MBO (management by objectives) is a powerful tool for directing and controlling people resources, and can easily be misused. In extreme cases, employees and their management alike can play games by manipulating plans to show they always meet their objectives. Their weekly goals may have been set so low that their success is virtually assured, while more ambitious staff members set personal goals beyond normal reach. The objective of every dedicated employee should be to become fully productive, and not to use the MBO approach to make himself or herself look good at the expense of his organization.

   Goals should be required on every weekly report, but they must be closely monitored by the immediate manager. A true MBO program helps both staff and managers improve their own performance, while rewarding superior effort. It never encourages or allows employees to use weekly reports to polish their public image.

Useful status reports come in many shapes and sizes. Figure 4.6 presents a weekly status report for a staff professional who has multiple assignments, such as a programmer/analyst performing production support tasks. Figure 4.7 is a status report for an individual who has consistent job responsibilities from week to week, such as a data control technician or computer operator. Figure 4.8 is a status report for professionals engaged in high level systems design, consulting, research, or management. The entries on each form are designed to match the typical activities of each group.

Notice that all three formats contain specific instructions as a part of the actual form, which eliminates the need to have separate documents for instructions.

These three formats force employees to define their roles or primary function, duties, and the relative priority of their assignments. Managers

Figure 4.6 Weekly status format for a multiple assignment professional

Wonderful Widgets, Inc.
Management Information Systems Division
WEEKLY STATUS REPORT

Name_____ Section_____ Date_____
Period covered: Week_____ Month_____ Other_____
Primary assignment_____
Do you want this report routed to anyone else? Who?

_____   _____   _____

1. List the tasks you have completed this week, which have taken more than two hours of
   your time. Estimate the hours used. If you have notified the user or requestor that the
   task has been completed, check the user column. Check the follow-up column if you need to
   spend additional time this week on that task.

Task	Start Date	End Date	Hours Used	Notified User?	Follow-up Needed?

2. List in general terms the tasks which have taken you less than two hours. Count the
   approximate number of times you performed the task this week. Indicate who or where
   the task came from, if that is appropriate. List any additional information in the comments
   column.

Task	Times Performed	Source	Comments

3. List the tasks in progress which will take more than two hours. Fill out the start date,
   estimated end date, a percent complete estimate (in tens of a percent), and a comment in
   the current status field that best describes your progress.

Task	Start Date	Est End Date	% Complete	Current Status

4. Are you waiting for assistance or information from any other section, department, unit, or
   vendor, that is holding up any of your assignments?

Figure 4.6   *(Continued)*

5. List any roadblocks or potential roadblocks that were not listed in Question 4.

6. What are your goals for this next reporting period? (Do not repeat information from Question 3.)

7. Prioritize your assignments.

8. Do you want to talk to your supervisor about this report?
   Yes_____   No_____

9. Do you have any other important information about this past reporting period that has not been mentioned?

are forced to rate their own time management skills on a weekly basis. The type of question asked on any status report should reflect the organizations's concerns.

EXPERIENCE EVALUATION FORMS

One of the first responsibilities of the senior staff is to accurately measure the experience and skill levels of new employees. Many experienced MIS managers feel that even detailed interviewing during the hiring process does not give supervisors a reliable picture of the potential employee, except in very general terms. Although progressive installations are now implementing careful prehiring screening techniques, other organizations still rely only on the classic interview activity to categorize future employees. But without a standardized evaluation procedure, it may take weeks or even months for a supervisor to discover the true capabilities of the newly hired professional. This delay is both unacceptable and avoidable.

Figure 4.7   Weekly report for consistent type positions

Form: DP-6

Wonderful Widgets, Inc.
Management Information Systems Division
WEEKLY STATUS REPORT

Name_____ Section_____ Date_____

Period Covered: Week_____ Month_____ Other_____

Primary Assignment_____

1. List your general duties under the task column. Enter the approximate percent of time
   you spent last week on that task. Use the A-B-C priority code, with A the highest and C
   the lowest. Use the comments space to provide additional information.

Task	% of Time Spent	Prty	Comments
_____	_____	_____	_____
_____	_____	_____	_____
_____	_____	_____	_____
_____	_____	_____	_____
_____	_____	_____	_____
_____	_____	_____	_____
_____	_____	_____	_____
_____	_____	_____	_____

2. Did you have any task not completed on time? If so, list the task and the reasons, if known.

   _____

   _____

   _____

3. List any roadblocks or delays in completing your assignments.

   _____

   _____

   _____

4. Do you have any additional information regarding the last reporting period, or any
   suggestions?

   _____

   _____

   _____

   _____

5. Do you want to talk to your supervisor about this report?
   Yes_____   No_____

Management also needs to periodically study the existing employees to
determine both ongoing training needs and possible staff reassignments.
By evaluating employees in a standardized manner, the results can be
compared from year to year or even quarter to quarter. Such surveys also
demonstrate individual growth and progress and may be used during
performance reviews.

One technique to evaluate both new and current employees is through a
written skills survey or experience evaluation. The title of the document is
not important, but the purpose is vital: to capture a technical "snapshot" of

Figure 4.8   Weekly report for a manager or senior professional

Form: DP-7

Wonderful Widgets, Inc.
Management Information Systems Division
WEEKLY STATUS REPORT

Name_____ Section_____ Date_____
Period covered: Week_____ Month_____ Other_____
Primary assignment_____

1. In priority sequence (A-B-C), list your personal assignments. Estimate the percentage of the time you spent on each task. Briefly summarize the status of each assignment.

Assignment	% Time	Status

2. What problems did you have last week that affected your work or your group's performance?

3. Rate your own time management skills during the past reporting period.
   Good   _____
   Adequate   _____
   Unsatisfactory   _____
   Explain the reasons for an unsatisfactory rating.

4. What scheduled assignments did you complete last week? Do not include tasks assigned to subordinates or others, and do not list projects that are reported in other documents. List only personal accomplishments.

5. List any personal time critical assignments due during the next four weeks.

6. If you manage people, are you caught up with your administrative requirements?
   Yes_____   No_____

7. Do you have any additional information that should be discussed with your own manager?

each employee so he or she can be directed to the right training program or job assignment. The experience evaluation form can also be used as an interview screening device, if approved by the company's legal department. Any interview material should not violate or even appear to violate federal equal opportunity provisions, although documents that deal only with technical matters usually have no problem in that sensitive area.

Figure 4.9 is a sample skills survey or "experience evaluation" form that can be used to screen new employees, analyze the current MIS staff, and look at potential reassignments. The example is oriented toward a large IBM mainframe installation with IMS and IDMS, and the survey used in other types of organizations would reflect their own technical environment.

Figure 4.9   Experience evaluation form for the systems and programming staff

Form: DP-8

Wonderful Widgets, Inc.
Management Information Systems Division
PROFESSIONAL SKILLS SURVEY

Name_____ Date_____
Section_____ Manager_____

This questionnaire is not a test or performance evaluation. The purpose is to help us understand the training and experience needs of our professional staff. Please fill out Sections I through IV, and return to your manager within five working days.

Thank you.

PROFESSIONAL SKILLS SURVEY

Section I. General Technical Experience

1. Check the operating systems you have used, and select the term that best describes your experience level.

System	Extensive	Moderate	Minimal
MVS/XA	_____	_____	_____
VM	_____	_____	_____
DOS/VSE	_____	_____	_____
DOS/SSX	_____	_____	_____
Others			
_____	_____	_____	_____
_____	_____	_____	_____

2. What computers have you worked with?

Manufacturer/Model	Years Experience
_____	_____
_____	_____
_____	_____
_____	_____

Describe any mini-, microcomputer, or workstation experience (other than word processing). Include hardware, software, and languages.

_____
_____
_____
_____

Figure 4.9 *(Continued)*

If you have never worked with a micro or mini, are you interested in a future opportunity in the mini or micro areas?

_____
_____
_____

4. Have you ever done any system software work, such as operating system or compiler "gens?"

_____
_____
_____

5. Have you ever worked with IBM MVS utility programs? If yes, describe the hardware/software configuration.

_____

Check the utilities you have successfully used.

IEBPTPCH	_____
IEBCOPY	_____
IEBCOMPR	_____
IEBDG	_____
IEBGENER	_____
IEBISAM	_____
IEBUPDTE	_____
IEHLIST	_____
IEHMOVE	_____
IEHPROGM	_____
IDCAMS	_____

Which ones are you most confident with?

_____

Have you had any formal training in utilities? If not, would you like a course or instruction in their use?

_____

6. If you have worked with IBM MVS JCL, check the areas, items, and concepts you are familiar with. Select the rating that best describes your experience level.
   1 = Very familiar
   2 = Can handle most situations without assistance
   3 = Have some experience, but occasionally need help
   4 = Very little experience, reading knowledge only

AREA	RATING
Instream procs	
Catalogued procs	
JCL overrides to procs	_____
Generation data groups	
Written procs from scratch	
Worked with tape files	
Worked with disk files	
Partitioned data sets (PDS)	_____
ISAM	
VSAM	
Direct access files	
Reruns of production jobs	
Restarted production jobs	_____

AREA	RATING
Written procs from scratch	_____
Worked with tape files	_____
Worked with disk files	_____
Partitioned data sets (PDS)	_____
ISAM	_____
VSAM	_____
Direct access files	_____
Reruns of production jobs	_____
Restarted production jobs	_____
Written restart instructions	_____
Used symbolic parms to pass information to a proc	_____
Modified production procs	_____
Calculated disk space requirements	_____
Determined backup/restore requirements	_____

7. Check the software packages you have worked with.

LIBRARIAN	_____
ROSCOE	_____
RPF'S	_____
PANVALET	_____
TSO	_____
TSO/SPF	_____
CLISTS	_____
CICS	_____
IMS DL/I	_____
IMS DB/DC	_____

Other data bases or TP monitors?

_____

_____

_____

SAS	_____
FOCUS	_____
EASYTRIEVE PLUS	_____

Other report writers or mainframe software packages?

_____

_____

_____

8. Have you worked on systems requiring teleprocessing?
   If so, please describe_____

   _____

9. Have you worked with any other hardware/software combinations not listed above, such
   as point-of-sale, direct order entry, CAD/CAM. optical memory, or bank automated
   teller terminals?

   _____

   _____

10. Have you ever supported production jobs, such as Payroll or General Ledger? If so, list
    the systems and describe the extent of your involvement.

    _____

    _____

    _____

Figure 4.9 *(Continued)*

11. Have you ever been "on-call" in a production environment? If yes, describe your experience.

_____

_____
_____
_____

12. Are you interested in the hardware aspect of data processing? If so, please explain.

_____
_____
_____

13. Have you interfaced with an operations section? If so, describe your involvement.

_____
_____
_____

14. Have you had design experience with:
Program or module design   _____
Integrated modules   _____
Complete systems   _____
Summarize your design experience.

_____
_____
_____

15. Over your entire career, how much direct user interface have you had?
None   _____
Limited   _____
Significant   _____
Extensive   _____

Describe your user contact. Was it problem resolution, consulting, systems design, training, etc.?

_____
_____
_____
_____
_____

16. Have you worked with any purchased application system packages? If so, list the package, vendor, and your involvement.

_____
_____
_____
_____

17. Have you debugged programs using core or memory dumps?_____
If yes, rate your skill at solving problems through a core dump. Mention any automated packages or debugging tools you have used.

_____
_____
_____

18. Have you written any system design proposals, or done any feasibility studies? If so, describe your involvement.

_____
_____

---

19. Please summarize your *previous* DP experience:

Years	Company	Company Business	Duties
———	———————	———————	————————————
———	———————	———————	————————————
———	———————	———————	————————————
———	———————	———————	————————————
———	———————	———————	————————————
———	———————	———————	————————————

Section II. Languages and Data Base

1. If you are now using PL/I, or have used PL/I in the past, please answer all the questions in this group:

   How many years experience do you have with PL/I?_____

   What version(s) have you used?_____

   Check the terms you can define and discuss in detail.

   Based variables   ———————

   Controlled storage   —

   Index area   ———————

   Fixedoverflow   ———————

   Oncode 8097   ———————

   Pointer   ———————

   Static   ———————

   Dynamic allocation   ———————

   DSA   ———————

   TCA   ———————

   Regional(1)   ———————

   Recursive   ———————

   Aligned   ———————

   External variable   ———————

   Order/reorder   ———————

   Are you familiar with these concepts?

   Based I/O   ———————

   Record I/O   ———————

   "By name" option   ———————

   Label variables   ———————

   Substr   ———————

   PLIRETC   ———————

   PL/I internal sorts   ———————

   Allocate   ———————

   2 dimension tables   ———————

   How do you rate your general knowledge of PL/I?

   (Check one of the following five statements.)

   1. Can handle almost all requirements of PL/I ———————
   2. Can handle most PL/I requirements   ———————
   3. Good knowledge of PL/I, but need help   ———————
   4. Can read PL/I and understand logic   ———————
   5. Minimal knowledge of PL/I   ———————

   How good is your ability to read and debug PL/I core dumps?

Figure 4.9 *(Continued)*

6. What do you need in terms of PL/I training? Please be as specific as possible.

_____
_____
_____
_____

2. If you are now using ASSEMBLER, or have used it in the past, please answer all the questions in this group:
   How many years ASSEMBLER experience do you have _____
   On what operating system(s) _____
   Which instructions can you use?

MVC	____	IM	____	BAL	____
BALR	____	CVD	____	CVB	____
SRDL	____	BCT	____	EDMK	____
MVI	____	LR	____	STH	____
LM	____	EX	____	MP	____

In a core dump, can you pick out zoned decimal, packed, and binary numbers?_____
Are you familiar with any of the following?
Packed decimal arithmetic   _____
Fixed point arithmetic   _____
Boolean logic and its use   _____
Variable records   _____
PDS's   _____
Direct access files   _____
QSAM   _____
BSAM   _____
QISAM   _____
QTAM   _____
EXCP coding   _____
TCAM   _____
Graphics access method   _____
Changing a JFCB   _____
Writing your own macros   _____
Reentrant coding   _____
What are your strongest areas of ASSEMBLER programming?

_____
_____
_____

In what areas do you need more training or experience?

_____
_____
_____
_____

3. If you currently use COBOL, or have used it in the past, please answer all the questions in this group:
   How many years of COBOL experience do you have?

_____

What version(s) of COBOL have you used? Under what CPUs and what operating systems?

_____
_____
_____

Check the terms you can define and discuss in detail.

comp	————	comp-3	————	comp-2	————
tallying	————	occurs	————	exit	————
renames	————	move	————	perform	————
search	————	set (index)	————	compute	————
group indicate————					

Are you familiar with these topics?

Report writer	————
ISAM files	————
Direct access files	————
Calling ASSEMBLER modules from COBOL	————

How would you rate your COBOL skills? Are they adequate to perform your current job functions?

_____

_____

_____

What would you like to see in terms of COBOL training?

_____

_____

_____

Can you debug COBOL modules from a core dump?_____

If you have used IMS, please answer these questions:

Check the terms you can discuss in detail.

Root segment	————	Command code	————
PCB	————	PSB	————
SENSEG	————	PSBGEN	————
GU	————	GNP	————
DLET	————	ISRT	————
Unqualified SSA	————	Qualified SSA	————
Multiple PCB's	————		

List the four types of IMS access methods.

1. _____

2. _____

3. _____

4. _____

What would you like to see in terms of additional IMS training?_____

_____

_____

_____

If you have used IDMS, please answer all the questions in the group.

Check the terms you can define in detail:

Currency	————	DML	————
Occurences	————	DMCL	————
Junction record	————	Record locking	————
LRF	————	Mapless dialog	————
Owner	————	Subschema	————
Get next	————	Schema	————
Calc key	————	Application	————
Area sweep	————	Index	————
Walk the set	————		
IDD			

Have you written ██████████ ———— How many?————

Have you written ██████ s?———— How many?————

Can you read a Bac██

Figure 4.9 *(Continued)*

Section III. Development Life Cycle Experience

A. Life Cycles

1. What formal life cycles (SDLC) have you used?

_____
_____
_____
_____
_____
_____

2. Can you explain the rationale and benefits for an SDLC?

_____
_____
_____

3. Can you list projects or situations where a formal SDLC is not appropriate?

_____
_____
_____

4. Have you used a prototyping tool? If so, explain the circumstances.

_____
_____
_____

B. Structured Analysis and Design

1. Have you created any of the following?
   Data flow diagrams
   Entity relationship models   _____
   Environmental model   _____
   Process specifications   _____
   Event list   _____
   Structure charts   _____
   Context diagrams   _____

2. Have you used a CASE tool for any of the following?
   Analysis   _____   Product: _____
   Design   _____   Product: _____
   Reverse engineering   _____   Product: _____
   Code generation   _____   Product: _____

Section IV. Application Systems Experience

Use the following scale to rate yourself on a combination of experience and knowledge of business application systems. Remember that different companies have different names for the same business function.

Your rating should include both current experience and previous employment.

0 = None
1 = Very little
2 = Some experience but limited knowledge
3 = Practical working experience
4 = Good experience and knowledge
5 = Excellent experience

A.	Payroll	0	1	2	3	4	5
B.	General Ledger	0	1	2	3	4	5
C.	Accounts Payable	0	1	2	3	4	5
D.	Accounts Receivable	0	1	2	3	4	5
E.	Profit and Loss	0	1	2	3	4	5
F.	Inventory Control	0	1	2	3	4	5
G.	Open Orders	0	1	2	3	4	5
H.	Sales Reporting	0	1	2	3	4	5
I.	Forecasting	0	1	2	3	4	5
J.	Order Processing	0	1	2	3	4	5
K.	Warehouse Control	0	1	2	3	4	5
L.	Warehouse Scheduling	0	1	2	3	4	5
M.	Billing/Invoicing	0	1	2	3	4	5
N.	Purchase Orders	0	1	2	3	4	5
O.	Bill of Materials	0	1	2	3	4	5
P.	MRP	0	1	2	3	4	5
Q.	Shop Floor Control	0	1	2	3	4	5
R.	Automatic Data Collection	0	1	2	3	4	5
S.	Automated Storage Retrieval Systems	0	1	2	3	4	5

Check the terms you can define:

A. Purchase orders _____

B. Open order _____

C. Billing invoice _____

D. Warehouse slot _____

E. Back order _____

F. Journal entry _____

G. Chart of accounts _____

H. General ledger account _____

I. Payroll check register _____

J. Offsetting entry _____

K. Picking document _____

L. Wholesale distributor _____

In general, how do you rate your current knowledge of the application systems you are working with? Would you like any specific training or education?

_____

_____

_____

_____

_____

_____

Section V. Training Needs

Please list any ideas, comments, or suggestions for a training and internal education program, especially as it relates to your own situation.

_____

_____

_____

_____

Thank you. Please return this form to your manager.

Figure 4.9 *(Continued)*

Section VI. Manager's Comments

(To be filled out by the employees supervisor or manager)

Please review the ratings and information in the first four sections. Can you add any more detail or suggestions for this individual?

_____

_____

_____

_____

_____

_____

_____

_____

MONTHLY AND QUARTERLY REPORTS

Mention the subject of monthly or quarterly reports to most managers or senior level staff members and they will frown, complain, groan, moan, or change the subject (or some combination thereof). Periodic status reports are looked upon as the price one must pay for holding a supervisory or management level position. Even a company president must prepare a monthly, quarterly, and yearly report for the board of directors or similar group. Of course, senior level company executives, such as company presidents, may have assistants to handle such dirty work, but typical line managers have only themselves.

The job of writing a progress report is another opportunity to improve communication throughout the department. Managers who effectively communicate the status of their section (which includes successes, failures, and everything in between) are looked upon by their superiors as managers who successfully tell their story. Senior company management frequently complains that data processing executives live in their own independent worlds, and one example is the poor communication skills of many MIS managers. Logically designed monthly and quarterly reports will help reduce that serious communications gap.

The underlying tone of a monthly report is very important. The author must honestly state the situation without painting either too bleak or too optimistic a picture. Effective monthly reports avoid emotion, present the facts objectively, and allow the readers to draw their own conclusions. Some managers try to use their monthly or quarterly report as a tool to intimidate or blame others in the organization. This approach rarely works; in many situations it will earn a poor reputation for the writer and outright sympathy for the victim. The author who has accusatory or similar statements, should save them for private documents. As a general rule, writers should only make statements in a report that they would feel comfortable making directly to another person. If a statement (or accusation) fails this test, it should be removed from the monthly report.

Section, unit, and departmental reports should be public documents if at all possible. With the recent trend toward participatory management and the desire to improve the flow of communication between management and employee, the author should distribute the report to at least the next level down in the corporate hierarchy. Second- or third-level managers can also give each member of their group an individual copy of their own reports. While management experts differ as to the amount and type of information that should be spread throughout the organization, most executives believe that a monthly or quarterly status report should be given to the manager's immediate subordinates.

Formal monthly reports must have correct grammar, syntax, and logical paragraph structures. The managers who do not have the basic writing skills to create a readable document should either develop those skills before the next month end report or ask a qualified person to edit the work. No matter how productive and impressive the accomplishments, a poorly written progress report will always leave feelings of frustration and disappointment.

A monthly or quarterly report longer than two pages needs a short summary as the first entry. The size of the pages or the amount of information packed into each page makes little difference: Many people prefer to read summaries rather than detail, and two pages seems to be the "cross-over" point. Monthly reports are usually given to other managers or even employees outside of the MIS department who may not have the desire or time to read a four-page monthly report. Frank Flowchart may write his monthly report for MIS Director Sherman Super, but he may also give copies to Tina Template and Larry Ledger. Both Tina and Larry will learn more about Frank's work from a short summary they actually read than from a four-page report they throw in the wastebasket. *People generally do read summaries.*

The following is a general purpose format that can handle a wide variety of MIS activities, including production support, project development, and operations. Again, senior management must require all departments and sections to follow a standard format so that reports from one level can be combined with other reports to feed the next higher reporting level. The programming managers should be able to easily combine and condense the reports from their three unit managers into their own departmental monthly report. The MIS directors should also be able to combine and condense the four department reports into their own final divisional monthly report. This practice works successfully only if the management teams use standardized report formats.

I. *Summary* (if needed)

II. *Major accomplishments:* A major accomplishment is one that required significant effort or had a definite impact upon the department, a customer, or the end product. In some installations the term *major accomplishment* varies so much from manager to manager that one report may list ten pages of major accomplishments while another mentions only three items. Did the department with ten pages of major accomplishments always do a better job than a department with only three major tasks? Obviously not. Unless senior management carefully defines and enforces the category of major accomplishments, the individual monthly reports may be worthless for comparison purposes.

III. *Major project status:* Most units in MIS have at least one important project that will take more than one calendar month. Such projects need a separate discussion in the monthly report that does not repeat information in the major accomplishments section, but rather summarizes the general status. The writer also states if the project is on, ahead of, or behind schedule, the budget situation, and the reasons for any deviation from the latest approved plan.

IV. *Activity summary:* This section analyzes the time spent by the group or unit in terms of planned and unplanned activities. Training, vacations, and education are known events that can be planned for with appropriate scheduling. Unplanned events such as an illness or a sudden request for a programmer's time to help with a critical data base abend cannot be anticipated, but do help explain how employees spent their time.

The activity summary is often difficult to write, but it can be the most enlightening. After all, company management continually asks the question, "How do all those people spend their time?" The activity summary should answer that query.

V. *Major goals for the next period:* A goal section should be the manager's "latest best estimate" as to the objectives that can reasonably be expected by the end of the next reporting period. If the goals are not reasonable but must be scheduled anyway, the employee should categorize the goals as time critical. This alerts all readers of the sensitive commitment, and leaves no room for ignorance. Only important goals that meet the requirements of section II should be included. The exception may be those relatively small but critical objectives that impact other departments or which have contractual obligations.

VI. *Progress toward quarterly or yearly goals:* Section VI will analyze the progress made toward meeting those goals. If no progress has been made, or if the department is falling behind in meeting those objectives, this section can discuss the reasons. The purpose is to ensure that all units in the division are both aware of their long-term goals and are periodically evaluating their progress toward those same objectives.

VII. *Problems:* All problems are not equal. This section lists the problems or roadblocks that have surfaced in four areas:

Planned intermittent
Planned reoccurring
Unplanned intermittent
Unplanned reoccurring

Planned implies the manager knew in advance of the situation. *Intermittent* suggests a problem that occurs sporadically or on a one time basis. *Reoccurring* describes a problem that has occurred more than once during the reporting period.

This four-way separation of problems forces the writer to categorize those roadblocks in terms that will help him effectively plan for the future. After listing the problems, authors can either propose solutions in their monthly report or in another document.

VIII. *Conclusions:* The last section answers the general question, "How is the department doing in relation to its objectives?" While the other sections concentrate on facts and measurable events, the conclusion section is the appropriate place for value judgments. Ideally, the previous factual statements will support those conclusions.

Since a monthly or quarterly report should be a public document, the author should avoid appearing either too pessimistic or overly optimistic. Rather, the author's attitude should be one of positive professionalism.

MEMOS

If written communication is the lifeblood of modern business, the common memo is the energy that keeps the body going or the garbage that clogs up the arteries. Some companies have so many memos floating from person to person that employees spend more time writing memos than performing their job functions. Other organizations discourage memos and rely upon verbal communication.

It is easy to overuse memos and ignore the telephone or face-to-face communication. Personal discussions can solve many problems, obtain information, and present ideas in a relatively friendly manner. Verbal communication is best used for taking preliminary steps toward an agreement that will eventually be documented. Memos, however, are another method of explaining, presenting, and settling the important issues in the MIS division.

Memos cause work, not only for the author but for the reader as well. The recipient may wonder what to do with a particular memo. Is it for information only, or does it require a reply? When should the response be made? Is the memo time critical? Must the entire memo be read, even if it contains five pages of boring detail the reader barely understands? How does it affect the reader and the reader's work? Employees dealing with a flood of paperwork and reports can waste incalculable hours pondering those questions, even if they are never verbalized. When busy people receive another memo, their first reaction may be: What do I do with it? Such questions not only waste time, they often lead to the wrong course of action. Productivity is enhanced when the recipient knows immediately how to handle a piece of paper.

The solution is twofold. First, the author of the memo must tell the recipient the expected response. If the author does not know what action is expected, then why send the piece of paper or electronic message? Second, the format of the memo must communicate in a simple and non-threatening manner. The recipient may not agree with the disposition suggestions of the author, but at least the author should establish a starting point.

Figure 4.10 presents a memo heading format that allows the writer to express action recommendations for recipients.

Using the requested disposition feature is complicated when writing to a nonsubordinate. The author cannot simply order the respondent to reply by a certain date; one does not tell a person higher in the pecking order or in another department what to do and when to do it. One can avoid the problem by leaving the date blank in the heading but suggest a date in the body of the text. If the date is phrased in the form of a question, the recipient will not be insulted. For example, one might say, "If possible, can you respond by September 14?" When writing to colleagues, a systems analyst would specify a requested disposition date, but when writing to the

Figure 4.10   Standard internal memo

		Form: DP-9

Wonderful Widgets, Inc.
Management Information Systems
INTERNAL MEMO

To:_____ From:_____ date_____
Subject:_____
Filing subject if different_____
Distribution list:

Name	Dept	Requested Disposition		
		Reply By	Action By	FYI Only
_____	____	_____	_____	_____
_____	____	_____	_____	_____
_____	____	_____	_____	_____
_____	____	_____	_____	_____
_____	____	_____	_____	_____
_____	____	_____	_____	_____

MIS director, the analyst would suggest a date in the memo. Tact is always wise, especially when writing to one's own manager.

Memos should contain a filing subject heading, because the subject listed may not indicate the overall category under which it should be classified. Standardized filing subjects allows employees to set up filing systems that match those in the rest of the company. If all memos that pertain to the Worm Farm Management System project are not categorized by the authors, one staff member will keep those memos in a file called "Worms" while another saves the documents in a file labeled "Muddy Flats, Iowa, Project."

The body of a memo should use an outline form. The sequential nature of an outline communicates more efficiently than straight text. A memo should rarely be written in narrative prose; rather, it should be similar to a user manual, with frequent headings, clearly delineated sections, and no unnecessary words and phrases. A good memo may even seem choppy during the first reading, but that feeling of conciseness does not interfere with communication. Memos should never use excess words! They should be brief, concise, and relevant.

Any memo longer than two pages requires a summary. Busy managers and professionals will often choose between reading a summary or tossing the memo unread into their in-baskets. Summaries are read more often than complete memos. Writing the summary also helps the authors condense their thoughts and focus on the true purpose of their documents.

UNPLEASANT NEWS

Every professional eventually faces a situation in which they must inform their manager or another executive of bad news. Such information may concern a cost overrun, a system design that overlooked a key point, a rejected idea, or an opinion that goes against the manager's thinking. Although some human relations experts suggest that bad news is best given in person, there are many occasions when those embarrassing cost overruns or equally embarrassing system design deficiencies must be discussed in writing.

The first rule for delivering nasty information is to proceed cautiously. Never write a memo or report when angry, upset, or frustrated. Most organizations do not need memos that sound angry, upset, or frustrated, because such documents trigger unproductive emotional responses. The only thing worse than an angry employee is an angry employee facing an equally angry manager. Both may be losers in the end.

The second rule is to gently prepare the reader before the paperwork arrives. The author should warn the recipient that a memo or report with unpleasant news will be arriving and should request a meeting to discuss the problem. Suddenly handing a senior vice president a memo stating that the new order entry system is $200,000 over budget and may be six months late will certainly trigger a negative emotional reaction. A carefully planned phone call to warn the reader will usually defuse a potentially explosive situation.

The third guideline is to use a style that does not blame or condemn. If the author must contradict the manager's statements, the memo can mention both sides of the issue. People respond better when the written word does not threaten or attack them personally. Above all, never insert comments that can be interpreted as personal criticism. In the world of internal company communications, each matter should be judged on its own merits.

SUMMARY OF KEY POINTS

- Internal forms and documents are a direct reflection of management policy—if the formats are ineffective, management itself may be equally ineffective. Well designed forms will help implement management policy.

- The user service request form needs a simple identification scheme that conveys more than the sequence in which it was received.

- A service request form should come with detailed, explicit instructions. Some users will not automatically understand.

- Project control status reports have two purposes: to help staff members accurately pinpoint their status and to communicate that information to management.

- The project management form should be easy to fill out, positive in nature, and professionally prepared.

- A standardized task control method is essential for employees who have multiple assignments. Don't allow busy staff members to keep everything in their heads.

- Professionals with differing responsibilities need different weekly report forms. Requiring all employees to use the same weekly report form is a mistake.

- The manager should provide weekly feedback on the employee's weekly report. Never let a report go unanswered.

- Interviews alone do not give employers an accurate picture of a potential employee's technical skills. An experience evaluation form will quickly fill in the details. Those forms should also be part of a continuing program of employee measurement.

- The author of a memo should indicate in the heading exactly what action each recipient is expected to take, along with a target date for that action.

- Before giving unpleasant news in a memo, the author should prepare the recipient verbally. One should never compose a memo while in an angry or emotional state. Technical and business documents should be built on facts rather than emotion.

5

User Manuals— Preparation

User manuals come in several forms: the traditional paper document, online HELP functions, and computer assisted instruction. Yet they all require the same degree of careful preparation and planning. Chapter 5 shows the technical writer methods to learn the subject, understand the limitations and capabilities of the audience, and obtain willing cooperation from the users. The chapter reviews the serious questions of "Who controls user manuals?" and "Should manuals be standardized?" Technical writers, systems analysts, users, and MIS managers will find the correct procedures for starting a user manual documentation project.

Requirements documents and business plans are more visible, but the often underrated user manual can make the difference between the ultimate success and failure of a computerized system. Even the best application, product, or device is worthless unless the users can operate the system effectively. User manuals should never be an afterthought. Too many MIS directors and managers classify a project as complete even if the manual phase is not finished or the final document itself is unacceptable to the end consumers. MIS as a profession is painfully learning that true service to the user includes providing him with high quality operating instructions and training.

Many user complaints about an application come from misunderstanding or confusion about the capabilities and restrictions of the product. The application may actually work perfectly! Observers declare that much of the expensive, unnecessary maintenance effort in some installations is caused by a lack of practical user documentation. Maintenance project leaders report example after example of wasted programmer effort because the user did not "understand" his system. The fault may not lie with the users—if MIS has not delivered good documentation, the users have nothing to work with. From a long-range management viewpoint, *MIS can often justify projects to develop user manuals on the basis of reduced maintenance costs.*

A common problem with user manuals is their lack of currency. A manual that was accurate five years ago may lead users merrily down the wrong path if the manual was not kept up to date. Other manuals may be current but the technical writer or other author did not understand the system. Simply having a manual is not enough. *Incorrect user instructions are often worse than no instructions at all.*

TYPES OF USER MANUALS

User manuals are not limited to the traditional hardcopy format. The "online" style of user documentation has proven quite successful. One early example of this approach is the HELP facility of IBM's widely used TSO application, development, and support product for the MVS operating systems. Using HELP, the computer user (who may not be technically oriented), progresses through various levels of instructions that relate to TSO features. If the user needs assistance while using a specific option, he presses a key and the computer provides him with online documentation. In effect, the user manual has been put online and gives "direct access" to the user. HELP (and similar online facilities) are still a form of user manual, and have the same problems as their cousins stored on traditional paper notebooks.

Computer assisted instruction (CAI) is now being implemented, and may soon trigger a revolution in both training and documentation. When combined with direct frame access laser videodisc, CAI can not only "teach a subject" but will provide an efficient way to deliver needed information to a user. In fact, one can foresee the day when "online manuals" and CAI/videodisc will replace most hard copy manuals—paper, after all, is only a communications medium, and technical writers may discover a better approach. Paper replaced the stone tablet and it may be time for something else to replace paper!

Manuals—both hard copy and online—range in size from multiple volumes explaining a general ledger system to one-page descriptions on how to hook up a CRT. The difference is quantitative rather than qualitative. While the author of the three-volume general ledger documentation faces additional problems dealing with large manuals, the technical writer scribbling one-page quicky instructions has the same goal: *User instructions must give users what they need, no more and no less.* Deciding what they truly need may be complicated, but the principles and considerations behind effective user communication remain the same. One project may take six months while another takes six minutes, but both have the same objectives.

TECHNIQUES TO LEARN A TECHNICAL SUBJECT

Before technical writing became a separate profession, programmers were often drafted to write user documentation. In other cases reluctant users volunteered to write their own manuals, and the results were predictable. The programmer knew the application (perhaps even wrote it!), but did a poor job communicating knowledge. The user knew only specific aspects of the system and also communicated poorly. In the 1990's the situation is reversed: Technical writers and systems analysts have the writing skills, but they often lack a detailed understanding of their topic. Most professional writers have neither the technical ability nor the time to read program code and decipher a system from start to finish. Even programmers assigned to an application seldom accomplish that feat. Then how can a writer learn a system, application, or new computer in a reasonably efficient manner?

The first step is to contact a wide variety of acknowledged "experts" in the particular application. Most MIS departments have programmers, analysts, managers, data entry clerks, computer operators, or secretaries who have worked with the system and have some understanding of the product. They may know only portions of the application that relate to their particular job function, but they can be valuable allies. If the MIS organization functions in a closed manner and does not encourage "knowledge sharing," the technical writer must work through official channels to obtain commitments from other managers. A technical author must utilize all available internal MIS resources before going outside the department.

The more information authors possess before going to the users, the more efficiently they will relate to those users and understand their problems. *Nothing infuriates a busy user more than MIS professionals who have obviously not done their homework.* The MIS staffers—whether they are programmers, analysts, technical writers, managers, or MIS directors—make both themselves and the department look unprofessional if they have not previously gathered basic information. Since technical authors need user respect when working on such projects, they must avoid looking incompetent.

The second step is to play "detective" and locate all written documentation on the system within MIS. Despite loud protests from cynical programmers and analysts, most shops have some written documentation on virtually every production system. It may be written on five year old paper yellowed with age, or typed by a sleepy programmer at three in the morning. It could be scribbled on tab cards, stuck on a bulletin board, or forgotten in an old online library. But written information usually exists, and those notes, memos, and assorted documents are a valuable reference tool. The information may be out of date or even totally incorrect, but the terminology, descriptions, and attitudes will prepare the technical writer for discussions with internal MIS staff and users. Discovering hard-to-find and unorganized documentation is often a challenge, but the results are worth the effort.

As a supplement to taking notes, the best tool for a technical writer is a tape recorder. If approached cautiously (and if allowed by company policy), many MIS employees will agree to a recording session if their statements are used only for information purposes. *The technical writer must never violate this trust.* A programmer, for example, may have a deep understanding of the system flow but hesitate to document his or her knowledge. With a microphone the technical writer can often get large amounts of information from these "experts" on tape while concentrating on asking the questions rather than transcribing the answers.

A third step is to schedule formal discussions with internal MIS experts, and to plan the questions before the meetings. This is an excellent opportunity to verify facts listed on those assorted notes, memos, and documents. But the primary purpose of these short discussions is to prepare the writer to meet the users. The programmer, analyst or manager can answer questions such as:

> What is the purpose of the system?
> How long have you been involved with it?
> What is your function in relation to this system?
> Can you summarize the processing from an MIS perspective?
> Can you summarize the processing as the users see it?
> Do you have any written information about this system?
> Do you know anyone else who has written documentation?
> What are the major strengths?
> What are the major weaknesses?
> Do the users like it? If not, which ones?
> Does MIS have any special problems with it?
> Do the users need information about other systems in order to use this system?
> What changes have taken place during the past few years?
> Do the users have any ongoing requests or serious complaints relating to this system or its operation?

Many of the answers do not directly affect the creation of a user manual. Yet the information is just as critical as a list of transaction codes or error messages, because virtually every user documentation project requires the author to develop a positive relationship with the user community. In most cases, *unless the author understands the "total" situation, he will not receive full cooperation, and his project will suffer*. The author must know that MIS has been promising the Accounting Department a new General Ledger system for the past five years, before strolling into Accounting and ask for help documenting the current general ledger system.

Meetings with internal experts should be an hour or less to avoid monopolizing technical personnel. Associates are usually willing to donate a quick hour or so to help a colleague, but a requested three-hour session may be put off until the next cold day in August. Even if the expert did agree to a three hour intensive session, the technical writer himself may be unfamiliar with the terminology and concepts, and will develop "information overload" very quickly. Short, informal discussions are most productive for everyone.

UNDERSTAND THE AUDIENCE

"Know your audience" may sound like a trite, simplified command similar to "know yourself," but preparing to write a user manual requires a detailed understanding of potential readers. The analysis is not difficult, if the author follows a standardized approach (see Figure 5.1):

1. *Have they ever used the application, computer, or system?* If the users have no direct or recent experience, the author will be writing for naive users and must anticipate very basic questions. Sophisticated users do not generally need such detailed assistance.

Figure 5.1 Understand the audience

> ✔ Ever used the system?
> ✔ New or experienced users?
> ✔ All have same level of experience?
> ✔ What judgment is needed?
> ✔ Users dedicated to system?
> ✔ Other help available?
> ✔ Motivated users?

2. *Will all the audience share the same level of experience?* If the manual is for new users as well as "experts," the author should consider a "two level approach" where the manual has separate sections for both types of users. Each section can have a different vocabulary, sentence structure, and degree of detail. Another solution is to write *two* user manuals. Whatever the approach, authors cannot write for new users in the same way they communicate with sophisticated users. It doesn't work.

3. *How much judgement is required in using the system?* Application systems differ significantly in the degree and nature of the judgment exercised by the users. For example, a technical writer creating a manual for a decision support system (DSS) used by a CPA or MBA would use a different "mind set" than when developing a manual for warehouse forklift operators. Both groups make decisions when working with various screens on their computer terminals, but the CPAs and MBAs should be more familiar with complex logic interactions. The author of the forklift operator manual will define the alternatives in detail when the operator discovers an "out of stock" condition, The writer of a DSS manual would assume readers will develop their own alternatives. This may be an extreme example, but the principle is valid: The technical writer must estimate the decision making ability of his audience because it will partially determine both the information he provides and his literary style.

In most cases, the degree of decision making increases as computer applications move away from the so-called "bread and butter" systems such as payroll and general ledger to the more sophisticated packages such as merchandise analysis or decision support systems. Even the technical world is changing. Programmers use complex relational data base calls that require careful analysis before they begin coding. The way one codes a DB2 program, for example, can dramatically affect the operating characteristics of a major update or inquiry module.

As the applications themselves become more complicated, technical writers find themselves relying more on the programming staff for answers. A good example is a software house technical writer developing a manual on data base design: The author may need to depend totally upon the experts.

4. *Are the people reading the manual fully dedicated to the system?* An order entry clerk who enters customer orders must be approached differently than a nurse in a medical office who operates a microcomputer on an occasional basis. The amount of dedication partially determines the amount of detail and the degree of repetition in the manual. The less time a user consistently spends with the task in question, the more detailed instructions he needs.

The situation is more complicated when the user must juggle several tasks at the same time, and technical writers must *put themselves in the user's position.* The pediatric nurse answering a phone with one hand and taking the temperature of a screaming 3-year-old with the other does not have time to, "Go back to section III-A when the invalid patient number message" appears. What does the nurse actually need at that point in time? Can the documentation provide enough detail in a condensed manner so he or she can handle the phone conversation, quiet the screaming 3-year-old, and correct the CRT error simultaneously?

In such hectic environments, the user should have virtually standalone sections which provide all required information in one place. The author must repeat essential information when necessary. *Although the concept of standalone sections repeats information and introduces the problem of maintainability, the practice is more than justified: The technical writer pays the price rather than the user.* However, when writing for dedicated users who will be thoroughly familiar with both the application and documentation, the author can legitimately send the reader back to other sections for additional information. Repetition can then be avoided.

. *Can the users get help easily, and what form will that help take?* Consider a technical writer documenting a microcomputer based inventory control system. The package will be sold with the hardware as a turnkey system, and the users may be three thousand miles away. The software company has a "hotline" but wants to reserve that function for serious problems. Should the manual be as complete as humanly possible? Of course!

Other writing assignments involve situations where the user facing the computer monster does have access to people who can answer questions. A bank teller having trouble with an online cash transaction certainly has knowledgeable supervisors who can provide additional information or advice. While the author should still provide a relatively complete set of teller oriented documentation, he can assume that his user will never be totally alone.

. *Are the users motivated?* If the typical users of a particular system are generally unmotivated, the technical writer can perform a service to his company by adding both spirit and humor to the documentation. Who says the *Guide to Ajax Software General Ledger and Window Washing System* must be totally boring? Humor—as long as it does not interfere with communication of essential facts and ideas—is perfectly acceptable.

Why can't the manual have a comical story about Joyce Journal who can never balance payroll entries, or about Gary Gremlin who occasionally causes the little red light to appear on the disk drive control unit? To make Gary Gremlin go away, the user may simply hit the reset button and reboot the system. The average nontechnical user would rather read about a red light called Gary Gremlin rather than about a channel control interface warning light or CCIW. Obviously, the manual must also have the correct name for reference purposes. Computers—like technical documentation—are not required by a law of nature to be dull. Each one of us has a little child in him or her, and a touch of humor in a user manual can actually help frustrated users view their jobs with a more positive attitude.

GETTING COOPERATION AT THE START

The success of many technical writing assignments ultimately depends upon the cooperation of the users. As technical writers follow their own professional path and move away from the traditional programming and systems background, they will need even more help.

Theoretically, obtaining cooperation from users should be easy. Many writing assignments deal with revising and updating existing user manuals, and the readers are personally interested in having better documentation. They never hesitate to point out problems and suggest improvements. In many cases they will demand rather than suggest!

Occasionally the technical writer will face an uncooperative or negative user who hinders the project rather than helps. The cause may be a dissatisfaction with the current user manual or even with MIS in general. Frustrated users who are negative toward MIS will transfer their hostilities to the smiling technical writer standing in the doorway. Such situations are complex, politically dangerous, and personally frustrating for the writer. In many cases, the author must simply do the best job possible under very difficult circumstances. As a last resort, he or she can ask for management pressure on the reluctant individuals.

Getting off to a good start with users requires a logical plan of action that recognizes their responsibilities as part of an interdepartment team:

1. *Notify the appropriate individuals and their managers of the project.* The technical writer should never rush over to a user, announce the start of a project to upgrade their system user manual, and demand instant suggestions. The notification process is somewhat involved, because the writer must not only give the users time to think about revisions to their manual, but must verify that the *correct* users are brought into the picture. Even the boss may not be the best user of a particular application.

   Depending upon their particular management philosophy, some managers consider themselves experts in all aspects of their department's operation and *will ignore staff people who may be the most qualified users to help with a documentation project.* The implications are serious! A technical writer forced to work with a manager or supervisor who is a casual user will often miss useful information. The writer should gently encourage the manager to allow the technical writer open access to those employees who can truly provide assistance. If the user manager insists upon dealing with the technical writer himself when he is obviously not qualified, the MIS employee should discuss the problem with his own management. Postponing or even cancelling the project is then an unfortunate but logical alternative.

2. *Schedule a meeting to present the purpose, nature, and scope of the documentation project.* The writer needs a carefully prepared one-page summary or at least a topic list to distribute at the meeting. Allow every person to make suggestions, express concerns, and ask questions. A good leader always treats suggestions in a positive and supporting manner, even if they are totally ridiculous and must be quietly ignored before someone else jumps on the bandwagon and paints MIS into the proverbial corner with no exit.

   After several working days, the technical writer should contact at least one key user for additional discussions. A formal meeting, however, is not necessary and may even hinder progress! Usually a simple telephone call or informal chat in the company cafeteria will help the user remember those points missed during the meeting. Sometimes the best suggestions come from people sitting in a noisy cafeteria or standing around the coffee pot. Successful technical writers (and systems analysts) learn to use a combination of formality and informality: The trick is to decide which is appropriate.

3. *Provide the users with a projected timetable for the entire project.* The schedule will include checkpoints when user assistance is required, along with an estimate in work hours of their effort. It is unreasonable to ask busy user (or anyone else) for help, if one cannot provide users with a rough estimate of their contribution.

   Estimating dates is a combination of art, science, politics, and black magic. Writers should always stress verbally and on paper the "tentative" nature of their timetable, since many factors are beyond their personal control. This is especially true when authors require detailed assistance from other groups.

4. *Report progress regularly.* Users will feel a personal interest and commitment when they can see the project unfold before their eyes. The status report can also remind users of imminent checkpoints that will require their assistance. Good communication will encourage cooperation and prevent those minor but annoying disagreements caused by the notorious "But I thought" syndrome. The motto of the technical writer who deals with users should be, "No Surprises."

By following those steps, both the end users and technical writer should share a sense of accomplishment. Instead of having MIS personnel thrust a completed manual in their hands, the users will become true participants in the design, development, and packaging of their own manual. The results will be worth the effort.

WHO CONTROLS USER MANUALS?

The single document in MIS that causes the most confusion concerning the ultimate responsibility dilemma is the user manual. Who makes the final decisions regarding the need to update, reprint, or modify a company's user manuals? Does MIS have the right to refuse or postpone a "legitimate" request? Can the Accounting Department require MIS to make corrections if the manual has errors or major omissions? What happens if the order entry manager says flatly, "It's not good enough. Do it over."

The immediate solution of asking higher management to arbitrate is not practical. Imagine the MIS director and accounting manager asking the senior vice president to judge each sentence in a documentation manual! Only in rare situations is it reasonable to proceed up the chain of command to settle documentation issues, and then *only* at the policy level.

Technical writers have discovered that unless an organization has a definite plan for documentation responsibilities, the burden often falls directly upon them. *They* must negotiate, explain, and satisfy the users, while always careful to incorporate reasonable suggestions from the people who actually use their products. In reality, technical writers often work for two areas, even when they report to MIS. Their "political" ability to satisfy their own management—who often gives them relative freedom—and their user base is critical to their success. Many technical writing specialists have more daily contact with users than with their own MIS colleagues or management!

The long-term solution is to develop a firm management policy regarding documentation responsibilities. Whatever the outcome, the agreement between MIS and the user departments should accomplish the following objectives:

1. Assign one group the responsibility for the mechanical aspects of documentation (i.e., creating, updating, and distributing),

2. Grant one group the authority to accept or reject the documentation, with a *definite plan to make the documentation acceptable* (a "we don't like it" is not good enough).

3. Establish a "user/MIS documentation committee" to oversee documentation projects and recommend priorities.

4. Provide a periodic review process by both areas to examine user documentation and discuss problems before they become serious political issues.

If the technical writing staff reports to MIS, the MIS director must have final decision making ability: Likewise, if the staff works for the users, the appropriate user manager must have ultimate control. But successful technical writing is more than the ability to discover information and transfer it clearly to paper or CRT. It is the ability to negotiate, arbitrate, and satisfy people who come into a situation with differing goals. Human relations is often just as important as sentence structure!

DOCUMENTATION STANDARDS FOR USER MANUALS

Standardized user manuals—having the same format, organization and style—have several advantages:

1. A user who transfers to another area is automatically familiar with the format of his new manual.
2. The technical writing staff becomes more proficient with one approach to documentation.
3. New technical writers will not (or at last should not) spend time searching for or developing another format.
4. Routine maintenance is often easier.

But in the real day-to-day world of MIS, standards that appear great on paper do have disadvantages:

1. The single format may not fit all situations, and some user manuals may suffer in quality.
2. The technical writers may not develop their craft by "experimenting" with new styles and formats.
3. Some users may not like the standard, and will push strongly for their own ideas.
4. Technical writers who do not like the standard (or believe it does not fit their specific project) may not do a thorough job.

Installations with years of experience creating successful user manuals may have enough knowledge to select one or even two formats that seem to fit most situations. By trial and error, they have discovered formats that work and other formats that confuse more than they help. Other organizations who are relatively new to professional user documentation *should refrain from setting standards for the sake of standards*. Those shops need a certain amount of real world experience (which includes both successes and failures) before they can jump into standardized user manuals.

SUMMARY OF KEY POINTS

- User manuals require extensive preparation before the writing begins: They must be planned like any other MIS project.

- User documentation can often be justified on the basis of reducing maintenance costs.

- Before contacting the user, the technical writer must learn everything he can from internal MIS sources.

- Even when everyone says, "There is no documentation!" there usually is. The author must play detective and find it!

- If allowed by company policy, the technical writer should use a tape recorder during interviews. It is difficult to accurately record every response from a subject, especially when the interviewer is not familiar with the topic.

- The technical writer should constantly put himself/herself in the position of the user.

- User manuals can be lively and even a little entertaining: Humor is justified if it does not interfere with communication.

- Follow a plan to obtain and hold user cooperation.

- A company needs a firm policy on user documentation which defines ultimate responsibilities and procedures for resolving disputes.

6

User Manuals—
The Mechanics

Chapter 6 has proven methods to prepare a successful user manual, once the initial planning and research is complete. You should know the information in Chapter 5 before reading this material. This chapter explains the macro-to-micro, or general-to-specific, approach, in which the author provides a logical framework before presenting detailed information. Sections describe the purpose and functions of the overview, and explain the hierarchical approach to organizing user manuals. User documentation must fit the reader's job responsibilities and not into the structure of the MIS development team. Technical writers, systems analysts, users, and MIS managers can use these suggestions and guidelines to create efficient, well organized user manuals.

Once the technical writer the evaluated his audience and gathered information, the second task is to plan the internals of the manual. Thorough planning is just as important to a writer as to a systems analyst, programmer, or manager. Indeed, many costly mistakes could be avoided if technical writers view their assignments as a series of projects, with all the requirements of true project management. *Good manuals simply do not just happen—they are planned.*

One example of planning is the prerequisite page. What do the readers need before they open up the manual? Is there another document they should have read? Do they need a basic knowledge of accounting, retailing, manufacturing, or data processing? Many user manuals assume some level of prior experience or study, but few clearly specify these requirements on a separate page. The manual should also repeat the prerequisites at critical points throughout the text, because some readers may ignore or forget the information on the prerequisite page.

OVERVIEWS

Every user manual longer than two pages needs an overview or summary, which introduces the manual, describes the purpose and intended audience, and prepares the reader for efficient use of the manual. Starting to read a user manual without an overview is like jumping into a swimming pool filled with ice water: The effect is not very pleasant.

There is a serious educational justification for always using an overview: a summary or overview fits into the macro-to-micro approach to education and training.

Humans tend to understand a subject better when they proceed from the overall or macro level to the detail or micro level. *Details are often difficult to understand when the reader does not have a mental framework to hold those facts.* One should not expect an accounting clerk to immediately jump into the proper use of transaction code 491 when he or she does not realize that transaction code 491 is one of seven accounts payable operations. People learn best when they appreciate the *relationships* between the details. Both training and documentation should proceed from the general to the specific. The big picture approach is not a matter of courtesy, but simply a technique that reduces the learning curve. In the decade of the 1990s, time is money.

The nature of an overview varies according to the situation. A manual designed to teach an order entry operator the correct operating procedures for a minicomputer would need a relatively short overview. The documentation instructing the accounting staff how to use a new general ledger system would need a longer, more complex overview. In the latter case, the author may compose two or more separate overviews for the generic types of people who will be reading the manual. Accountants would need one approach while accounting clerks might appreciate another style and slightly different set of facts. *The overview should be tailored to the audience or audiences.*

Even experienced writers with excellent skills at explaining details shudder at the thought of writing an overview. While the author of a system design document usually writes his or her summary as the last step in the development process, the author of a user manual should create a skeleton or rough draft of the overview *before* he or she starts the body of the manual. This exercise will help focus the authors' attention on the key points involved in creating a user manual. After the manual is complete, the author can revise the overview based upon the actual contents of the manual. Without this initial effort, the writer may forget or misinterpret key points that will seriously damage the value of the project.

A good overview answers the following questions:

- What is the purpose of the manual?
- Why do I need to read it?
- What exactly is the application (or system or product)?
- How will it help me do my job?
- What are the most important points to look for in this manual?
- Is there anything special I should understand about this application, such as its value to the company?
- How does this application fit into the organization?
- What are my duties as it relates to this application?

The information will give the reader a friendly orientation to the task of reading the manual. Consider the following overview from an inventory control systems manual:

> This manual is for buyers, assistant buyers, and senior buyers who work with the Inventory Control System (ICS). The purpose of ICS is to monitor the movement of merchandise from the vendors to the warehouse to our retail stores in the Midwest. ICS automatically captures purchases, sales, returns, and adjustments, but depends upon the buying staff to audit the daily and weekly error reports. They must also submit file maintenance transactions to keep ICS correct. The buying staff analyzes the weekly stock status and other reports to spot trends and discover problem situations in each store and district. ICS is the only link between the warehouse and retail stores. It is vital to the entire vendor replenishment process, as well as to the accounting systems it feeds.

The overview helps the reader understand the nature of the system and his or her general responsibilities. It also stresses the importance of ICS to the entire organization, which may improve the employee's motivation and job performance.

ORGANIZATION OF THE USER MANUAL

While a logical organization or structure is vital to the success of any user manual, there is no single organizational scheme that will fit every situation. A technical writer should rely on personal experience and the examples around him or her to select the most effective structure for that specific project. What is suitable for one manual may be inappropriate for another, and significant changes to a system or product may justify an entirely new arrangement.

The *hierarchical* approach is the most common. This method divides the system into logical components that have a definite relationship to each other. For example, if a user manual breaks down the system or product into four major topics, the user manual will have four chapters. Each chapter may then have individualized sections.

While simple in theory, a good hierarchical approach is often difficult to implement because there are multiple ways of breaking down any subject. The author may view an application as consisting of logical sections A, B, and C, while the user actually works with the system in terms of D, E, and F. The difference is subtle but important, because user manuals *should be designed to fit the hierarchy as seen by the user, not the author.* A logical outline to one person may be nonsense to another.

For example, many existing user manuals have separate chapters for transactions, reports, and internal processing. Is that approach logical? Yes, from the system designer viewpoint, but not for the consumer who actually uses the application. Each member of the inventory control staff deals with job responsibilities rather than traditional MIS activities. That is, an "item add" transaction is part of the normal daily file maintenance procedure, and the manual therefore needs a chapter on daily file maintenance. Users demand documentation that follows *their* working habits, rather than an analysis of the system in technical terms. The best user manuals are often designed for individual job functions.

MIS typically designs systems in pieces. One programmer creates the transactions, and another develops the screen formats. But the typical user could care less! He sits down at a CRT to perform daily file maintenance, not to enter transactions.

A typical (but not totally efficient) user manual may follow the classical format:

1. Introduction

2. Transactions

3. Error reports

4. Standard reports

5. User modifiable reports

6. Production cycles and options

7. Index

The preceding organization will eventually provide the needed information, but the users would describe the manual as a puzzle, until they were thoroughly familiar with the contents. The information is present, but it is not organized according to the users normal activities.

A better structure is shown for a purchase order system:

1. Triggering purchase orders

2. Creating manual purchase orders

3. Paperwork disposition

4. Modifying the report formats

5. Error conditions with purchase orders

6. Relationship to open orders

7. Cancelling or modifying purchase orders

This hierarchical table of contents does not separate the efficient transactions created by Randy Record from the artful screens developed by Carol Cathode from the aesthetically pleasing reports written by the plodding but ever faithful, Charley Cobol. Instead, when the clerk needs to cancel a purchase order, he will go directly to section 7 which will tell him to use Randy's transaction 401 in Carol's INVMT screen and check faithful Charley's 801 hard copy report. The manual has been designed for employees working with purchase orders, not for the MIS professionals who developed the system.

Even in departments with few employees, the gain in productivity is startling when user manuals are organized according to job function. The gains are even more impressive for large companies who make a sincere effort to organize user manuals around their daily activities. The hierarchical approach is logical, as long as the author remembers to arrange the hierarchy from the users perspective.

INTERNALS OF THE USER MANUAL

The body of a user manual should proceed in a macro-to-micro approach, and every chapter or major section requires an introductory paragraph that explains the purpose and organization of the chapter. Readers want to know *why* they should read that section and *how* it is arranged. Good authors will try to *sell* the material to their customers, because getting people to actually use a manual is like trying to sell them vitamins: The introduction tells readers why the product is good for them.

Descriptive titles can help the reader quickly identify key portions of the text. For those user manuals not written in narrative style, a title for each paragraph may seem to interrupt the smooth flow of the manual. But the convenience of quickly locating specific topics more than justifies the choppiness of the frequent headings. Other manuals are written in narrative form and the headings can then be confined to major section breaks. A manual needed for quick reference will need more headings than a manual needed for general understanding. Again, defining the purpose of a user manual helps the writer select the correct number and placement of headings.

Authors must continually put themselves in the position of the end user of the application, system or product. What does he or she need to know to accomplish the task? The truth may surprise even an experienced systems analyst. For example, an accounting clerk may need the procedure for turning on a CRT before entering data. The warehouse supervisor may not know instinctively how to power up the minicomputer, disk drive, and printer. Such details may be obvious to the analyst or technical writer, but not to the end user! The message is clear: Think like a user, not as an MIS professional. This shift of orientation must apply throughout the writing process.

To visualize the situation from a user's perspective—especially the more naive or unsophisticated ones—often requires the writer to spend significant amounts of time working with the user in his or her environment. There is no substitute for visiting a department, taking a detailed tour, and then simply wandering around the area informally chatting with people. This rule applies not only to the information gathering stage, but also when the author is busy creating the manual! In addition to picking up valuable information, the technical writer will eventually judge the level of data processing and business sophistication of future customers. The author will also learn more about the problems, feelings, and frustration levels of the audience.

When creating the manual, the author should put error codes, warning messages, and error recovery procedures where they will be needed *if* the user is following detailed instructions. For example, a programmer using a data base host language interface "open" routine may get a program termination with a code A456. A technical writer could easily document the error codes in the appendix (and probably will), but should at least mention the most common open errors in the section describing the open instruction. In many real life situations, typical mistakes, errors, and omissions can be accurately predicted, and the technical writer who can anticipate the most likely mistakes will help increase user productivity. A programmer seeing the explanation for A456 on the same page as the open command will not shift mental gears by browsing through the appendix. The gain in productivity is significant—not just because of the time saving, but because the user did not change his mental orientation or mind set.

The audience for a technical manual often consists of both experienced and naive users, and the writer has the obvious problem of trying to satisfy both groups. The author who has decided to create one manual (a common practice because of time constraints) must allow the sophisticated user to skip over unnecessary information. Helpful statements include "If you know how to operate a 3278 CRT, go to paragraph C4" or "If you understand the difference between LIFO and FIFO, go to section B in the next chapter." It is also reasonable to change the writing style in paragraphs or sections that are directed toward naive users. For example, a reader who has never worked a 3278 CRT may need a detailed, forgiving, and simplified writing style. The section explaining LIFO and FIFO can be written for someone who has never taken an accounting course.

Both technical MIS manuals and business system manuals often depend upon information in other documents. Therefore, the technical writer should carefully list references to other manuals or documents. For example, when confused by a statement in the inventory control manual, a retail company buyer may not automatically turn to the Order Processing Manual for an explanation of "retail price rounding." The inventory manual should direct the user to other documents. The author should never be afraid to insult readers by explicitly listing other references or places to go for assistance. This practice is one trademark of good user documentation.

Manuals are more interesting and effective when the author uses terms familiar to the user. To an MIS professional, the physical location where customer orders are processed is simply one desk out of ten in the Order Entry Department on the west side of the fifth floor. But to anyone in the section that special desk is called "order control." The employees may refer to it as "OC" or some more colorful term. Manuals for users should contain their own buzzwords and colloquial expressions if they have stood the test of time. One would not include casual expressions used only by one individual. The manual will then seem more natural or custom designed, and therefore more relevant to the reader.

What happens when the manual cannot explain a particular problem or address a complex issue? Users are further puzzled if the manual does not provide them with specific instructions. The documentation should direct them to the next logical place for assistance, if it is another manual, the MIS systems group, or the vendor. *It is unreasonable to expect a user manual to solve all problems*, and the body of the text should contain frequent comments regarding outside assistance. If the trial balance report is incorrect because an account number rejects, should the accounting clerk call MIS or talk to her supervisor? If the manual directs her to call MIS, does she first call Operations, The MIS Help Desk, Systems and Programming, Quality Assurance, the Office of the Director, or the MIS secretary she had lunch with last week? Problems will develop in any computer system, and the manual should honestly tell the user how to resolve those problems.

When writing the body of the documentation, the author should maintain a relatively consistent format, style, vocabulary, and writing technique. The exception is when the author provides separate sections for naive and sophisticated users. But within a section or chapter written for the same generic audience, the author should maintain consistency. If several technical writers and systems analysts join forces to create a large manual, the manager or senior writer should verify that all writers have a similar, or at least complementary, style. A manual that has widely differing styles will frustrate many readers.

The index is the final cross reference feature and should be developed with great care. With a complete index, users can go directly to specific areas of interest. Often a user who is already familiar with the system can evaluate the completeness of an index and suggest improvements. *The index should be as carefully prepared as the overview or introduction.*

FIELD TESTING THE MANUAL

Inexperienced technical writers deliver a completed user manual to the Accounting Department and proudly declare "I hope you like it!." *Hope* is not an appropriate businesslike statement. The users should have been examining, criticizing, and approving the manual as it was developed. If the user department did not participate in the development, they could have at least approved the manual on a chapter-by-chapter basis.

But even with the closest cooperation between MIS and the users, one final step remains. Just as computer programs must be tested before production, user manuals must be field tested with the same care given to a new application system. A program, system, or electronic device rarely works perfectly the first time, and user manuals are no different. All parties involved—including MIS and user group management—must understand clearly that even if the manual is "accepted" by the users, a field test is absolutely necessary. The project is not complete until the field test has uncovered the inevitable errors and omissions.

The concept of acceptance is often misunderstood by those who still believe that a strict dichotomy exists between nonacceptance and acceptance of a system, application, or product. This theory is not valid for most complex MIS products. Users cannot possibly verify every feature in a complex or sophisticated application, and neither can they verify every section, sentence, and word in a user manual. The long awaited words "I accept" should be changed to "I tentatively accept," and the field testing procedure should be an integral part of that acceptance procedure.

Field testing requires cooperation between MIS and several volunteer users. In some cases, the manual will be the first documentation they have seen, and therefore the entire process of using documentation will be new. Even new users can still provide helpful comments and suggestions. The friendly interaction between technical writer and user will help clarify points that were not properly understood.

The volunteers should provide constructive feedback to the technical writer, and not suggest a complete rewrite or major changes to the manual. Rather, users can identify missing pieces, suggest changes in wording or terminology, or propose a rearrangement of the material. The field testing phase should last as long as the production cycles involved with the application. That is, if the user manual describes a system that has daily, weekly, and monthly cycles, the field testing phase should carry through beyond the next month processing. Of course, one cannot always carry this guideline to its logical conclusion: A chapter on year-end processing may need to wait until the following year end for evaluation. The rest of the manual can certainly be tested, modified, and approved. With most production business systems a five- to six-week testing phase is adequate, if the users are truly working researching the manual and providing regular feedback.

REVISIONS

Documentation must evolve along with application system enhancements, hardware improvements, and personnel changes. Even with perfectly stable business systems, as the user staff gains more experience with both the product and manual, they will find areas that need improvement. MIS needs an easy-to-use procedure that will allow all interested parties to suggest, monitor, and implement changes to completed user manuals. The procedure can involve a special form, a memo to the technical writing staff or application support group, or a joint MIS/user committee who oversees user documentation.

Manuals need a *change page* which lists the purpose and nature of the latest modifications. For example, revision 3.0 of an accounts payable manual might list the following changes:

- Added new purchases reconciliation subsystem.

- Upgraded edit screen error messages.

- Deleted obsolete reports 401, 402, and 403.

Giving people a new manual is like giving them a new car, desk, or office. Their initial reaction is, "What's different from the old one?" By identifying the changes, the technical writer will save users the unnecessary time and frustration of discovering the differences for themselves. If the frustration level increases beyond a certain limit, some users have been known to ignore the revised document and use the old manual!

ONLINE USER MANUALS

User documentation accessed through a CRT has several unique requirements. Simply loading paper-oriented documentation into an online library is only the first step: The material should be revised to fit the needs of a viewer using a CRT.

Visible page size is an important factor. With hardcopy documentation, the user can easily flip back to see the start of a thought or topic on the previous page. Sentences and paragraphs frequently spread across two pages with little impact on the reader. We accept without question the need to occasionally span a page of a report, document, or a book. Users no longer have that luxury with a CRT display. They can page back to the previous screen, but there is often a delay of a second or more, and this time lag makes the process inefficient. Even a one-second delay is often enough to break a user's mental concentration. With online documentation, each screen should be a separate, easily understandable entity. The author should write documentation on a screen-by-screen basis as if the user could not return to the previous screen. This guideline (which is admittedly false) will help the writer compose each screen as a whole entity.

The second requirement is that every CRT screen inform users exactly where they have been, and where they are going. Traditionally, online systems use the standard procedures of "Press PF1 to Continue" and "Press PF2 to Return." This is not acceptable for online documentation. Users must know *where they have come from* and *where they are going*. A better message would be, "Press PF1 to See Screen 3-of-4 of Purchase Order Cancellation" and "Press PF2 to Return to Purchase Order Main Menu." The prompt should change with virtually every screen to tell the user his exact location.

SUMMARY OF KEY POINTS

- The overview helps the readers understand why they should study the manual, and how the subject fits in with their personal job responsibilities.

- The overview should be designed specifically for the audience. If there are two or more target groups, there must be two or more overviews.

- The hierarchical approach to user manual organization works well if the author uses the hierarchy of job functions relating to the user. Manuals should be organized around user responsibilities, not according to the MIS development team.

- Frequent descriptive titles should be used in the body of the manual, even if they seem to make the material "choppy."

- Each page of online documentation should be a complete thought, and not run over to the next screen, even if some pages are short.

- Each online screen must tell users exactly where they are according to the user manual organization.

7

Data Center Documentation

A data center depends upon procedures to manage computer processing, resolve the inevitable problems, and satisfy basic reporting needs. Procedures are defined through documentation. Many mistakes and production errors are directly or indirectly caused by incorrect or incomplete written communication. Chapter 7 provides sample run instructions and problem reporting logs along with the correct procedures for using them. It describes special procedures documentation and master system documentation books, both of which help control even the most complex environment. Data center managers and technical writers can use these sample forms and instructions to quickly improve both daily and long term operations.

Modern data centers are not simple black boxes that automatically accept data through one door and spew reports through another: Some data centers even function as a separate business unit. Others function under the control of an independent, outside organization. Most MIS departments require a large number of operations and support personnel, and those staff members communicate through specialized forms and reports. If their written communication is not efficient, productivity decreases and problems increase. A well managed data center has precise, exact, and concise communication both internally and externally. Even the movement toward automated scheduler and console operations (the so-called "lights out" data center) has still not eliminated the need for defined procedures.

RUN SHEETS

A technical writer or manager investigating the complex subject of run sheets quickly appreciates the historical problems associated with those documents—and the emotional opinions associated with them. Run sheets are known by many names in the same operations department, most of which should not be repeated around young children. Rarely does one find an organization who has successfully created a useful operational run sheet that helps operators rather than hinders them. One reason for this lack of progress is simply tradition or custom. Data center managers may be comfortable with an old, archaic format everyone knows is virtually useless, but the management is reluctant to change. Perhaps they fear any new format may be worse than the old one!

Run documentation invariably seems to be incorrect, confusing, contradictory, puzzling, or some combination thereof. When a production problem occurs, existing documentation seldom helps. Operators complain so much their suggestions are ignored or disregarded. Some operators revert to the time honored practice of calling another operator or the supporting programmer. If that fails, they may fall back upon the even older practice of trying solutions at random. Eventually one may seem to work, or the problem will become so confused they must turn the entire fiasco over to the production support staff.

But operational run instructions can be clear, useful, and informative if MIS management is willing to make good documentation a departmental priority. Even the best run sheets will never win a prize for creative writing, but they can indeed serve as the final authority for job setup, processing, and problem resolution. Run sheets can be useful, but the effort requires hard work and logical thinking.

The first step in creating good documentation is to define the basic purpose of operational run sheets (besides satisfying the requirements of the internal or external auditors). Run sheets should:

- Help in job scheduling.

- Inform the tape library which tapes need to be staged, and which will be created.

- Tell the operators which demountable units are needed during the job.

- Give the operations staff enough information to handle restarts and reruns without asking for assistance from either programming or technical support.

Operational run instructions that go beyond those four basic needs may have too much information. For example, some managers demand that run instructions list all work files and their space allocations for information purposes. This increases both the length and complexity of run sheets, and the data is seldom accurate. Management must strike a balance between what is nice to have and the effort needed to maintain those extra data fields. For example, the hardware analyst may wish to see run sheets that list the current space allocations of work files, but the burden of updating such information may cause the staff to ignore run sheets altogether. *Operational documentation should be designed with the goal of minimum effort.* The team designing the run sheets should verify that all proposed information is worth the effort. If Charley Channel, the hardware analyst, wants to see specific unit and device information about each job, how much effort will it require? How often does it change? Does anyone else really need that data? More importantly, do the people who actually use the run sheets on a daily basis need to know about unit and device information? If the answer is "no," the information should not be on the form. Let Charley get his own data.

Run sheets should be easy and quick to change. An online text editing system is an excellent method to develop and store operational instructions. Whatever the medium, run sheets should be relatively easy to modify by computer operators and tape librarians. While programmers will make changes as they install enhancements and new features, update control should not be left exclusively with the systems and programming staff. In an ideal situation (with reasonable cooperation between departments), all users should have the ability to update, correct, and modify operational instructions as needed.

Although groups should share the responsibility for updating run documentation, one manager or section must have final responsibility for verifying the final product and arbitrating the inevitable disputes. Normally, this is the operations director, but could easily be the programming or technical support manager. This person will need a mechanism to track which individuals made changes to the run sheets, and if that person distributed the revision to everyone who keeps hard copy listings. An alternative is to allow only one person to make the physical changes and control the distribution, but this approach must be simple and direct: If the change procedure is cumbersome, some employees will not make the effort, and the run sheets will never be maintained. Perhaps the best policy is to try unrestricted access and if serious control problems develop, appoint one person as "run sheet czar" to take charge of all operational documentation. In high-pressure data processing environments, this last method may be the only procedure that works.

Like other forms of documentation, run sheets should be periodically revised as the hardware and software environment changes, and as employees become familiar with the value of useful documentation. The act of continually using documentation is not only enlightening but educational: As they gain experience, they will make positive suggestions.

Another problem with run sheets is that traditional formats seldom allow free form expressions. To a certain extent, every production job is slightly different and requires special instructions regarding restart, rerun, timing, or job resource allocation. Every form needs space for overflow information. For example, if the rerun procedure requires more space than the "Rerun" section allows, the form should have considerable additional space for "Comments." The "Comments" area can be used for many valuable tidbits of information.

Run sheets formats differ for each operating system, and Figure 7.1 illustrates run documentation for an IBM/MVS installation. Any additional software used by the Operations Department will affect the information on the form. A restart management system, for example, which automatically resets generation data groups and scratches unneeded data sets, will reduce the amount of restart information.

Should IBM/MVS restart and rerun instructions reside in the run documentation or should it be listed as comments in the JCL procedure? The arguments are strong on both sides of the issue, but a number of operations managers feel that step level restart instructions should be in the procedure rather than in separate documentation. If a job in an IBM/MVS installation abends, the shift supervisor, support technician, or operator will usually examine the hard copy JCL (IBM job control language) listing. Therefore, it is more efficient for most MVS shops to keep their step level restart instructions in the procedure. For rerun documentation the opposite logic applies. If a job is complete and must be reran, the operations staff should go to a separate set of instructions (such as run sheets). Rerun procedures can also be more complicated than restarts, and may require long narrative explanations. Comments are excellent documentation in JCL, but the JCL procedures are no place for long narration!

Whatever the decision, all jobs should follow the same standard approach. For example, all step level restart instructions should reside in the procedure, and all rerun information should be in the run sheets. Without standards, the operations staff will be confused when it comes to the typical restart/rerun questions that always arise. Mistakes will be painful.

Operational documentation such as run sheets should be designed as an extension of management policy, just as system design documents or feasibility statements carry out management directives. By using carefully engineered formats, MIS management can decide those nagging questions such as, "Whom do I call when something goes wrong?" These puzzles should be answered in writing as the result of a thoughtful decision rather than at 2:00 A.M. during a busy month end weekend.

Figure 7.1   Run sheet for an IBM MVS installation

Job Name _____

Description _____

Date Revised_____ By_____

System_____

Alternate Names for Job

_____

Purpose of Job

_____

_____

_____

A.   Setup and Timing

A.1   Prerequisite job(s)

_____

_____

A.2   Following job(s)

_____

A.3   Frequency   Nightly____ Daily____ Monthly____ Weekly____
Biweekly____ Quarterly____ Request____ Yearly____
Internal need____
Other_____
If "request" or "internal need," who provides the decision? How does the
information get transmitted to the operator?

_____

_____

_____

A.4   Normal processing time (in hours) _____
Maximum   _____

A.5   Normal run schedule
Start time_____ Stop time_____

A.6   Special requirements (not tape or disk)

_____

_____

_____

_____

_____

A.7   Input tapes from other jobs? yes_____ no_____

DSN	From Job	To Step	Step	Disposition
_____	_____	____	____	Scratch____ Save____
_____	_____	____	____	Scratch____ Save____
_____	_____	____	____	Scratch____ Save____
_____	_____	____	____	Scratch____ Save____
_____	_____	____	____	Scratch____ Save____

Figure 7.1 *(Continued)*

A.8 How many scratch tapes are needed?_____

A.9 Any removable disk devices needed? yes_____ no_____
If yes, which packs? _____   _____   _____

A.10 Any other special setup requirements?

_____

_____

_____

_____

B. Processing

B.1 Tape and disk

Step	Description	Input Tape dsn, Output Tape dsn or Removable Disk Removable Disk
____	_____	_____
____	_____	_____
____	_____	_____
____	_____	_____
____	_____	_____
____	_____	_____
____	_____	_____
____	_____	_____
____	_____	_____
____	_____	_____

B.2 Control parameters? Yes_____ No_____
Describe format

_____

_____

_____

_____

_____

Who prepares the control parameters?
Shift supervisor_____ Data entry_____ User_____ Operator_____
Other_____
Who answers questions about the control parameters? _____

B.3 Console messages and replies

Message ("I" if information only)	Response
_____	_____
_____	_____
_____	_____
_____	_____
_____	_____
_____	_____

_____   _____
_____   _____
_____   _____

B.4   Any special processing requirements not yet listed?

_____
_____
_____
_____
_____
_____
_____

C.   Rerun Instructions

Rerun procedures are often based on a specific reason. Please locate the problem and use that procedure.

C.1   Why do you need to do a rerun?

Reason	See Procedure
_____	_____
_____	_____
_____	_____
_____	_____
_____	_____
_____	_____
_____	_____
_____	_____
_____	_____
_____	_____

C.2   Specific procedures

Number	Action
_____	_____
_____	_____
_____	_____
_____	_____
_____	_____
_____	_____
_____	_____
_____	_____
_____	_____

C.3   General comments on reruns (cautions, potential problems, etc.)

_____
_____
_____
_____
_____

Figure 7.1   *(Continued)*

D.   Additional Information

D.1   Report distribution: _____Priority _____Normal _____Overnight
_____Standard paper _____Form number
_____Number of copies
_____Outside fiche tape
_____COM
_____Number of parts (if not 1)

original

To: _____ Dept:_____
Copy 1 to: _____ Dept:_____
Copy 2 to: _____ Dept:_____
Copy 3 to: _____ Dept:_____
Copy 3 to: _____ Dept:_____
Copy 4 to: _____ Dept:_____

D.2   User notification? _____yes _____no
Name_____
Office_____ Area_____
Phone _____
Name_____ Office_____
Area_____ Phone_____
Notify immediately? _____yes _____no
Notify via _____

D.3   Balance procedures? _____yes _____no
Describe_____
_____
_____

If out-of-balance, describe action_____
_____
_____
_____
_____

D.4   Quality control:
Check JCL listing? _____yes _____no
Condition code check _____
Sort counts _____
Record counts _____
Check anything else?

_____
_____
_____
_____

JCL disposition: _____Normal or send to: _____

D.5   If this job abends and cannot be restarted, what action should be taken?
_____Save until next working day and send to Systems
_____Call Systems immediately
_____Call on-duty analyst for that application immediately
_____Call Systems in the morning
_____Postpone the following jobs/Schedule ID until resolved
_____ _____ _____

What is the impact if is this job is not completed on schedule?

D.6   If the job is not complete during the shift, who else should be called?

_____

_____

when? _____immediately _____morning _____next working day

The same form can also be used by both the tape library and the forms distribution section. Some installations utilize separate forms for Operations, the Tape Library, and Data Control, which becomes confusing and eventually causes duplicate information.

A good run sheet is a reference tool rather than a narrative document. The difference is subtle but critical. The tape librarians who need setup information should know that section A will always give them tape information. The computer operator should know that section C always contains rerun information. If computer operators need tape information, they also know where it is located on the same form.

Well designed run sheets acknowledge that reruns are a fact of life in MIS departments, and that _good documentation prepared before the rerun helps reduce serious problems._ If a job is important enough for a computer, it is important enough to deserve advance planning for rerun purposes.

The following comments help explain the philosophy behind selected entries in Figure 7.1. A form is more useful when all those concerned understand the purpose!

Heading

Every document (including a run sheet) should have a _date revised_ field. The last person to change the run sheet should also list his or her initials along with the change date.

The _alternate name_ space prevents misunderstanding when installations typically have more than one informal name for the same job. The jobstream that creates purchase orders may be called _PO Generate, Purchase Orders, Process PO Master,_ or _PO4440_ or simply _PO._ They all refer to the same job but are used by different people in different departments.

The _purpose_ summarizes the job and its relationship to the application system.

Section A: Setup and Timing

Question 3 reduces the mystery concerning production jobs that are run on specific request or because they simply "must be run." A large number of production jobs rely upon someone's instinct rather than upon specific instructions.

Section B: Processing

Question 2 defines the origin, use, and disposition of control parameters.

Section C: Rerun Instructions

The first question requires the operator or supervisor to define the reason for a rerun, because the most appropriate rerun procedure may depend upon the cause of the problem. If job Y abends because of a bad tape from job X, the operator may follow a different procedure than for a program error. Incorrect or inappropriate rerun procedures are a curse in many computer centers, and most of those periodic disasters can be avoided by careful planning before the inevitable problems arise.

Section D: Additional Information

Quality control checks and balance information are vital to many production jobs, and should be documented directly in the run sheets. The computer operator or control clerk needs definite instructions on handling errors: Who do they contact? Can they continue? What are the effects? These questions should be resolved in a quiet conference room during the day before slightly panicky computer operator must make their best guess at 2:00 A.M. Murphy has proven that slightly panicky computer operators at 2:00 A.M. are not the best decision makers.

PROBLEM REPORTING LOGS

Whenever a significant problem occurs in a large, multi-CPU data center, or even in a small minicomputer operation, the response should be the same: The problem should be efficiently logged, evaluated, and resolved with a minimum of human and computer expense. That scenario does not always happen. Some data centers are looked upon as the weak spot in the chain that links the customer to the finished product. And efforts to resolve that weak link are frustrating. Frustrated MIS managers frequently describe the computer room as a mysterious black box which devours phone calls. Memos and verbal questions disappear into that gray area of "No, I don't know where it stands."

Formalized problem reporting logs combined with a firm commitment to use them correctly will help reduce that confusion. When a problem appears that cannot be solved immediately, the problem log will start the tracking process and verify that the staff moves toward an eventual resolution. People can always say, "I didn't know about that," or "I forgot," but those excuses become very shaky when the problem has been immediately logged on paper or into an online text editor. When excuses melt away, efficiency quickly rises!

Implementing a problem log procedure (sometimes called an "interrupt" or "situation" procedure) requires careful planning by the Operations staff. MIS management must insist that all areas of the organization faithfully follow the problem log reporting procedure: The concept is useless unless people let the system work!

The four keys to a practical and successful system are:

1. *Make the form easy to use, with checkmarks, circles, or single key entries replacing most of the writing.* Busy operations personnel do not have time for long sessions with a CRT or a pencil when disaster strikes. If the form requires too much time, they will usually handle the problem and fill out the form after the fact. This common but unfortunate approach reduces the value of any problem tracking system. The form should be used *as the problem is happening.*

2. *Teach the staff to evaluate the priority of each problem, which includes an immediate estimate of the possible implications.* The employee investigating the situation should have enough experience to judge the seriousness of the problem. Deciding severity by user reactions is always dangerous, since one user may complain bitterly about an incorrect figure of little importance, while another user may casually mention an incorrect week number in a heading line that indicates the entire weekend processing is wrong.

3. *Create a workable but efficient paperflow.* A computer operator will not willingly stand at a copy machine making 17 copies of a problem log. Nor will they chase three managers for their signatures every time a problem occurs. The workflow must be simple and fast.

4. *Encourage the entire MIS department to view problem logs as helpful tools rather than another paperwork curse, or as a document that points the accusing finger of guilt.* Poor management practices will cause problem reporting logs to be more trouble than the original event.

Problem logs are most useful when everyone in the organization understands when they are needed, and when they are quite literally a waste of time. Making that distinction is often difficult! Management should create a policy document listing specific examples where a problem log is needed and other situations where they are not justified. Certainly the MIS management team does not want a document for every phone call or request that comes into a data center, Help Desk, or computer room, but only for those significant interrupts. The term *significant* is virtually impossible to define, since it varies with the environment and degree of control that management wishes to exert. The best guidelines—or perhaps the only ones that actually work—are those that give realistic, understandable examples.

Figure 7.2 illustrates a problem log designed for an IBM/MVS data center with online and overnight batch applications. One form can handle both types of situations, although the nature of online interrupts is qualitatively different than overnight batch problems. While this suggested format does have most of the information needed for many organizations, a problem reporting log always demands some customization.

Figure 7.2 Problem log

Number_____ Date_____ Logged by_____
Time_____
Original_____ Corrected copy_____ Refers to #_____
Date corrected_____ Corrected by_____
Section_____
** source******   **** priority****
Job   _____   Scheduled   _____   Informational _____
User   _____   Non-scheduled _____   Normal   _____
Internal   _____   Serious   _____
MIS info   _____   Critical   _____
           Route   Software   _____
           Copies   Data control   _____   (D/C keeps original)
           to: applications   _____
                      user: Finance_____ Order control_____
                                     Dist_____
                                     Administration_____ Warehouse_____
                                     Sales_____ Planning_____
                                     Other_____

Note: Copy all serious and critical problems to MIS Director.

A.   General Information

Name_____ Abended?_____ Abend code(s) _____
Messages_____
Action taken_____
_____
_____
_____
_____

Probable cause_____
_____
       Application_____ Disk_____ Tape_____ Operator_____
       User input_____ Documentation_____ JCL_____
       Unknown_____ Other _____
Final cause: determined by_____ date_____
Section_____
       Application_____ Disk_____ Tape_____ Operator_____
       User input_____ Documentation_____ JCL_____
       Unknown_____ Other_____
Critical path problem?_____
Restart time_____ Restart date if different_____
Assistance required during restart? From whom_____
On-site_____ Time notified_____ Notified by_____
Arrived_____
Restart documentation correct?_____ If not, what was wrong? _____
_____
Comments:_____
_____
_____
_____
_____

B.   Online Application

Task name_____ System_____
Abend code _____ Console message _____

Date base abend flag set?_____
    If yes, what time did you start checkpoint recovery? _____
        What time did recovery complete? _____
        What time as task restarted? _____
Probable cause: Application_____ Disk_____ Operator cancel_____
        File lockout_____ Loop_____ Data_____ Unknown_____
        Other_____
Final cause: Determined by_____
        Date_____ Time_____
        Application_____ Disk_____ Operator cancel_____
        File lockout_____ Loop_____ Data_____ Unknown_____
        Other_____
Comments:_____
_____
_____
_____
_____

C. Other

Rerun needed?____

Job ran incorrectly,
But no rerun needed_____

Output from job#____ Lost____

Printer malfunction,
Cause_____
_____

Missing tape_____

Hardware problem?
Tape drive#_____ Down?_____
    Malfunction_____
    Notified vendor at_____
    Responded at_____
    Fixed at_____
Disk drive #_____
    Code_____
    Malfunction_____
    Notified vendor at_____
    Responded at_____
Explanation_____
    Fixed at_____

Additional recovery needed?_____

Incorrect report?
    Notified by_____
    Investigated by_____
    System_____
    Possible error in job#_____
Action taken_____
Other problem:

_____
_____
_____
_____

UPS problem?____
Condition _____
Called service at_____
Responded at_____
Fixed at _____

Communications problem?
Line #_____
Error code_____
Intermittent?_____
Times retried_____
Down time_____
Up time_____
Corrected by_____
Cause_____
_____

The entries in a problem log are usually self-explanatory, if the designer used descriptive titles that are meaningful to the operations staff. Of course, some instructions are still needed. Like all other forms, a problem log must be tested on the actual users in a production-like situation. This test will determine the level of documentation needed. The following explanation will give MIS management a basic understanding of the reasoning behind some of the entries and sections in Figure 7.2.

Heading

Problem logs are often corrected after the fact, or as new information is developed. Analysts or managers can then check the "corrected" copy entry, list their name, and note which original problem the revision applies to. A frequent complaint among operations managers is that incorrect problem logs are never revised. For example, if a production abend is initially charged to a program error, but further research points to a transient hardware problem on a tape drive, the real cause of the problem may never be communicated. If a problem is important enough to need a written problem log, it is important enough to be updated with correct information. The purpose is never to place blame, but simply to communicate the facts: The Operations staff should know that a transient hardware error caused job number 456 to abend last night, so they can watch for additional problems on that tape drive or controller.

Many problem logs are for information only, and employees should not waste valuable reading time on those frequent but annoying troubles that routinely arise in a busy data center. They should, however, know that the problem happened. The operator who checks this entry should be reasonably sure that no one else in the organization needs to follow up on the problem, although it is still an individual responsibility to audit any suspicious looking problem log.

A *serious* interrupt means that a production jobstream is holding up subsequent jobs or may not meet its assigned completion schedule. A *critical* problem implies that unless the situation is resolved immediately, the major production schedule in the shop will not be met. An example is a disk failure that destroys an important data base, requiring quick action in restoring the file, reprocessing updates, notifying the users, and bringing up the online tasks. Another example is a bad input tape in a job that starts the entire overnight critical path, and the tape cannot be recreated through normal means. Unless the problem is resolved, all overnight critical path jobs will be held up, which will delay startup of the online day. This type of situation could be devastating in a banking environment.

The originator of a problem log should determine who else should review the interrupt. Not everyone in a large organization should receive all interrupts, so a single individual (either the originator or an *interrupt controller*) must decide who gets copies of each interrupt form. However, there must be one physical location (such as a common file cabinet or computer file) where a copy of each interrupt is kept, so any authorized person can research previous problems.

Probable Cause

When a problem occurs, the operators may not have enough information to pinpoint the cause. Later, however, as the job is restarted or as they learn more about the situation, they may change their classification. The *final cause* entry is used only when the operator, originator, or other staff member discovers the true nature of the problem.

Since operators occasionally discover that restart documentation is nonexistent or incorrect, the problem log allows him or her to note that condition.

Online Application Problem

Since online processing varies according to the hardware, software, and systems in use, the problem log suggested for an online type of interrupt in Figure 7.2 must be revised to match a specific environment.

Other Problems

Since the number of possible interruptions in a data center is virtually infinite, this section lists only a few of the more common. Again, the format allows the originator to use check marks or a single stroke on the keyboard rather than words or even phrases. By reducing the manual effort, this approach encourages the operations staff (and others) to fill out problem logs faithfully and accurately.

SPECIAL PROCEDURES DOCUMENTATION

Run sheets and problem logs are not enough to run a data center, because many serious real life situations cannot be traced to particular production jobs or specific problems. For example, a disk head crash that has destroyed several critical permanent files will require a detailed recovery plan and a realignment of the subsequent production schedule. The implications are both serious and complicated. The only thing worse than a head crash is a hastily prepared recovery plan that restores the wrong files at the wrong time! A once-a-year event such as warehouse physical inventory will need detailed task lists so everyone involved knows his personal specific responsibilities. Both of these examples are usually looked upon as potential crises by operations managers, since they are invariably the source of irritating and continuing problems. But the event itself does not cause the irritation, rather, it is the lack of planning and lack of documentation. For many companies, taking a once-a-year physical inventory is like a bad dream, but taking a physical inventory when the important players are confused, is a nightmare.

To reduce this confusion, managers and other employees can predict worst case scenarios and prepare for those situations by careful documentation. The act of creating documentation forces employees to prepare for all eventualities. Too often the operational management team looks at planning as an activity restricted to yearly budgets and future hardware upgrades, but good planning covers all areas of data center activity.

Perhaps the lack of forethought is caused by a reluctance to envision the worst. No one likes to anticipate a head crash on the most important pack in the shop, and no one cares to think about what *can* go wrong during a yearly physical inventory. Optimists may be fun to be around at parties, but one or two pessimists are more valuable during the planning process.

One deliverable from this enlightened preparation approach is the *special procedures documentation* manual which contains solutions and answers for those generalized problems that may occur. This collection of information will become just as important to the data center as the book containing detailed run sheets, and should be treated with equal respect.

The subjects in a special procedures manual depend upon the activities of the particular shop. Some common events which can be included are:

- Disk crashes on the permanent production packs:
  What recovery method is possible?
  How many application systems are involved?
  What departments should be notified?
  What other systems are not involved and can be ran normally?

- Once or twice a year systems that need coordination within the data center or with user departments:
  Who schedules the activity?
  How does the data center fit into the picture?
  What planning meetings are necessary, and who should attend?
  What department or section has the experts who can provide additional information?
  Does the data center need any special staffing to handle this event?
  Should the tape library or technical support be involved?

- Situations where the entire overnight batch or weekend batch integrated systems must be reran:
  Who or what group should coordinate the effort?
  What reports and/or files are wrong and should be discarded?
  What should the users be told? Can they use any information from the incorrect reports?
  What unusual problems can be anticipated from the rerun procedures?
  What steps in the rerun can be skipped?

■ An out-of-balance condition that holds up critical path processing:
   What steps should the operator take to solve the problem?
   What are the likely causes?
   What are the risks if the shift director ignores the out-of-balance and continues with production?
   Is the magnitude of the out-of-balance important?
   Who should the shift director contact if he cannot solve the problem?
   How much delay can he accept before calling for help?
   If the decision is to ignore the message and continue, what should the users be told? Should they be asked to help in the problem analysis?

■ A key production support person who cannot be reached:
   Who is the next in line to be called?
   How long should the shift director wait before calling the next individual?
   Should any management level personnel be notified of the problem?

■ A sudden lack of material such as paper or tapes:
   What are the names and phone numbers of the regular suppliers?
   Are there any local companies who provide materials on an emergency basis? What paperwork is necessary to purchase supplies on the weekends?
   Should the shift director make the decision or call the manager?
   Can a shift director ever make that decision himself or herself?

A special procedures book should be in a looseleaf binder with tabs so the operations personnel can quickly locate needed information. Staff members should review the material at least quarterly so they are aware the information exists. It is not necessary to memorize the details, but simply to know that such facts are available and where to find them. Operations managers should verify all employees in their section who may be involved in special problem type situations have actually reviewed the manual.

Some installations put their special procedures book in an online text editing or program development system. This will eliminate the problems associated with paper. If, however, the online system is down or unavailable due to serious hardware problems, the special procedures documentation will be unavailable. For example, a shift supervisor might need to study the recovery procedures for a head crash on the same disk that supports the online text editing system, but since the online application is down, the material itself is unavailable. The hardware problem could prevent employees from seeing the solution! Most installations who store vital documentation on disk also print a hardcopy backup just for these rare but always possible situations.

Updating a special procedures book is just as important as updating run instructions. As the hardware, software, or applications environment changes, the special procedures book will need new sections as old topics are deleted. It is important for the operations manager to critically examine the book and make changes when appropriate. Too much useless information is as bad as not having enough useful facts—the net effect is the same.

AUTOMATED OPERATIONAL DOCUMENTATION

Creating and maintaining operational documentation such as run sheets, problem logs, and special procedures manuals is a costly and time consuming project. Busy employees must be taken from other assignments and given enough resources to develop the initial documentation. Operations and programming management must continually insist that each staff member meet his or her personal commitment to keep the documents current. This is expensive in people time, and data processing experts have traditionally suggested the computer as a way to automate tasks that need large amounts of human effort. Several software companies have recognized this need and developed automated packages that provide run sheets, flow charts, and other operational documentation based on the job control language (or JCL in IBM terminology). But automation is not always the answer to everything, as many systems analysts and frustrated users have discovered over the years. Can those packages actually help a data center? Or are they little more than expensive glitter?

The benefits from such a computerized system can be impressive, especially if the product uses the actual job control language and its run time parameters to produce the documentation. A good software product will allow the operations department to choose documentation output that is very detailed or very summarized, depending upon the particular need and circumstances. Eventually these products will allow the operations and programming staff to actually design the formats, in the same way that fourth generation application development systems let users design their screens and hard copy reports. A good product will allow online storage, maintenance, retrieval, and comprehensive search facilities.

Automated systems can have disadvantages, primarily when the operations staff cannot effectively use the documentation formats without major changes. While it is always possible to force computer operators to accept what is available, such pressure will lower morale and create resentment. If management decides to impose a specific form or system upon the operations staff without allowing them to participate in the design and testing phases, the operators may respond by ignoring the documentation. The advantage of an inhouse-designed form for run sheets, problem logs, and associated documentation, is that the staff can help mold the output into a form that is useful for them and their environment.

Although a purchased package can be a major breakthrough for a shop which has limited or virtually nonexistent documentation, operations managers should carefully compare the benefits from a package with the advantages of a system designed specifically for their particular hardware, software, and applications environment. A ready-made product is easy to install, can produce documentation quickly, and usually takes less clerical effort to maintain. The inhouse-designed forms (which can also be made into an automated system) will have a format designed for an individual data center, but requires more work from the operators and programmers to set up the initial documentation. Fortunately, some vendors will provide a free trial period to evaluate their automated system, which makes the comparison project relatively straightforward. As these systems become more sophisticated and flexible, they will become more and more attractive. But until these products do possess this flexibility, MIS managers must take a close look at the benefits of a package compared to the inherent advantages of an inhouse designed system. The choice may be difficult.

MASTER SYSTEM DOCUMENTATION

Run sheets and assorted documentation are easier to use when organized into a manual (either hard copy or represented by a file on disk) related to each application or to each logical unit of operation. Most business data processing installations use a specific application system as the unit of work, such as general ledger, inventory control, and accounts payable. These application specific manuals allow immediate access to information when a question or problem appears.

But run sheets themselves do not allow operators and programmers to understand the flow of data between specific jobs, or between different production schedules. In a typical batch environment, daily jobs produce data which is fed into other daily, weekly, or monthly jobs. Problems and misunderstandings develop because the staff does not understand this data flow or system integration. Indeed, those employees in a data center rated as most knowledgeable may be those who have mastered this data flow concept! Therefore, another document called the *system flow* should be the first entry in the master system manual, and it should be designed for operators rather than programmers. Although the programming staff obviously needs similar information, their style and level of detail will probably be much different. Of course, any document that describes the operational data flow will still be helpful to new programmers or those employees who wish to learn the basics of the technical side of an unfamiliar application system.

Analysts traditionally use the standard flow chart to describe a computer system. This format works reasonably well if the writer spends considerable thought selecting the appropriate level of detail. *The common mistake that renders many beautiful flow charts useless is that they possess too much detail for an operator.* Like run sheets, the guideline for a system flow diagram should be, "What does the operator need to know?" and the answers are never obvious. With too little information the document will be unsatisfactory, and too much detail will obscure the important facts. The solution is to ask the operations staff to make detailed suggestions and recommendations based on their own experience. Simply asking a new operator who is trying to learn the systems is an excellent way to obtain feedback. Involving the operational staff will help the writer or manager select the optimum level of detail needed by the employees.

DATA CENTER STATISTICS REPORT

Business analysts look at the typical data center or operations department as an information factory, and suggest measuring the input and output of the computer room as one captures the performance of a manufacturing plant. Performance statistics are a concise, easily understood way of comparing the activities of the data center from one period to another. Without such measures, it becomes impossible to answer the question, "How is the Data Center doing?"

The answer is to publish a weekly and monthly statistics report that captures the most relevant data available. This allows MIS management, data center management, and key user managers to understand the workload, problems, and production aspects of their data center. Figure 7.3 is a sample Data Center statistics report that can be modified to fit most environments. This report should be issued weekly, and for a monthly cycle should be accompanied by a one- or two-page narrative that mentions the significant points. Statistics and raw numbers are important, but the narrative explanation will put those measures in the proper perspective.

SUMMARY OF KEY POINTS

- Run sheets should contain only the facts needed by the people who actually use them, such as computer operators and tape librarians. They should not have information for nonusers such as programmers and data analysts.

- One group or individual must have primary management control over run sheets, and monitor the updating and distribution process. If no one is responsible for run sheets, no one will maintain them.

- Run sheets should answer the questions everyone knows will arise, but are afraid to ask. For example, when this job fails at 2:00 A.M. for this specific reason, what should the operator do? What are the effects if it cannot be resolved by 3:00 A.M.?

- Every significant problem in a data center should be tracked through a problem reporting log that is easy to fill out and use.

Figure 7.3 Data center statistics report

	Current Week	Last Week	Month to Date	Previous MTD	This Year YTD	Last Year YTD
Production:						
Jobs complete on time	___	___	___	___	___	___
Jobs restarted	___	___	___	___	___	___
Lost time for restarts	___	___	___	___	___	___
Reruns	___	___	___	___	___	___
Nightly critical path complete by 0600	___	___	___	___	___	___
Nights critical path late	___	___	___	___	___	___
% critical path on time	___	___	___	___	___	___
Total interrupts	___	___	___	___	___	___
Hardware	___	___	___	___	___	___
Application	___	___	___	___	___	___
Software	___	___	___	___	___	___
Unknown	___	___	___	___	___	___
Others	___	___	___	___	___	___
User response time						
0800	___	___	___	___	___	___
1030	___	___	___	___	___	___
1200	___	___	___	___	___	___
1400	___	___	___	___	___	___
1600	___	___	___	___	___	___
1800	___	___	___	___	___	___
Batch turnaround	___	___	___	___	___	___
Payroll hours	___	___	___	___	___	___
Illness	___	___	___	___	___	___
Overtime	___	___	___	___	___	___
Training	___	___	___	___	___	___
# employees	___	___	___	___	___	___

- It is difficult to separate significant from non-significant problems. Expect mistakes. Provide realistic examples as guidelines.

- Run sheets are not enough to handle every situation that will arise in a data center. A special procedures manual should contain information that tells how to manage actual and potential problems. This manual can also be the disaster manual, although it describes other situations, such as taking a once-a-year physical inventory that seriously affects the data center.

- Automated operational documentation can help, especially for shops which have virtually no existing documentation.

- Run sheets and other documentation should be organized into a master system log for each specific application or logical unit of processing.

- The data center statistics report is a simple but effective way to communicate some of the important measures of data center performance.

- The monthly statistics report needs a description of the important facts that affected the statistics: Raw numbers (even when they show trends) need some explanation.

8

Software Acquisition Documents

Buying ready made software is a common practice: Most companies purchase their "bread and butter" applications such as payroll and general ledger, and some organizations buy virtually all their core business systems from software vendors. Choosing the best package is not easy. The success of any selection process depends partially upon the quality of the written communication that flows between the vendor and MIS. Chapter 8 has four carefully designed documents that will fit into almost any software methodology: a vendor evaluation survey, sample letter of reference, user questionnaire, and software comparison chart. Systems analysts, technical writers, users, user department managers, and MIS executives can use these forms with only slight modifications.

The term *acquisition* immediately conjures up visions of legal contracts and purchasing agreements, but there is more analysis in the software acquisition process than in writing or revising a contract. Everything involved in acquisition is complicated, but the procedure has a greater chance for success if the team performing the package selection uses carefully engineered documents. Precise technical writing prevents problems and reduces the risk inherent in purchasing a software package.

Conversely, inadequate written communication can lead to poor MIS and user decisions. Purchasing the wrong package can be a fatal error.

Software contracts themselves *are* complicated and require legal expertise. The trade journals often report companies suing vendors over packages and systems that did not perform according to expectations! In most situations, *the problems did not originate with the contract, but with the preceding software acquisition process itself*. The selection group made a mistake, and the best contract in the world will not rectify that original error. For every business that sends its lawyers to the courtroom, there are fifty others who were equally disappointed by a software package but decided not to go through a long, expensive legal drama.

Even the best lawyer cannot save a company from the ongoing pains of a poor software selection. The organization may survive, but the staff will still pay a heavy price in terms of user dissatisfaction and MIS frustration. Effective technical communication during the selection and negotiation phase will help prevent those "incorrect selections." Like system design documents, internal and external vendor related materials should be part of a well thought out *software acquisition methodology*. Too often, however, MIS staffers are given only theoretical approaches and not sample formats they can modify for immediate use. This chapter provides documents that will fit into most software acquisition methodologies. For those companies who do not have a formalized approach, these samples will help develop a rational and logical method to selecting software.

VENDOR EVALUATION FORMS

Once the project team selects the final packages for consideration (or even during the initial screening) they require detailed information about the vendor. When a company purchases a software package, they are also buying the people and organization behind the system. The larger the package, the more important the vendor's capabilities. When selecting a $200 microcomputer application, MIS will generally be satisfied if the system works! But when selecting a two hundred thousand dollar manufacturing system that takes months to install, MIS will be vitally concerned with the vendor's ability to support their investment. Large, expensive, and complex applications require large, expensive, and complex installation efforts: The vendor may be a key to success or failure.

Figure 8.1 is a "vendor evaluation survey" that will uncover basic information about the company behind the product. This form can also gather information about organizations who are being considered for service contracts or consulting awards. In terms of software acquisition, this document has enough information for the team to judge the vendors on the four critical support criteria:

Figure 8.1   Vendor evaulation survey

INSTRUCTIONS TO VENDOR:

Please complete this survey and return to the address listed on the cover letter within three weeks. Also, please attach any material requested, or other documents you feel support your qualifications. Thank you.

Your Name_____ Title_____

Company: _____ Division:_____

A. FINANCIAL BASE

1. How long has your company been in business?_____

2. Has ownership changed during the past five years? If so, explain the timing and circumstances.

   _____

   _____

   _____

   _____

3. Are the current owners contemplating selling the business?

   _____

   _____

4. How many employees do you have now? _____
   How many do you plan to have in one year?_____

5. How many employees have you hired during the past twelve months? _____

6. How many employees have you lost during the past twelve months? _____

7. How long has the CEO been with the firm? _____

8. Are you in litigation? If so, list each action and describe in an attachment.
   yes_____ no_____

9. Are you taking legal action against any other company? If so, describe in a separate attachment.
   yes_____ no_____

10. Are you a public company? _____
    If so, enclose last years annual report.

11. List your gross sales for the past five years:

Year	Gross Sales
_____	_____
_____	_____
_____	_____
_____	_____
_____	_____

12. In what year was your first software sale? _____

13. What is the total value of all software sales made since your company began? _____

14. What is the sales forecast for the next fiscal year? _____

Figure 8.1 *(Continued)*

15. List five trade publications that you advertised in:

_____

_____

_____

_____

_____

16. List the name, address, and phone number of your bank.

_____

_____

_____

17. What is your Dun and Bradstreet number? _____

B. THE PACKAGE

1. When did you first sell this product? _____

2. Did you develop it yourself or did you purchase it from another company? _____

_____

3. When was this product first developed? _____

4. How many major releases have you provided since it was first sold to customers?

5. How many installations do you have of this product?

_____

6. How many employees serve on "product enhancement" or development teams specifically for this product? _____

7. When is your next planned major release? _____

8. What are the next planned enhancements?

_____

_____

_____

_____

9. Who represents you (e.g. your own people, independent sales organizations, consultants)?

_____

_____

10. Do you have a 24-hour hotline? If so, what type of people handle phone calls? _____

_____

11. Is there an extra charge for hotline support?

_____

12. Who backs up the hotline staff? _____

_____

13. What type questions will the hotline staff *not* answer?

_____

_____

_____

14. List the five best aspects about your system.

_____

_____

_____

_____

15. List five weak points reported by customers.

_____
_____
_____
_____
_____

16. Will you provide a complete client list?_____
    If yes, please attach.

17. List five reference sites we can contact. We will need names, addresses, and phone numbers.

_____
_____
_____
_____
_____
_____
_____

18. To your knowledge, has anyone purchased your package but failed to install? If so, please describe.

_____
_____
_____
_____

C. SERVICES

1. Do you have multiple site leasing agreements? _____

2. Do you provide consulting services? _____
   At what rate? _____ Expenses _____
   For what purposes: _____

_____
_____
_____

What is the background of your consultants?

_____

During the last calendar year, about how much revenue did you derive from paid consulting services? _____
List two companies who have purchased your consulting services during the past two years. Please provide name, address, and phone number of someone we can contact.

_____
_____
_____

3. Does the product have a User Group? _____
   During the last calendar year, how many times did the User Group meet? _____
   Does the User Group control all or part of your development effort? If so, please explain.

_____
_____
_____
_____

Figure 8.1 *(Continued)*

When did the User Group form? _____
Who can we contact in the User Group? _____
_____
_____

4. When customers discover problems, who do they first contact? _____
   For source code changes or fixes, do you give customers line number fixes, or do you send a complete new module? _____
   Besides major releases, do you have revisions? _____
   If yes, how often do they occur? _____

D. MANUFACTURING EXPERTISE

1. How many APICS certified employees do you have? _____

2. How many others are enrolled in the certification program? _____

3. In what positions are the certified employees?
   _____
   _____
   _____
   _____

4. How many Class A users do you have? _____

5. How many users do you have in the process industry?
   _____

6. How many of your users have purchased your other packages? _____

7. What is the average time to fully implement your MRP? _____

8. What is the longest time taken to install your MRP?
   (Ignore companies who stop and start the implementation project). _____

9. Do you provide guidelines (such as suggested task lists) for implementation? _____

10. Has your inventory control module ever interfaced directly with an Automated Storage/Retrieval System? If so, please describe.
    _____
    _____
    _____

11. What auditing firms have inspected and/or approved your suggested physical inventory accounting procedures?
    _____
    _____

■ Financial base

■ Experience level

■ Staff qualifications

■ Ability to respond

Written responses also furnish additional legal protection, because documents have some binding authority. Unfortunately, the degree of legal impact varies with each situation. In some cases, they have no legal standing! Nevertheless, experienced systems analysts and managers have learned that salespersons who tend to exaggerate slightly when chatting amiably over a two martini lunch, will lose that tendency when they must put their answers in writing.

Before using this questionnaire the project team should eliminate those questions that do not apply to the system under consideration, and add statements that reflect upon the specific application. Section D of Figure 8.1 concerns a manufacturing environment and was designed for a project team considering an MRP-II (Material Requirements Planning) package. By replacing Section "D" one can adapt the form for other business or scientific systems. These specific sections do not replace the detailed requirements, but rather summarizes them in a format that can be easily understood. If this section expands, it will eventually become a request for proposal (RFP). But for a vendor evaluation survey or initial screening procedure, only the important requirements are listed. The purpose of a vendor evaluation survey is to narrow the field as quickly as possible.

LETTER OF REFERENCE

Once the final candidates are selected, the project team often calls or writes existing customers of each vendor. Analysts typically use phone calls or letters. Which one gives the most useful information? Or should the systems analyst use both? A phone call is obviously less work for both the analyst and customer, and can often elicit opinions that many people will refuse to put down on paper! On the minus side, however, even the best prepared phone call cannot answer every detailed question. Also, verbal discussions are transitory, and unless the listener records the conversation, he may forget critical items.

The best approach is both: Use a phone call to contact the person, follow up with carefully designed letter and questionnaire, and then call again to verify the responses and gain additional opinions.

Letters and survey documents require effort, but are more permanent than a phone call. Unfortunately, such letters also have a frustrating habit of being ignored. Some companies who send out ten letters of reference will feel fortunate if three are returned. This throw-it-in-the-wastebasket attitude is not simply random, but is predictable. For example, the spirit of cooperation rises with the cost and complexity of the package: A manager responsible for a $5,000 utility may be less likely to respond than one who uses a $200,000 manufacturing package. Companies with complex purchased applications will often furnish information to other organizations if their comments will not get them into legal difficulties. Their motivation may come from a desire to help fellow professionals, establish friendly contact with other companies, or simply to get back at the vendor for a poor job. *The initial phone call should attempt to uncover that motivation.*

Having a company respond to a questionnaire is encouraging, but the actual value of the information partially depends upon their personal attitudes.

The accompanying questionnaire should be brief: Most ten-page questionnaires automatically wind up in the wastebasket. Busy MIS professionals and users often refuse to spend their valuable time completing long, involved documents that will never help them directly. A one-page questionnaire is ideal, although two pages are usually acceptable. Anything over three pages may disappear forever!

It is difficult to determine the best person in an organization to contact. Sales representatives may provide the name of the person they are most familiar with, or someone who is unlikely to criticize their product. In the same company, however, *one may find differing opinions on the same product*. The director of manufacturing may not be satisfied with an MRP system because it does not give him adequate production reports, while the purchasing manager may think the system is the greatest invention since fast food hamburgers. The software analyst may hate a disk space utility software package at the same time the operations manager extols the virtues of the system that saves him one hour during the overnight processing. Letters of reference and survey questionnaires are valuable, but they should not always be taken literally: Everyone who relies on such information must understand their limitations. *The opinions expressed in questionnaires are a function of the individual's personal experiences, his job responsibilities, his familiarity with the package, and the amount of sleep he got last night.*

The way to handle that potential problem is simple: Send the material to at least *two* people in the same organization, preferably in different departments. Although those two or more individuals may collaborate, the project team has a better chance of getting a more valid opinion. If responses from those individuals differ greatly, the analysts may wish to recontact them by phone for further details.

Figure 8.2 is a reference letter to a person previously contacted by phone, and Figure 8.3 is the corresponding questionnaire. Every survey document should be designed for both the specific application and the type of respondent. Some analysts create an all purpose form that can be answered by several groups of people. This shortcut is a mistake! The respondents are doing the project team a favor, and should not be forced to search through extraneous information. If the team needs answers from the viewpoints of MIS, payroll, accounting, and internal auditing, they should provide a custom designed questionnaire for the contact. The payroll manager does not want to be bothered reading questions on data base access efficiency meant for the software expert.

Figure 8.2 Letter of reference

Mr. Gary Grimy
Production Manager
Dirt Enterprises, Inc.
9046 Yucky Avenue
Muddy Flats, Iowa 40567

Dear Mr. Grimy:
    Thanks for your offer to give us your opinions on the Worm Farm Management System you had developed by your parent corporation, Wonderful Widgets. As I mentioned, Wonderful Widgets has now turned WOFAMS into a package we at Consolidated Widgets may use for our own worm subsidiary. As you know, it's hard to know which end is which in the worm farm business, and we need every bit of computerized help we can get.
    Attached is a short questionnaire and self-addressed stamped envelope.
    For your information, we have also sent a questionnaire to your controller Terrance Tightwad III, for his evaluation of the financial reports.
    Again, thanks very much for your help. We greatly appreciate your cooperation.

Sincerely,
Bernard Brown
Senior Systems Analyst
Division of Worms

SOFTWARE COMPARISON CHART

Once all the information has been compiled from letters of reference, requirements documents, RFPs, and detailed discussions, the project team summarizes the important points in comparison documents. These handy charts compare each package according to the most important criteria determined by the team. The value of a comparison chart depends upon the thought put into the document. A good chart will allow the decision makers to visually scan the document and rate the possibilities in a logical manner. A poorly designed or executed chart can waste weeks and months of effort by confusing an already complex situation. *The job of a software acquisition team is not only to gather all important information about the packages and vendors, but to present those facts, opinions, and judgments in an easy to understand picture.*

    System analysts and technical writers always have a serious responsibility to the companies that pay their salaries, but even more so when performing software acquisition studies. By manipulating software comparison documents, an analyst can easily slight one vendor and give an unfair advantage to another. This is unethical at the very least (if not illegal), and violates the basis of professional responsibility. Because most senior managers and users would rather read summaries and comparison charts than detailed requirements, the ultimate choice may be affected by the implied tone of the chart or summary. Every software acquisition and

Figure 8.3 Sample questionnaire to evaluate a package

---

1. When did you first install WOFAMS? _____

2. How long did your installation take? _____

3. Did you have any unexpected problems with the installation process? _____

4. Please rate WOFAMS, with 5 the highest and 1 the lowest:

General effectiveness	1	2	3	4	5
System accuracy	1	2	3	4	5
Ease of use	1	2	3	4	5
Reliability	1	2	3	4	5
Completeness	1	2	3	4	5

5. What is the best thing(s) about WOFAMS? _____

6. What did you like least about WOFAMS? _____

7. Are you satisfied with the production reports?
   Daily _____
   Weekly _____
   Monthly _____

8. Are the data entry screens easy to use? _____

9. Are you satisfied with the online edits? _____

10. Are the audit trails satisfactory to your production people? Do you have any suggestions for better auditing? _____

11. Is your online response time acceptable? Is it always less than three seconds? _____

12. Did you work with Wonderful Widgets during the installation phase? _____
    If so, did they meet your needs? _____

13. Have you worked with them since installation? _____
    If so, please comment upon their service _____

14. How would you rate their user documentation? _____

15. In general, on a scale of 1 the lowest and 5 the highest, how would you rate WOFAMS as a generalized system to handle the Worm Farm Business? _____

Thank you very much for your comments.

---

vendor contact document should be reviewed by at least one other professional to verify its objectivity.

Although requirements are often developed by discussions, arguments, and eventual compromise, a good comparison document goes beyond those specific requirements and looks at a software acquisition from a company-wide perspective. That is, the document evaluates the software package based upon five critical factors:

■ How does each package satisfy the A-B-C requirements for the user and MIS?

■ How does each vendor rate in terms of probable support?

■ How does each software package fit in with other projects, activities, or purchases as listed in the long range MIS plan?

■ What are the relative risks of each package and vendor?

■ What are the total external, internal, and ongoing costs of each system?

A document that specifies only user requirements is therefore presenting only one fifth of the software acquisition circle: The other four fifths may actually determine which system is best for the organization! Software purchases are business rather than purely technical decisions. User requirements are certainly important and should be give a prominent place in the comparison document, but other factors are equally important and must be included in the comparison. If the chart ignores vital business oriented considerations, the senior decision makers may eventually ignore the comparison document. This is equally frustrating to the project team and the managers who appointed them, even if the analysts and technical writers have done an outstanding job analyzing and categorizing user requirements. Their only mistake was to underestimate the scope of their responsibilities.

Are the five factors of requirements, vendor support, long-range fit, risks, and costs always necessary? In any given situation, one or more of those considerations may not apply, or perhaps another one should be substituted. Selecting the critical factors that will determine the ultimate choice is not as simple. The technical writer should carefully poll the decision makers before creating a document to obtain their actual criteria for making final software decisions. If they reply with the obvious statement, "Why, on the basis of user requirements, of course," the technical writer should repeat the question. Either they did not understand the request, are being evasive, or are not true decision makers. If the analyst team fails to get cooperation, they must make their own guesses, but they must always go beyond user and MIS requirements in their summary documents.

For both user and MIS requirements, comparison charts can use either a simple "yes/no" answer or a more sophisticated ratings matrix. There are at least two ways to quantify judgments.

First, one can say that category A requirements are obviously more important than category B requirements. (This chapter assumes the analyst team is using the classic "A-B-C" approach to requirements definition as explained in Chapter 3.) The technical writer can assign a weight of 3 to all category A requirements, a 2 to category B, and a 1 to category C. These relative weights are purely arbitrary: One could assign category A a value of 6, category B a weight of 3, and category C a value of 1. By using the "yes/no" checks, if a package meets six category A requirements, it will receive a score of 18 (6 × 3) for category A. If it meets 12 category B requirements, it will receive a rating of 24 (12 × 2) for category B compliance. This method is superior to counting the number of check marks in each category.

The *double ratings* method assigns weights for each requirement *within* a category. For example, a specific payroll system (which involves transmission of confidential information) may provide "adequate" data security, which constitutes a one line category A entry in a requirements document. But another package may have sophisticated security procedures that should be rated outstanding. The yes/no method would compare both systems equally (each would receive a score of 3 for data security). The analyst, however, needs a simple way to explain that one package is superior, and to include this advantage in the total score.

By using a one to three scale *within* the category, he assigns a value of 3 to the package that has superior data security features. Then, the score for data security becomes 9 (3 × 3). The first 3 is the standard rating for all category A requirements, and the second 3 is the value for this package because it has exceptional data security features. Other packages that only meet the basic data security requirement would receive the standard 3 (3 × 1), because default value would always be 1. The double ratings approach provides more accurate totals for comparisons, and also helps the entire project team by forcing the analysts and users to understand the relative value of each requirement.

Figure 8.4 illustrates a software acquisition comparison chart using the five basic considerations for selecting the best fit software package. The User and MIS requirements section uses a double ratings method. The total score in the requirements section explains the relative fit of the most important requirements. This matrix format takes more time, but the results are always worth the effort.

SUMMARY OF KEY POINTS

- When buying a software package, the organization also "buys" the vendor: their people, resources, and degree of support. Using the Vendor Questionnaire helps the team discover strengths and weaknesses.

- Before sending a letter of reference to gather opinions about a package or vendor, call the person and ask permission. Ask about his or her general attitude toward the package. Don't depend upon the phone call, but use these verbal comments to supplement your understanding of his or her responses.

Figure 8.4   Software comparison chart

This chart was developed by the Software Acquisition Team of Consolidated Widgets, for the purpose of selecting a comprehensive Worm Farm Management System. Our three finalists are WOFAMS (from Wonderful Widgets), SLIME (from Muddy Data Systems), and ICKY (from Underground Systems, Inc).

Explanation: This chart compares our finalists in five areas:
—User and MIS requirements (broken down by A-B-C priority)
—Vendor support and performance
—How each package fits into our Long-Range Plan
—Risks
—Costs, including direct, indirect, and ongoing

I. User and MIS Requirements	WOFAMS	SLIME	ICKY
A. Inventory Control			
Category A (required—			
base value = 3)			
Real time updating	1	1	0
Inquiry by length of worm	0	1	1
Physical inventory capability	3	2	1
Random locator system	1	2	0
Parent-child access	3	1	2
Group item numbers	1	1	1
Interface to purchasing system	2	0	0
MIS: relational data base	1	0	1
MIS: at least 6 CRT's online			
simultaneously	1	0	1
Category B (suggested—			
base value = 2)			
Inquiry by color	1	1	1
Update by color group	1	1	0
Average costing by worm	2	1	0
MIS: automatic backout			
by tran code	1	0	1
MIS: inquiry by tran code	0	2	1
Category C (nice to have—			
base value = 1)			
Accidental death history file	2	0	2
Suggested replenishment by warehouse	3	2	2
MIS: transaction history file	1	0	0
Total raw scores for			
inventory requirements	13	8	7
Scores with weights for			
A(3), B(2), and C(1)	55	36	31

II. Vendor	WOFAMS	SLIME	ICKY
In business more than 5 years	yes	no	yes
In business more than 2 years	yes	no	no
Number of employees	79	32	12
Dun and Bradstreet trend	up	down	up
Dun and Bradstreet general evaluation	good	risky	good
Hotline support	no	yes	no
Consulting support (chargeable)	yes	yes	no

Figure 8.4   *(Continued)*

	WOFAMS	SLIME	ICKY
Number of major releases	6	3	2
Client survey	good	fair	mixed
Annual sales (in millions)	45	18	6
Next year sales forecast (in millions)	49	23	18
MIS comfort level with technical reps	good	good	poor

III. Interface with Our Long Range MIS Plan	WOFAMS	SLIME	ICKY
Supports at least two other data bases	yes	no	yes
Other data bases	yes	no	no
Vendor has purchasing system available now	yes	no	no
Handles multiple worm farm locations	yes	yes	yes
Could use MIS Information Center	yes	no	no
Runs on minis (distributed option)	yes	no	yes
Vendor provides contract programming	no	yes	yes
Vendor has accounting systems ready	yes	no	no

IV. Risks	WOFAMS	SLIME	ICKY
Vendor going out of business (estimate)	nil	maybe	low
Package will be obsolete in 3 years	no	maybe	no
Could handle government regulations if worms become controlled substance	yes	yes	maybe

V. Cost	WOFAMS	SLIME	ICKY
Purchase (in thousands)	120	94	75
Interface to existing systems	59	40	65
Vendor maintenance per year	12	12	7
Internal installation cost	10	10	10
Total direct expense to vendor	120	94	75
Internal MIS expense	69	50	75
Total indirect and direct	189	144	150

- Send the reference letter to at least two people in the same organization: Never depend upon one response. Select people in different areas who use the package. Follow up with a probing phone call if the responses differ greatly.

- After collecting all information about packages and their vendors, use a Software Comparison Chart to present the findings. The Chart must include non-technical factors (such as cost) as well as user/MIS requirements. Reviewers need to see each candidate in a side-by-side format.

- The Software Comparison Chart should be checked by professionals outside the project team to verify that it does not give unfair advantage to one vendor.

- The classic A-B-C requirements should be weighted, so that category A requirements are worth more than category B. The Double Ratings method uses weights within a category to further differentiate between packages.

9

Programming and Technical Documentation

MIS professionals complain about the sad state of their own technical documentation. Yearly internal and external audits repeatedly point to inadequate or out-of-date internal documentation. Even organizations which pride themselves on the quality of their user documentation may neglect documenting systems for their own employees. Chapter 9 describes the purpose and business justification for documentation, and emphasizes that internal documentation must follow predefined standards. Internal documentation has three objectives: assist system maintenance, aid research or investigative work, and prepare for eventual program replacement. The Answer Book and System Log will provide a safe resting place for other important but often overlooked information. This chapter is for all technical employees, technical writers, and MIS managers.

Well written and useful technical documents are so rare they are often treated as works of art, and are shown proudly to important visitors. Even software companies who sell complete application systems as their primary business often admit their own internal documentation is vastly inferior to their user documentation. The key term is *useful*, for much of the documentation that does exist was never designed according to logical rules and procedures, but simply *evolved*. Internal documentation that is not carefully planned is about as useless as a payroll system thrown together without precise rules. Both are more trouble than they are worth. Computer hardware and software have come a long way from the 1970s, but the same complaints of those early programmers are still heard in the 1990s. If documentation exists, it must help the MIS staff in their day-to-day work assignments. If it fails that test, the documentation has little practical value.

Many of the same considerations that apply to such diverse documents as feasibility statements and requirements definitions, should apply to program level documentation. The principles of effective written communication are just as important when one programmer writes information for another.

Why does one document a program? The reason must justify the time and expense of creating the documentation. The classic premise for providing internal documentation is that the original programmer and analyst team will not be supporting the program forever. Other employees will assume responsibility, and they will not have the same intimate familiarity as the original group. Without such detailed knowledge of the program and system, the new supporting team will require longer time to correct problems and provide upgrades. This scenario, however, is only one justification for internal documentation.

There are three basic reasons for documenting a computer program or unit of software:

1. Help with the inevitable maintenance effort, by quickly imparting at least a generalized understanding of the module to other programmers or analysts.

2. Explain the details of processing (or logic), which will answer questions posed by users and other MIS employees.

3. Identify information about a program so it can be eventually replaced.

In any given situation, a program or module may fall into one or more of these conditions. Perhaps the analyst predicts that the "purchase order generate" program will be subject to periodic maintenance requests. The internal documentation should therefore be pointed toward the specific needs of a maintenance programmer. Or the program logic in a pricing program may be very complex and the original programmer can visualize many requests from the users to clarify the options or costing logic. Complex programs need documentation that explains the processing in easy-to-understand terms so a programmer is not forced to laboriously trace logic paths in the code. In other cases, a manager may know that a given program is slated for replacement in the near future, and he should direct the programmer to provide enough details so that future analyst teams can use that information as their base requirements. The latter justification truly demands a long range management viewpoint.

Unless the programmer or manager who supervises the technical staff understands the specific justification (or justifications) behind internal documentation, he may waste valuable time and resources. Documentation styles, content, and format will differ for each of these three purposes. If, however, any of these reasons do not apply, the effort may not be justified. For example, if management is relatively certain a particular program will not need maintenance or enhancements, the first reason is eliminated. If the processing logic is simple or thoroughly documented in a user manual, the second reason is not valid. And if that same piece of software will most likely never be replaced, internally documenting that particular unit of software is not justified. Obviously, this example is extreme, but the principle is correct: A programmer should never start documenting until he knows *why* he is doing the documentation. Understanding the purpose will help make the documentation meaningful.

Defining the purpose helps the programmers analyze their audience. Like a system design proposal or user manual, every piece of technical documentation is written for specific groups of people having particular needs. If the purpose in documenting a program is to help with future maintenance problems, the programmers assume they are writing for other programmers working in a maintenance rather than development environment. The audience will need information that helps them analyze the program and make changes safely. If the original programmers place themselves mentally in the position of a maintenance programmer, they can direct their documentation toward the unique and sometimes high pressure needs of maintenance.

Standards for internal documentation are not simply "nice-to-have": They are necessary. Technical documentation is seldom read casually: Rather, it is typically used in time critical situations. Programmers must quickly understand how a module works, and they should not spend valuable company time adapting to a new style of internal documentation before they can understand the program. If programs are internally documented in varying styles, there is a significant relearning period every time a programmer moves to a different module, and the frustration factor increases with every format change. Every program or module written in a specific language should use the same format for its internal documentation. A programmer who has gone through one module should find the next one slightly easier if the internal comments and documentation follow the same general format. If they have differing styles, each attempt to understand a module will be more difficult. Consistently applied standards will help programmers, analysts, and managers realize the potential advantages of internal documentation.

JUSTIFYING INTERNAL DOCUMENTATION

Before internal documentation can become a routine departmental policy, management must evaluate the economic value of good documentation for programs and modules. MIS management should apply the same type of cost and benefits analysis they apply to user projects. The financial exercise to justify documentation is healthy, and one should never accept documentation merely because the "experts" say it is needed. Why should MIS, for example, spend a week of additional programmer time on a project that is done just to develop internal documentation? If the users are satisfied with their application, is it necessary to spend 40 hours on documentation when there are always high priority projects waiting in the wings? Does it make good business sense?

If the rationale falls into one of the three previously mentioned categories, the answer is a definite yes, especially in regard to routine production support. Maintenance consumes a large portion of many MIS budgets, and one direct cause is that programmers assigned to application systems have a difficult time understanding the source code. It is not due to incompetence, poor training, or lack of effort, but rather that most application systems are written in third generation languages such as COBOL, and are difficult to understand.

Internal documentation—when properly done—helps remove the mystery and speeds up the maintenance effort. While it is difficult to provide quantitative justification, senior MIS management should have enough personal experience with production support requirements to understand the validity of that argument. Internal documentation is a good investment when *analyzed via the MIS long range plan as a technique to reduce the maintenance effort*. If, however, management takes only a narrow short term view, internal documentation is a losing investment. If MIS management is truly to develop business skills, they must stop looking at their departments with a day-to-day orientation and discover the long range business advantages. Internal documentation is simply another business investment.

THE DATA DICTIONARY

The heart of any business application system is the collection of data elements used to reflect both permanent and temporary information (i.e. fields which are calculated or serve as "work variables"). A data dictionary describes data elements in the following terms:

- Descriptive name
- Identification name or number
- Range values

- Internal structure (i.e., format used in the computer)
- External format (i.e., format or formats available for display)
- Editing characteristics
- Allowed alternate names
- Business definition
- List of modules that use the element

An application system written without a data dictionary may have different names for the same field, or the same name may refer to different data elements. The size of a data element passed from program to program may vary. Perhaps each programmer invented fields he believed were meaningful but are actually confusing to users or other programmers. While data base management systems help solve such problems by enforcing a common file or data structure for permanent data fields, only a comprehensive data dictionary will give true control over the companies entire information base.

The advantages of a data dictionary are:

- Each program will use the same data element name, which prevents confusion.
- Programmers should take less time to develop programs, since data has been predefined.
- Data has the same characteristics throughout the application system or systems.
- Both users and technicians share a common definition of each data element.
- Library scans will pinpoint all occurrences of a specific data element, which will help in both maintenance and development projects.

While simple in concept, implementing a data dictionary for existing application systems is a major commitment of time and resources. Should management require a retrofit of all production systems to use the data dictionary? The answer depends upon the degree of disorder. If the original programmers attempted to use some degree of consistency for names and definitions, the project may be costly but feasible. If, however, the developers followed their own whims, the project is virtually impossible. But even if technically feasible, senior management will seriously question the payback of a retrofit: In many cases, a data dictionary should be used only with new applications.

An *active* dictionary is an integral part of a system development procedure—the programmers must use the dictionary to create programs and data structures. A *passive* dictionary is a voluntary reference tool and its value depends upon how well the developers adhere to the dictionary. An active dictionary is the better choice.

DOCUMENTING PROGRAMS FOR MAINTENANCE PURPOSES

In COBOL programs the IDENTIFICATION Division is the obvious starting point for easy to find documentation, but other languages do not have such formalized locations. However, programs written in PL/I, BASIC, and ASSEMBLER can easily provide similar information, and in the same general sequence as COBOL.

Every program needs two titles: a technical name that describes the module from the traditional MIS programming viewpoint, and an application title that explains the business purpose. This second title (often used as a subtitle) should be meaningful to a user or systems analyst. It is difficult to develop a single title that is meaningful to everyone. Usually both titles will convey enough information for the two groups who typically inquire about programs. Titles are not cast in stone. As programs evolve (usually to encompass more functions), their titles should be changed to match their new orientation. Changing a program name that has existed for ten years does cause confusion at first, but the situation is even worse for programmers facing a new program with an incorrect or inappropriate title.

Classic MIS texts insist that programs need the name of the author and date written, but such facts are only marginally important. In a typical maintenance environment—once the system has been turned over to a maintenance team—few people will care when a program was written, and even fewer know or care to know the name of the original author. Once a programmer has completed a module and turned it over to another person or group, he is generally free of any responsibility.

The purpose of a program is often partially explained by the titles, but the programmer should write several sentences fully describing the purpose of the module as it relates to input and output. For example, the purpose of program PO9000 may be to accept purchase order transactions from the user, apply them against the item and vendor data base, create written purchase orders, and generate open order transactions. This statement not only summarizes the logic, but gives the reader a basic understanding of *why* the program is important or "what does it do?" If the programmer does not grasp the purpose behind the program, he is missing the essential ingredient that will allow him to understand how the program fits into the application system. Without that basic understanding, maintenance will be even more difficult and frustrating. Comprehending a program is like learning brain surgery: The student does not simply pick up a scalpel and start slicing away before he knows how the brain fits into the overall body scheme. The macro-to-micro or general-to-specific approach is still best.

The programmer also should describe the *inputs* in another paragraph. Most computer programs have inputs from users, transaction files, or master files. If any documentation does exist in the typical MIS department, it is usually information about data, but existing file documentation is often confusing. Too often a programmer will simply list the seven files into a module, but actual file names are meaningful only to technical people who already understand the program. Instead, input should be described both in technical terms such as specific file names, and as "types of information." A purchase order file can be called "MPO9170" and can also be described in data terms as "a transaction file having user item level and header PO triggers." Both are correct, but they convey different meanings. It is relatively simple to judge the completeness of a paragraph describing input. If a sophisticated user cannot understand the "data flow" portion of the internal documentation, the comments in the program are not satisfactory.

The *processing* should be described in overview terms, even if it duplicates information provided in the "purpose" section. Important transactions should be mentioned (it is usually impractical to list them all inside a program), along with their effects on the output. For maintenance purposes, the programmer should give only a brief summary of the processing logic, since many standard maintenance requests deal with input and output rather than detailed logic changes.

The *output* should be documented in the same manner as the input, with two ways to describe each output. For example, the programmer would describe the PORPG file in technical terms as a variable length report file that is passed to a sort utility, and describe the same file in "application" terms as a file having Purchase Order header, item level, and trailer report records. Users in the purchasing department may not relate to "variable length files and sort utilities" but they can understand purchase order header, line item, and trailer records. Programmers writing documentation must think like technical people one moment and as users the next. By providing internal documentation that focuses on these differing "mind sets," the original programmer will be doing his department a valuable service.

DOCUMENTING PROGRAMS TO EXPLAIN LOGIC

In many complex business or scientific applications, programmers are required to "explain" the internal logic or trace specific conditions within a program. Maintenance and production support in many installations has been jokingly referred to as the "tell-me-why" function! The best way to avoid this time consuming task is to create specialized documentation in the logic sections, which is usually updated as programmers discover new information about a module.

For example, a frequent request in many purchasing systems is to explain a calculated item cost when the vendor provides various levels of discounts, such as quantity and price breakpoint. The results on the purchase order are often hard to understand when there are multiple factors that affect the final item cost. While the original system design document may have specified the "planned" logic, the programmer may have misunderstood or found additional combinations not covered in the original document. Even if the system design was virtually complete, applications grow of their own volition as the business environment becomes more complex. Program logic often becomes more involved every year. Each program or module in such applications should have internal comments labeled "processing," and as new facts are discovered, the programmer should faithfully add them to the module. The programmer's concern should be for the long-range benefit of his or her professional associates. For example, if the programmer discovers the program gives precedence to the weight breakpoint over the quantity discount, that piece of information should be preserved by internal comments in the logic section. *Every investigation that takes more than 30 minutes of actual programmer or analyst time should be documented directly in the program.*

Even in the best managed installation with a consistent program of updating user documentation, the results of such investigations are not always reflected in the user manuals. Therefore, the programming and technical staff must preserve their own investment in resources by capturing the results of their many research assignments permanently in the source code. If documented neatly, such comments will not clutter up a program. Six months or a year later, when another user asks the same question, the information will be readily available in the program. It still requires a programmer to find the correct module, but he/she will not need a day, a week, or a month to trace the code and determine the priority of price discounts. The next user will be happier than the first who had to wait a day, a week, or a month. The programming manager will be happier because he/she did not expend significant programming resources to answer "another darn fool question that must have been asked ten times during the past five years." By simply talking with programmers, MIS management can estimate the time savings with this type of internal documentation. Answering questions that have been answered before is both frustrating and unproductive.

Internal logic documentation should explain the options available in a program. User options are often the hardest to understand. As new options are added to a system, the user documentation may fail to list them, or not specify all their effects. The option itself may be simple but the ultimate results may be confusing! Identifying such information in the source code itself is often the only way that MIS can preserve those clinical facts.

FLOW CHARTS

The ubiquitous flow chart is controversial. Some MIS professionals believe they are *obviously* required to understand a program, module, system, or entire business application. Others approve of flow charts in theory but in practice find them either too detailed or not detailed enough, or too simple or too complicated to decipher. The same programmer or analyst may think they are wonderful one day and a waste of time the next! Their actual value lies somewhere in between. Flow charts can be valuable when *the originator understands the purpose of each flow chart and writes for the appropriate audience.* Like internal documentation, flow charts should come in two varieties: one for the technical expert and another version for those who wish to understand data flow or general business function. Flow charts as a tool are not intrinsically useful or useless, but it is their suitability for a specific purpose that determines their ultimate value. It is difficult to create a single flow chart that can be understood by more than one type of person, except for a very high level overview. So-called "generalized flow charts" that should appeal to everyone actually help only "generally," and MIS is not a "generalized profession."

Traditionally, programmers and systems analysts have used their trusty template and sharp pencil to produce flow charts. For obvious reasons, the eraser was often used more than the pencil. But flow charting has long been a mechanical, time-consuming, and often tedious job. Developing the information necessary to create a flow chart may have been challenging, but the laborious process of slowly drawing a square, rectangle, or circle has caused many programmers and analysts to take shortcuts. Some postponed drawing flow charts until the manager or supervisor forgot about the documentation assignment. Others conveniently forgot some details that should have been left in.

Even more difficult than creating the original flow chart is making changes to an existing handwritten chart! What programmer wants to redraw an entire page of symbols merely to insert a newly added file or logic option? Even if accurate flow charts were created when the program was put in production, they are seldom maintained. Therefore, many programmers routinely avoid using existing flow charts because they are usually inaccurate. They would rather work laboriously through the code themselves. Flow charts may be useful, but mechanical difficulties make them hard to work with.

The solution is an automated graphics package which can place standard

EDP flow charting symbols on a screen. The system should provide basic word processing printing facilities, such as printing specific pages, rearranging blocks, copying symbols, and global editing. Text and graphics must be on the same page (and CRT screen). Such packages are a virtual necessity in today's MIS organization.

Many CASE tools provide flow charting capabilities along with their structured analysis tools such as data flow diagrams. Structured analysis and design adherents propose models such as data flow diagrams, and state transition diagrams as replacements for the classic flow charts, but existing applications developed before CASE are seldom retrofitted. These production systems definitely need automated flow chart tools.

THE ANSWER BOOK

Every system, subsystem, or logical group of programs requires a document that answers routine questions about that business unit. Many problems or potential difficulties with a system are not related to actual program errors or mistakes. Rather, they pertain to the operational environment and are impossible to document in specific programs. These are classified as miscellaneous facts that a few key individuals keep in their heads, but are nevertheless important to maintenance programmers and analysts. This answer book is quite literally a life saver when it comes to serious production problems. Typical questions found in an answer book might be:

- Why does that system run so long?
- Can the run time ever be reduced? If so, how?
- When you rerun this application, what are the implications? What are the possible side effects?
- What research techniques are best when resolving a production problem?
- Who in the user community can or should approve program changes?
- Does this system or program grouping have any legal implications for the company?
- Why do these programs give us so many problems?
- Who is the current MIS expert on these modules?
- What are some good suggestions for testing program changes?
- Are there standard JCL test modules or reusable test conditions available?
- Are there any good ideas for improving the performance of this unit that have not been logged in the pending project file?

The answer book should be an informal document written strictly for the technical staff. Every time an answer is developed as part of normal production support the originator can simply add the question and corresponding answer to the book. A word processor or online text editor is always best, but the information must be accessible to any authorized member of the programming or systems staff at any time. A manual locked in a managers office is worthless at 2:00 A.M.! Miscellaneous information has solved many a crisis in the busy world of MIS.

THE SYSTEM LOG

Application systems are like living organisms: They constantly evolve through maintenance, enhancements, and modifications required by other projects. Users constantly demand improvements and changes, while MIS modifies applications for internal benefits. Changes to a system are the leading cause of production problems, user dissatisfaction, and unresolved questions, all of which consume large portions of valuable MIS resources. The actual change may work, but its impact may not be felt until the next weekly, monthly, or yearly processing cycle. Some mistakes may be caught years after the program or system has been modified or reran. The situation becomes more complicated when no one in MIS or the user community remembers exactly what happened. When did that particular change take place, and what was the purpose? When was the system last reran, and what steps were skipped because they were "not needed?" Human memory is fallible, and the staff may have turned over several times since the rerun last year. Only the written word survives.

The alternative is a *System Log* for every application system or subsystem. The purpose of this document is to track MIS history, because *history will often provide the answers, or at least a clue to the probable answer!* Simply having a time log of each major event relating to a systems life cycle is also helpful for planning and audit purposes.

A typical System Log might be:

04/09/92   Put in production by J. Kenney and W. Williams. Had to restore the I104 data base twice because of errors in update program PO50BA (skipped each receipt transaction).

05/03/92   Corrected errors in handling transaction code 04 and 05 (item level PO triggers) which were dropping off the last item in every PO. PO numbers 34000-34987 have been affected, and will not clear out for at least four months.

05/18/92   Bad tape on PO675 input caused abend, and we recreated all PO transactions. Had difficulty with warehouses 5, 6, and 8. Impossible to verify that every PO trigger was recreated. Expect nasty calls for several weeks. Users must audit report 560 and put in manual PO's if we missed their data during recreate. Sorry about that!

06/23/92   Implemented Phase II project which corrected seven major errors in PO445 and PO446. See Phase II project description (S. Benard) for details.

06/24/92   Phase II caused errors—PO's from three warehouses were on each others reports. Implemented fix (see fix log 92-129 in Operations for details). Had to backout data base updates for night of 06/23/92, and restored data base I1055 and I0195 to 06/23/92. Reran jobs 14, 15, and 16, but skipped 17. Will things ever get better?

The style of each entry is simple and direct. People who read system logs need only the basic facts. They want to know what happened, in what sequence, and where to go for additional detail. The value of a system log depends upon management's absolute insistence that it be kept up to date, and accessible to all authorized persons. The drawback with any system log is determining which events should be included: If some technical people incorporate every one-line fix, the log may become massive if there are many changes or problems with a given application. If that happens, one individual must assume control and insist that only "major events" be logged. Obviously, it is impossible to always predict which event has the potential of becoming a serious problem in the future, but someone must make the initial decision. After six months to a year, management can reevaluate the guidelines and expand or restrict the entries in the system log. Like other documentation, the rules for a system log are not etched in stone: they can and should be modified to match the current operating environment.

SUMMARY OF KEY POINTS

- Good internal documentation will help the MIS staff in their day-to-day and week-to-week activities by increasing productivity.

- Documentation will help reduce the maintenance effort, explain the processing of a program and system, and serve as "requirements" for the programs eventual replacement.

- All internal documentation must follow the same set of standards—even if the standards are not the best.

- Internal documentation is cost justified only when management takes the long-range view. Technical documentation for the staff should be looked upon as a long term business investment.

- A good data dictionary can link together all internal documentation and the actual source code. An active dictionary is better than the passive variety.

- The results of every investigation that takes more than 30 minutes of actual programmer or analyst time should be documented, either in a user manual, technical manual, or directly in the program.

- Automated flow chart packages are justified on the basis of increased productivity.

- Every application needs both an Answer Book and a System Log. The Answer Book holds valuable miscellaneous information that does not fit in other documentation, and the System Log lists important events in the history of that application. Both documents will dramatically assist the technical and managerial staff responsible for production support.

10

Strategic Documents

MIS is an expensive and critical pillar of many organizations, and senior management expects MIS to participate in formalized planning and control procedures. In the past, MIS departments have been criticized for what appeared to be unplanned, explosive, and unprepared growth. One glaring reason for this criticism is the lack of formal plans that can be measured and controlled. Another criticism is that MIS is often ill-prepared to shift directions quickly and support strategic organizational needs. This chapter introduces the strategic project plan, which describes a key project in relation to other projects and activities, and the strategic long-range plan, which combines major projects, long-term direction, and relevant organizational factors into a single document that serves as the long-range plan for information systems. Chapter 10 is for technical writers, systems analysts, and MIS managers responsible for planning activities.

A strategic project is any proposed MIS-related development or maintenance effort that may provide a competitive advantage for the organization. The advantage could be greater sales, lower costs, increased profits, or higher prestige. It may even protect an existing market situation, but in many cases a strategic project is an idea that allows a company to get ahead of the competition.

Timing is often the critical factor in strategic projects, since opportunities typically exist for a limited period. The chance to be the *first* to enter a new market is available to the first company who can put together an order processing and shipping system to serve that market need. An opportunity to form an operating partnership with a related but noncompetitive company may work only for the first or second successful mergers. An advantage that can dramatically increase sales and profits today may be an illusion tomorrow.

Figure 10.1   Strategic project plans

Section	Target
Section	*Target*
Summary	Senior Management
Body	Management
Introduction	Management
Benefits	Management
Operational considerations	MIS/Users
Conclusions	Senior management
Appendix	MIS staff

Strategic ideas may have more risk than other MIS projects and therefore appear glamourous or exciting. Everyone wants to be first, and company executives in difficult situations may see a strategic idea as a solution to existing problems. The document proposing a strategic project should always guard against over optimism, and should honestly describe the risks, disadvantages, and probable costs. Glamour has no place in any type of project proposal document.

The Strategic Project Plan consists of:

- Summary
- Body
- Introduction
- Benefits
- Operational considerations
- Conclusions
- Appendix (optional)

EVOLUTION OF STRATEGIC PROJECT PLANS

Often key individuals in the organization—such as marketing managers or sales directors—will create an idea involving information systems that could generate a significant benefit for the company. If they can gather enough initial support from management, and if their idea is not currently in the long-range plan, the idea is labeled as "strategic." Often seemingly valid suggestions sound impressive but fall apart during the preliminary evaluation. Others have obvious benefits but the cost in terms of information systems development is so high that the proposals are rejected.

For those ideas that survive the initial management screening process, a systems analyst or first level manager is usually assigned to write a strategic project plan. This document is different from a business plan, because business plans are generally limited to approved, defined projects. The strategic project plan is a unique combination of user request, feasibility statement, design document, and business plan. Since the situation justifies flexibility, the strategic project plan bypasses the usual documentation steps in the development cycle. It is by definition a rush document for a rush business priority.

The sponsor is the initial contact point for information, but should never be the only source. Sponsors differ in their understanding of their own proposal. Marketing Director Sally Smart may burst with enthusiasm and wisely make the effort to understand the order entry, accounting, and billing implications of her proposal. Benjamin Befuddled may be equally excited about his idea but not realize the profound effect on warehouse operations. Sponsors who have done their own homework present an easier assignment than those who have convinced management with little more than bubbling enthusiasm. A Strategic Project Plan must be built around facts rather than emotion.

Some excitable sponsors bristle with indignation at the first hint that their idea is not perfect or could adversely affect other departments. Such a person should be used only for high-level information. Senior management requires an unbiased, objective strategic analysis. Using a source who is obviously biased—either strongly in favor of the idea or strongly opposed—provides only biased information.

Gathering information about a strategic idea is very similar to traditional systems analysis. First the analyst identifies most or preferably all of the functional areas impacted by the idea. Managers or staff members in those areas must be contacted, informed of the idea, and asked to provide comments. The systems analyst needs to understand the overall effect of the proposal on each unit in the organization, but not to the degree needed in a systems development project. In the interviewing process, the systems analyst or technical writer is performing some aspects of the feasibility statement (see Chapter 3). The purpose is to gather general information on the specific idea and verify its practicality.

MIS area managers or senior professionals must also be interviewed. Their comments on the scope, nature, and probable cost will help determine if the idea is feasible.

FORMAT OF THE STRATEGIC PLAN

The Strategic Project Plan consists of a summary, a main body, and an optional appendix.

The *summary* often serves as a standalone document for management review, and should be written with great care. It is usually two pages or less, and begins with a one-paragraph explanation of the idea. Business terms rather than MIS terms are appropriate, since the audience will be senior management.

The next topic is a concise explanation of the benefits. The writer should emphasize the justification for the proposal. Will it increase sales? Will it protect a current market? Will it encourage future growth? Benefits should be stated in a positive but realistic manner.

The third topic describes the probable development cost for MIS. Like project proposals, this statement should provide comparisons to previous projects and avoid specific estimates in hours or dollars.

The final item in the summary should review the potential impact on the organization. Every strategic project varies in its affect on user areas, company policies, staffing allocations, and organizational control. It is important to identify each impact, and allow management to understand the true scope and complexity of the project. MIS is usually only one factor in a strategic project.

The *introduction* begins the body of the document. Generally it consists of one or two paragraphs that explain the purpose of the document, describe the goal of the project, recap the history of the analysis or research effort expended to create the document, and note any key factors in the project.

The *benefits* section tells the reader why the project is justified. Since the Strategic Project Plan is a business-oriented document, the benefits should be expressed in business terms understandable to senior management. Market surveys, research analysis, and sales projections are relevant to the benefits section. Graphs included in the text (through desktop publishing techniques) are an excellent way to communicate benefits.

The sponsor may have such information available, although after an interview the systems analysts occasionally find themselves with more wishful thinking than hard facts. In this situation, the author must formulate the benefits section so the predicted benefits are attributable to specific individuals *willing to be quoted in print*. Theoretical benefits should never be ascribed to the author of the document, but to the sponsor, a designate, or anyone who has an insight into potential benefits.

The next section explains the *operational* or functional characteristics of the project. It begins by reviewing the impact upon the business, and follows up by discussing the requirements from an MIS viewpoint. Staffing issues in the user areas and in MIS must be mentioned. If hardware or software questions materially affect the project, these should be discussed with alternative solutions. This section also lists open issues or questions that must be resolved if the project is approved.

The last paragraphs in the operations section should suggest a user project leader. A Strategic Project requires a manager who can cut through bureaucracy, rules, and procedures, and yet maintain positive relationships throughout the organization. Senior managers may not seriously consider a project unless the sponsor identifies an individual who is willing to take full responsibility for implementation. The systems analyst may need to gently encourage the sponsor to identify that person.

The *conclusion* is the author's opinion. If the results of the investigation are favorable, the document should formally recommend that management consider implementation. This assumes the idea is feasible, beneficial, and cost effective for the organization. This section should be only one or two paragraphs, but must realistically summarize the benefits, operational issues, and value to the organization. The sponsor should help write the conclusion, but should not add statements that are blatantly unjustified by the rest of the document. The purpose of this section is to persuade the reader that the project should be approved. If the systems analyst has done a good job presenting the facts, readers will draw their own objective conclusions.

The *appendix* is vital. Performing the research needed to develop a Strategic Project Plan often develops detail information that is not appropriate for the body of the document, but should be included for a specific reader who may want to review details. Also, since one of the goals of technical writing is to preserve knowledge gained at company expense, interview results, memos, and supporting documents can form the appendix. The systems analyst should verify in writing that the author of a memo or the subject of an interview agrees to have the document included in the widely distributed Strategic Project Plan. The information in an appendix may satisfy a detail-oriented reviewer who needs more facts that can be included in the body of the document. The appendix is usually distributed only to MIS recipients.

STRATEGIC PLANNING DOCUMENTS

Strategic Planning Documents are also known as Long-Range Plans, Strategic Information Systems Plans, or MIS Mission Statements. Sometimes they are called Five-Year Plans. A Strategic Plan is a document or series of documents that tells both the corporate community and MIS itself the direction and goals of MIS. It is partly a business plan for MIS, in terms of hardware, software, communications, staffing, and policies, and partly a publicity statement directed toward the rest of the organization. Such documents are valuable because they address such critical issues as distributed versus centralized processing, service levels, new technology, and the maintenance of current systems compared to the development of new applications.

Unless senior management specifically asks that certain topics be avoided, no subject that affects MIS should be automatically excluded from a Strategic Plan. The possibility of the company merging or buying another entity could be included as a contingency project in the Plan.

The need for a long-range planning document should be obvious, but some organizations still avoid planning because the process of long-range planning is subject to error. Or they may not be willing to allocate the significant resources necessary to create a realistic plan. As MIS grows in size and importance, more senior managers will demand some form of strategic planning document, and MIS staff will be forced into the complicated but important world of strategic planning analysis.

MIS needs a Strategic Plan for its own control. As a function, data processing of the 1990s is vastly different from data processing of the 1980s, and the changes in the MIS profession are increasing in depth and frequency. Job positions unknown in the 1980s are common today. Communication networks are forming the backbone of corporate computer systems. Factory automation is opening new windows of opportunities. Fourth generation languages, CASE products, and code generators are providing new development tools that improve productivity. All these alternatives and options are difficult to manage or even conceptualize without a single document that allows management to appreciate their interaction, relative value, and long-range potential. A Strategic Plan is the "sanity check" for MIS management.

Typically a Strategic Plan is written by an MIS manager or management team. The weakness of this approach is that readers will be reluctant to constructively criticize a document written by someone relatively high in the hierarchy. *The secret to a successful Strategic Plan consists of suggestions, joint analysis, and honest assistance from many others in MIS.* Assigning the job to a manager often prevents this unflinching cooperation. Even senior company executives will hesitate to question Donna Data's Strategic Information Systems Plan when Donna Data happens to be the information systems director and sits with them at the executive lunch table. Even if Donna assigns the work to her staff, a Strategic Plan with her name carries the personal authority of the information systems director. Personality has become more important than content, and communication between MIS and the rest of the organization suffers.

Instead, MIS management should assign the job to a senior systems analyst, with an MIS manager serving as sponsor. A staff member is less inclined to treat a Strategic Plan as a task that demonstrates management skill but as a challenging, team-oriented, information gathering exercise. Creating a Strategic Plan is difficult enough without ego factors interfering in the communication process. Managers can provide much of the input, but the Strategic Plan should be a staff-written document.

The role of the management sponsor is critical. He must insure the timely cooperation of other MIS areas and user departments, help the systems analyst avoid political battles, and referee disputes before they become traumatic. Planning MIS direction occasionally involves territorial questions in terms of staffing and responsibilities. The sponsor is an ally who helps the analyst complete an admittedly difficult assignment. The sponsor also serves as the ever present sounding board for the analyst. Strategic plans must go through several iterations and only a management representative can insure timely reviews by others in MIS.

Interviews, published documents about future projects, budget authorization memos, and minutes from planning sessions provide the raw material for the final document. The amount of information available is adequate only if planning has been a regular feature of MIS management activities. It is not feasible to prepare a Strategic Plan unless either the information already exists in other forms or if MIS management is willing to allocate enough senior level staff and management time to complete the planning process.

Systems analysts can approach the strategic planning process as they would begin any other assignment. They can investigate and list the requirements supplied by the users of the Strategic Plan. What do they want to know about MIS? Next they would collect the information and facts needed to meet those requirements. Strategic Planning cannot be accomplished in a few short meetings, but should extend over the entire year. Many organizations allocate a month each to collect and formalize planning information, but perform planning activities as a regular part of management duties. Successful MIS departments do not expect a systems analyst to create a Strategic Plan without some degree of planning already accomplished.

Strategic Plans are often strikingly consistent from year to year. The plan in 1993 may be similar to the plan from 1992 in everything except content, since MIS managers are reluctant to change a widely distributed document. It may not be very good, the unspoken logic goes, but at least everyone is familiar with the document format. Why change?

That attitude is opposed to the principles of good technical writing, good management, and good sense. A Strategic Plan is important, but it is simply another form of written communication that can always be improved. One could argue that if any form of technical writing requires regular improvement, the Strategic Plan fits that criterion. A poorly written Strategic Plan is little better than no Strategic Plan.

The author of the document should consider the complex readership of his final product: Strategic Plans are read by many individuals and referenced by an even larger number throughout the year. The company president, the systems analyst, and the user manager can all reference the document during its life cycle. All have different reasons, which may vary according to the situation. The company president may review the entire plan in January to correlate budgets with approved projects, and in June may study the plan for information on data base integration. A systems analyst may review the entire plan in March to locate projects of interest, and study the section on computer-integrated manufacturing in September. The order entry staff may examine the plan in April to prepare for discussion on warehouse modifications.

Analyzing the needs of a varied audience who use the Strategic Plans for equally varied purposes creates a formidable challenge for the most experienced systems analysts. How do they create such a versatile document?

The first step is to send a questionnaire to all recipients of previous Strategic Plans, asking them to suggest improvements. In selected cases (e.g., with users who depend heavily upon the Strategic Plan) an in-depth follow-up interview will provide additional information. The questionnaire should be less than one page, contain a minimum number of questions, and be sent in a format that allows the recipient to quickly fill in their responses and return the questionnaire with minimal inconvenience.

Questions should be customized to each organization's current Strategic Plan, user and MIS base, and corporate environment or culture. The key issues are:

1. How do you use the Strategic Plan?

2. How often do you reference it?

3. What parts or sections of the current Strategic Plan do you find the most helpful?

4. What parts or sections of the current plan do you find the least helpful?

5. Does the plan have too much detail or too little?

6. Are you satisfied with the terminology and vocabulary?

7. Is the Strategic Plan organized so you can find the information you need?

8. Is there any part or section you would like to see expanded?

9. If you have seen a Strategic Plan or comparable document for other companies, can you list any ideas that would apply to us?

10. Can you give us any suggestions for improving the Strategic Plan?

The next step is to categorize the responses by type of reader. The purpose of this analysis is to determine if the organization would be better served by two or more Strategic Plans. *A common mistake in many companies is the assumption that one document can be all things to all people.* Creating multiple versions of the Strategic Plan is an option in companies where people view the Strategic Plan as a working document. In organizations where the Strategic Plan is never referenced, this problem never arises. But when the Strategic Plan is valuable, a survey of the readership may indicate that two or more distinct audiences exist. Different readers deserve slightly different documents, and the Strategic Plan is not exempt from such an approach. It is better to have two documents that satisfy the majority than one document that satisfies no one.

For example, the survey may indicate that senior managers are best served by a document that emphasizes business terms and cost factors. The questionnaires may show that MIS managers and users need a version of the same material that emphasizes functional requirements. If such a dichotomy exists, MIS management should encourage the systems analyst to develop separate formats for each audience, and be extremely careful to insure that the information in the two documents is equivalent. The version for senior management may be called the Strategic Information Systems Business Plan, while the version for MIS management could be titled the Strategic Information Systems Technical Plan. It is possible that several specialized versions of the plan will be created for different interest groups, and that select recipients receive all versions.

A Strategic Plan should be in a looseleaf binder and include sections on traditional MIS considerations such as hardware, software, data base, distributed processing, major approved projects, staffing, and communications. Tabs should be used to divide the sections. Nontraditional subjects should also be considered. For example, a section devoted to organizational issues that affect MIS is appropriate. If the company is in an industry where mergers are frequent, that possibility should be raised as an issue, and a brief strategy described to meet that possibility.

A section on key MIS management concerns is always appropriate. Every MIS department has its own set of particular problems that should be analyzed in a Strategic Plan. Some departments allocate so many professional staff members to maintenance that development work suffers. This section could review the problem, discuss alternatives, and present a strategy to solve the problem. Other departments flounder because they use multiple technologies and do not have the resources needed to support diverse technical environments. Still other MIS areas face difficulties because the user groups fail to set realistic priorities. Whatever the problems, the Strategic Plan should at least acknowledge the situation: Preferably, it should propose a solution.

Many Strategic Plans have too much detail. A Strategic Plan is a management document, and should not be burdened with detailed information more appropriate for other documents. For example, a Strategic Plan may have one page listing projected staffing, by job title and by MIS area, for the next five years. Management level readers are generally not concerned with such details. Rather, they prefer to know total projected overall staffing levels for the next five years, and the *justification* for the increase. The same logic applies to such factors as disk capacity or CPU growth. Too much detail hides the essential information and confuses the readers who must make judgments or decisions. Details are appropriate for other documents.

There is another reason for not including details: Published management level documents tend to be "cast in concrete." A number or statement—no matter how obscure—published in the Strategic Plan may becomes law. MIS management finds it difficult to suggest changing a number, estimate, or even a CPU MIPS rating when it has been published in the Strategic Plan, for fear that a senior manager will challenge them for not following the plan. MIS management should include only statements or estimates they feel will stand for the life of the plan.

Major development or maintenance projects should be listed only in summary form, unless the information is definite. Detail that is not supportable is never appropriate. It is better to describe the proposed new order entry system as a purchased application package that will meet most of the critical MIS and user needs. It is asking for trouble to state that the new order entry system will meet 12 currently identified critical requirements, when those 12 were developed in 10 minutes for the purpose of completing the Strategic Plan. When the project begins, those 12 requirements may expand to 37, and someone must explain the additional 25. Adding detail just to make the plan sound better is a mistake. *Never include a statement, direction, or number unless it can be supported.*

Adding a glossary of technical and business terms helps many readers understand unfamiliar terminology. Some recipients of the Strategic Plan look on the document as a learning or education tool.

An appendix is not always needed. Detail does not belong in the Strategic Plan, although an appendix that refers to other published documents is sometimes beneficial. The personnel manager who wishes to see headcount projections by job title, by MIS area, for the next five years can look in the appendix and find a listing for a document titled "MIS Staffing Plans" published last month by the MIS Financial Planning Group. The order entry manager who needs more information about the Order Entry project can be referred to the "Initial Order Entry Scope Memo" written by Tina Template in June 1992.

If the Strategic Plan is to be issued in versions for distinct audiences, the document for senior managers and non-MIS readers should minimize MIS jargon and explain any remaining technical terms in the text. The document for technical readers should assume that the readers need some explanation of business terminology, but that the reader understands MIS jargon.

SUMMARY OF KEY POINTS

- A strategic project is a time-critical project that can provide the organization with a significant benefit, such as increased sales, improved market share, or new markets.

- Strategic Project Plans should have a summary that is a standalone document, a body with introduction, benefits, operational considerations, and conclusions, and an appendix.

- The Strategic Project Plan is a combination business plan, feasibility statement, user request, and design document.

- Strategic Project Plans should always address the issue of project staffing from the MIS and user areas. The plan should propose one individual who is willing to direct the project.

- Strategic Plans are also known as Long-Range Plans, MIS Mission Statements, and Five-Year Plans. Their purpose is to predict MIS business and operational growth and how it will be managed.

- Have an experienced systems analyst write the plan. Never assign the task to a manager, because a document written by a manager is often treated as a personal effort. A document written by a systems analyst is more likely to be a team effort.

- Have a senior MIS manager serve as sponsor, and allow him or her to encourage cooperation from other areas and individuals.

- The Strategic Plan should be improved from year to year. Use a questionnaire to all recipients to ask for comments and suggestions.

- If needed, create multiple versions of the Strategic Plan, such as one slated toward senior, nontechnical management, and another version for MIS and the users.

- Never load the Strategic Plan with more detail than it deserves; the plan should be a summary document. Too much detail confuses the readers.

11

Agreements for Outside Services

Contracting for services from outside software firms is an attractive option for a growing number of organizations. Consulting companies promise to study problems, analyze the causes, and recommend solutions. Programming houses offer the services of systems analysts, programmers, and project leaders for both short-term and long-term assignments in place of hiring additional permanent staff. Application software maintenance support firms claim they can provide production support services at less cost and greater efficiency than an internal MIS department. All such arrangements depend for their success on written agreements, and technical writers, managers, or systems analysts are often pressed into service to create an agreement document. This chapter describes the process of developing an agreement document for three types of outside contracts.

Many MIS managers, either willingly or through not so gentle persuasion, use outside firms to supplement their own internal work force. These may be consultants hired to solve a particular problem, or programming houses that provide additional assistance during peak development periods. Using outside firms can be lower in cost than additional permanent employees, if the need is temporary. Permanent employees cannot be terminated as easily as contractors, who can be dismissed when the project is over or the assignment is completed.

Yet there are many horror stories about outside firms brought into an MIS organization and disaster struck before the ink on the contract was dry. The complaints from both sides are classic:

The firm didn't do its job.	No one told the firm its responsibilities.
The hiring company failed to live up to its responsibilities.	Employees in the hiring company were never told their own responsibilities.
The firm did not meet the schedule.	The hiring company did not provide the firm with a schedule.
The firm did not have enough supervision.	The firm had too much supervision.
The firm did not live up to its agreement.	The firm had no agreement other than a letter with the hourly rate.

In many cases, the problem resulted from a poorly written or nonexistent agreement. Establishing a temporary partnership with an outside firm is a complex situation that demands planning and mutual understanding. Promises made over coffee in the cafeteria and confirmed by scribbles on a slightly soggy napkin are quickly forgotten. Commitments made by managers over the phone mean nothing to staff level employees who must work together on a daily basis. A firm handshake and a convincing, "Trust me, we know our jobs," usually leads to mistrust.

An agreement is not a contract. A contract is a legal document specifying terms of payment, general responsibilities of all parties, grounds for terminating the agreement, and other business matters. Agreements do not replace contracts, but supplement them. A contract should be written by or at least reviewed in detail by a lawyer. A technical writer, manager, or systems analyst can write the agreement if given the time and the requisite authority. In general, the agreement should precede the contract, and in many cases the lawyer will copy sections of the agreement for use in the contract. The legal status of an agreement varies, even if both parties sign the document. Nevertheless, no outside firm should start work until they have both a signed agreement and a signed contract. The agreement could be part of the contract if the reviewing legal experts are satisfied with the nature of the document.

Most companies also require an outside contracting firm to sign a letter of confidentiality before serious discussions begin. These are legal documents and should be prepared or reviewed by a lawyer. The letter of confidentiality also specifies the ownership of the work, consistent with the copyright laws.

CONSULTANTS

Consultants are hired by MIS departments to solve specific problems or provide information about a specific course of action. A good document describes the problem to be solved or need to be addressed, working environment, and the final deliverables. Many consultants—even the best—have their own interests at heart, and they make a profit by extending their stay as long as possible. The company hiring the consultant has an interest in minimizing his or her stay. When two organizations have opposing interests, a comprehensive written document is the best way to avoid disputes.

Creating an agreement document for consultants requires interviews. Rarely will a technical writer be handed detailed notes and asked to compile the notes into a formal agreement. Instead, the technical writer may be asked to arrange a meeting with the hiring manager and consulting representative at 1:00 P.M. and have a mutually agreeable document ready by 5:00 P.M. Impossible!

Before anyone can prepare the first draft, the writer must find answers to some or all of the following questions. The answers may not be definite, but they will provide a foundation for the document. Some information is better than none, and a lack of answers will alert management to potential problems.

Some of the questions to ask are:

What is the problem to be solved?

What are the deliverables expected by management?

When are the deliverables expected?

Who in the department will work with the consultant, and how much time will they spend with the consultant?

How will management prevent the consultant from monopolizing key members of the department?

Who will supervise or manage the consultant when a disagreement or conflict arises?

What documents should the consultant read to prepare himself for the job?

Will the deliverables be reviewed by any department members before final submission?

Will any staff member have editing or approval responsibilities before the deliverable is submitted?

Will the deliverable be confidential? If so, who is authorized to receive it?

Are there any checkpoints or milestones (such as briefings) required?

When is the final deliverable due?

Does the consultant have any responsibilities after the deliverable is accepted?

Are there any limitations or restrictions on the employees the consultant may interview?

Will the consultant travel, and if so, who makes, funds, and approves the travel arrangements?

If all the answers cannot be found, the technical writer can add a section to the agreement with unresolved issues. This section should alert the hiring manager that perhaps additional meetings are needed to better define the role of the consultant and the hiring department.

The format of the agreement should be simple, and can be a list of answers organized into logical sections. For example, Section A could include all known facts about the deliverable document (perhaps a recommendation for a new screening procedure for prospective programmer/ analysts). Section B could describe the working environment for the consultants, and identify the employees available for interviews and other operational matters. Section C could be a list of questions that have not been answered. An open issue page does not imply that the consultant should not be hired: Rather, it lists the unresolved questions that eventually must be answered.

APPLICATION SOFTWARE MAINTENANCE SUPPORT

A trend in MIS is to hire a specialized programming or systems support house to provide production support or maintenance services. Such a company will replace the maintenance function of the internal MIS department and allow them to devote their limited resources to new development. In other less happy circumstances the MIS department is unable to control the maintenance function, or senior management suspects the MIS department is not working efficiently. Occasionally an MIS department will lose several key individuals, and MIS management hires an outside firm to replace the services of the former employees.

Whatever the reason, outside software firms who specialize in production support do have advantages. They will often contract to keep the systems rolling for a fixed monthly fee. They allow the internal MIS experts to concentrate on development projects which usually include replacement of the older systems. The fixed price option is attractive to organizations who dislike large, unpredictable, and inevitably upward shifts in their maintenance budget. Outside companies may have special skills such as online debugging or data base management that are beyond the capabilities of the internal MIS department, and the organization does not wish to hire such individuals. The major advantage, however, is often the perception that production support will "become someone else's headache." Management believes they can unload a frustrating burden by simply writing a check once a month. Like many perceptions, this attitude can be wishful thinking. The difference between a headache truly gone and a new headache replacing the old one is *the quality of the agreement document signed before the transfer of responsibilities.*

Application software maintenance is a function that has been traditionally difficult to limit, hard to satisfy, and impossible to categorize. What a user considers maintenance is labeled "modification" by MIS, and what is called maintenance by MIS is termed "a waste of time" by the users. The accounts payable director may feel that a change to a heading is necessary, while the MIS manager may see the request as a low priority wish list item. Few people agree on what maintenance is or should be, and even if an organization laboriously hammers out a detailed definition of what is and what is not maintenance, disagreements will still occur. How then can a technical writer define an agreement to provide a service for a function that is so difficult to pin down?

Maintenance must be defined, not in the ultimate resolution of this old controversy, but as a series of specific requirements to be performed by an outside service. The difference is subtle but critical. Managers and employees who will energetically argue continuously about the true definitions of maintenance, modification, and development, find it easier to agree on specific responsibilities to be supplied by another company. Perhaps the difference is that specifying maintenance for a limited situation does not have political or jurisdictional implications. The author of the document should stress that the definition of maintenance for the agreement is only a matter of convenience. It is the responsibility of the technical writer to insist that all discussions on defining maintenance should limit themselves to the agreement under consideration. The problems of the world cannot be solved in a single document.

The resulting definition of maintenance depends upon the hardware and software environment. The following example for a large IBM mainframe installation lists problems to be fixed and other responsibilities of the maintenance firm. It also defines the interface with other groups such as development and technical support.

The outside firm will have the following responsibilities:

Fix any application software production job that abends during its second production run, with abend defined as a failure that prevents successful completion of the job (Development will support jobs until the first successful production run).

Correct any disk space, file allocation, or hardware error that prevents completion of a production job for the first or subsequent runs.

Implement changes to JCL identified by Technical Support that will increase efficiency or conserve resources, but will not cause any application program changes.

Make changes to application software necessitated by changes in hardware, such as installation of a new disk drive.

Perform reallocation and movement of files required by hardware changes, hardware replacements, or hardware failures.

Assist in reruns of production jobs requested by the Operations Shift Director or his designate.

Review all modifications made by Development and provide written analysis of the impact on production support.

Assign two representatives to the Disaster Recovery team who can participate in off-site drills, and who will travel off-site if a disaster occurs.

Generate the current set of daily, weekly, monthly, and yearly production reports for review by Operations Management.

Assist Technical Support in any changes that affect the application software, including conversions due to data base changes.

Make available to Development all test materials created during the maintenance function.

Document on form RS-298 each production incident and the final resolution, including source code changes and review signature by Development team representative.

Document on a form RS-299 any nonemergency change made to the applications, such as JCL changes made to increase efficiency.

Participate in structured walkthroughs as requested by the Development Manager or his designate, and review system changes for impact on production support.

Perform minor code modifications on an "as time permits" basis, with the Development Manager or his designate arranging the priority, and devote a minimum of thirty hours a week to such projects.

The definition of maintenance has not been resolved on a permanent basis, but enough to establish responsibilities for the length of the agreement. As circumstances change and agreements expire, the details can be modified.

The next step is to define the physical facilities provided by the hiring organization.

How many offices will the maintenance firm be assigned?

What terminals, printers, and cabling will be furnished?

Will standard office supplies such as desks, chairs, file cabinets, and paper be available?

Will secretarial support be provided?

What documentation manuals and application system documentation books will be allocated to the maintenance team?

What building access keys will be supplied, and how will the maintenance team account for them?

How will they be returned after the agreement expires?

The third requirement is to identify personnel considerations. How many people does the maintenance firm expect to have on site? The hiring company may want to screen maintenance candidates before allowing them on the company premises. Will the hiring firm have veto power over employees of the maintenance firm? Perhaps the hiring organization needs the authority to ban an employee of the maintenance firm who violates a company rule or does not get along with the other employees. Dress codes should be specified if applicable. A conflict will occur if the employees of an outside organization follow a more relaxed dress code than the employees of the hiring company. The same situation applies to work schedules: The maintenance team should use the same prime shift work schedule as the hiring company.

The fourth item to be resolved is the hours of support (such as 7 days a week, 24 hours a day) and procedures to notify the maintenance staff when a production problem develops. This question should be documented in detail. Will pagers be used, and who will furnish the pagers? Will a maintenance team member be on site 24 hours a day? What is the expected response time, and how will it be monitored for compliance?

A final matter to resolve is the procedure for amending the agreement. More than any other document written for outside services, a maintenance agreement will become obsolete after only a few weeks, because both participants learn by experience. Wisdom increases dramatically when the inevitable complications arise. If an agreement is signed on March 1, by March 10 both parties wish they could revise the agreement. A schedule and mechanism for changes must be identified. The situation is essentially collective bargaining, and both groups should compromise to meet their goals. By having the procedures for amending the agreement already specified, the maintenance firm and the hiring organization can proceed directly to the more important matter of negotiation.

APPLICATION SYSTEM DOCUMENTATION

Professional technical writing companies offer their services to MIS departments struggling to support application software that is poorly documented. According to their marketing brochures, high-quality technical and user documentation will reduce maintenance expenses and allow the users to solve their own problems. In many situations this logic may be valid, but it is the responsibility of the hiring organization to compare the costs with the benefits. One obvious factor in the cost benefits equation is the useful life of an application system: Documenting a 10-year-old order entry system that is scheduled for replacement in two years is questionable. Clearly, however, as distributed processing and departmental systems place more computer access in the hands of the user community, thorough, readable, and accurate documentation will become even more critical. Routine support of user systems, such as answering basic questions about system inputs or outputs, is becoming an increasingly large percentage of post implementation budgets. Good documentation does reduce that cost.

One approach to contracting with a documentation firm is to hire the company to supply technical writers or analysts who will work under the direction of an internal project leader. The employees of the technical writing firm perform specific tasks assigned by the project leader, and function as temporary employees. An agreement is still needed, even if the overall, day-to-day management will come from the hiring organization .

For example, an agreement could cover such points as the physical facilities allocated by the hiring organization, projected scope of work, tentative timetable, checkpoints for review, and general working conditions. A section describing the approved documentation format is always needed. The agreement should describe in general terms the nature and degree of suggestions expected from the technical writing experts. Perhaps they will supply a standard format for technical documentation and user manuals, or will suggest new forms for user input. The agreement should stress that the technical writing consultants will be supervised by the internal MIS project leader, but those consultants are expected to use their talents and experience to assist the MIS project leader.

The other approach is to give project control responsibility to the outside technical writing firm. The outside company manages the work effort with minimal supervision and direction from the hiring organization. This requires a more detailed agreement specifying the final product: It is easy to spend a large amount of money for a large amount of documentation that is not what the hiring company needs.

The technical writer, systems analyst, or manager assigned to write the agreement, will pose questions to both the hiring manager and the technical writing marketing representatives. Several discussions may be needed to develop an agreement that protects the hiring organization, but is flexible enough to allow the technical writing experts to do their job.

During these sessions the author of the agreement should encourage resolution of the following questions:

1. What office space, secretarial support, and production facilities will be provided?

2. What systems, applications, jobs, or functions are to be documented?

3. What skill levels and experience factors are needed by the employees of the technical writing firm assigned to this project?

4. Who in the hiring organization will be available for interviewing? How much time will be allocated for each person? What hours during the day will be allowed for sessions?

5. What mechanism will be used to document the material (i.e., specific word processing package, graphics, and hardware configurations)?

6. Who in the hiring organization will review and approve documentation efforts, and at what points in the project cycle?

7. If a document is not approved by the hiring organization, and the technical writing team does not modify the document to their satisfaction, what is the process for resolution?

8. What is the procedure for formally accepting a document?

9. Is the technical writing company responsible for document distribution or publication?

10. What format(s) will be allowed for documentation?

11. If a system, application, function, or process changes or is expected to change during the project, what is the procedure for notifying the technical writing staff, and who is responsible for notifying them?

12. What is the procedure for modifying the agreement, and when will modifications be discussed?

13. Will the hiring firm have the authority to edit the drafts on a line-by-line basis?

14. Does the hiring organization have the right to reject employees from the technical writing firm?

The format of the agreement depends both on the answers and specific situation, but should include at least three sections: an *administrative* unit that defines facilities, employee relations, and organizational concerns; a *document* section that describes the project deliverables; and an *appendix*, with sample documents in the format and structure expected by the hiring organization. The sample documents are critical to understanding the expected results. If samples are not available, or if the technical writing analysts are expected to develop their own, the agreement should provide for a formal review of the selected format.

Technical writing agreements should require at least one formal status meeting several weeks after the project begins. By its nature, technical writing assignments are often hard to measure, and a status meeting early in the contract allows individuals to share their experiences.

SUMMARY OF KEY POINTS

- MIS departments are turning to outside firms to supply technical experts to fill specific needs. A well defined agreement will prevent unpleasant surprises. A poorly written or nonexistent agreement is the foundation for serious misunderstandings.

- A contract is a legal document prepared by a lawyer, and often specifies payment, length of service, and business arrangements. The agreement can be prepared by an MIS professional or manager, and specifies the daily job duties of the outside firm.

- An *agreement* is a short but complex document that reflects intensive discussions, decisions, and assumptions by both parties. Management must allow the author sufficient time and support to develop an effective agreement.

- Consulting agreements emphasize the exact problem to be solved and the way the consultant will attack the problem.

- Software maintenance agreements require precise definitions of the work to be performed. Vague generalities cause confusion.

- Technical writing agreements define the application or applications to be documented, and should have examples of the proposed finished product.

12

Word Processing, Graphics, and Spreadsheets

Word processing (WP) may be as common as the telephone, but the benefits are not automatic. Selecting the best WP package is a tricky decision, and avoiding the problems that come with unplanned implementations is even trickier. This chapter shows techniques to manage the word processing function and provide useful guidelines for those who use word processing. Spreadsheets are another personal computer-based tool that require careful judgment in terms of documentation. This chapter is for anyone who uses a personal computer or network for word processing, spreadsheets, or graphics applications.

Word processing is the most popular function on personal computers, but only one of many applications now available. The explosion of personal computers in the office environment continues the trend toward distributed processing, where low-cost computer power either replaces applications on the expensive mainframe, or provides applications not suitable for mainframes or minicomputers. Local area networks have expanded the versatility of such machines by reducing the number of copies needed, allowing shared files, and providing easier upgrades. Word processing, spreadsheets, data base systems, and artificial intelligence are all on personal computers.

The value of good written communication applies equally to minicomputers and personal computers as well as to large mainframe business applications. Electronic spreadsheets, for example, may be perfectly designed for manipulating numbers, but the quality of documentation can make the difference between a usable spreadsheet and a spreadsheet that must be rewritten simply to change a few values. A single user data base application that tracks customer complaints may be fine until that particular user transfers to another department. Documentation is still important, even in the flexible world of the personal computer. Personal computers have not reduced the benefits of quality written communication—they have expanded the need.

WORD PROCESSING AND ELECTRONIC MAIL

Although word processing exists on mainframes, minicomputers, and personal computer networks, word processing applications on the personal computer present the most common challenge for those concerned with good technical communication. Personal computers are inherently more flexible, which provides the user with greater opportunity for error and consequently more personal responsibility for preventing mistakes.

The word processing features required by an organization depend on the users' needs. An MIS area that frequently produces large documents may require an automatic indexing facility, where the press of a function key compiles a list of all pages that reference a specified word or phrase. Word processing software has matured to the point where virtually all of the major full-function packages are reliable, flexible, and reasonably efficient. They differ in the degree of adaptability for desk top publishing, graphics, networking capabilities, ease of use, and external features, such as the ability to convert word processing files to formats that can be used with other personal computer packages. One direction is toward integrated packages that contain word processing, spreadsheets, graphics, statistical analysis, and data base components. When considering word processing packages, checklists of features are useful, although actual hands-on experience before purchasing is equally important. Individuals react differently to the unique styles and on-screen formats of each package. What is right for Frank Flowchart in MIS may not be comfortable for Joyce Journal in Accounting. If the organization decides to implement a single word processing standard for all corporate users, the needs of many employees should be considered.

Packages change over time. The major software vendors issue periodic releases, which contain significant improvements over the current versions. A decision to select package X and not package Y may be justified one year, but the next major release may give package Y badly needed features not present in package X. User needs also evolve.

Personal computer-based word processing and its instant availability places new demands on professionals and managers who formerly depended on a secretary to prepare their documents. There are numerous potential problems when professionals and managers perform their own word processing. Those in management responsible for personal computer word processing should never assume that they can simply load the personal computers with software and allow the users to charge ahead without guidelines. A little planning will prevent a lot of embarrassing mistakes. New users need more than quick demonstration of the keystrokes to bring up the main menu.

Guidelines for word processing and electronic mail are:

1. *Never write a memo or document when angry.* A writer who drafts a nasty memo and sends it to the secretary for typing has an opportunity to reconsider the decision when the draft is later returned. The delay allows the negative emotion to subside. Under the do-it-yourself scenario of personal computer-based word processing, authors can create the angry memo, distribute it themselves, and face an unpleasant situation, all within the space of minutes. Productivity triumphs, but the result is bad for all concerned. Electronic mail is even less forgiving. A writer with a personal computer must physically deliver the offending document to the mail slot, mail room, or other person. But with a simple push of a button, the electronic mail system will cheerfully deliver the angry memo. Some electronic mail systems do have a function key labeled, "I really didn't mean to send that memo and I want it back," but even that sophisticated feature does not work if the recipient has already opened the offending memo.

   Relatively instant communication can lead to relatively instant interpersonal problems.

Figure 12.1 Rules for using PCs

Personal Computers and Communication		
Never write when angry.	Take backups!	Beware of security with electronic mail.
Use software to verify spelling and grammar.	Use consistent formats.	Identify each page.

2. *Always use a spell checker or more sophisticated device to identify spelling errors, erroneous punctuation, and improper grammar.* Secretaries audit their own work and release to the originator only material they have carefully proofread. Professionals expect that no matter how bad their pencil copy looks, the secretary will produce final output that is virtually error free.

Executives and others who are suddenly given word processing or electronic mail capability may not realize the impact of misspelled words and grammatical errors in their own documents. A glaring spelling mistake in an otherwise well-written proposal will distract the reader, and can change a favorable opinion to an unfavorable response. Punctuation, grammar, and style are important, but spelling stands out for all to see. For those who are fortunate enough to have a strong sense of correct spelling, an automatic spell checker program is still highly recommended. It is essential for those not so fortunate. Every document or memo should be processed by a spell checker before distribution. If the word processing package comes with a feature that also checks grammar, complexity level, and style, the author should use that additional check for any memo or document that is more than a simple note.

Some professionals complain that spell checkers waste time because the software identifies technical words that are spelled correctly but not in the internal dictionary. Most spell checker packages allow the users to add their own technical vocabulary or buzzwords to the dictionary. Even if a spell checker does not have this basic capability, the experience of observing the software locate each instance of a technical word alerts the author to the number of technical terms in the document. Does the document have too many buzzwords for the audience?

As artificial intelligence is built into word processing software, aspects of technical writing such as syntax, style, vocabulary, and grammar will be analyzed. Many word processing packages now have an online thesaurus, which suggests alternate words. A frequently used word in MIS documents such as *problem* could be replaced by *disaster, difficulty, opportunity, challenge, situation, crisis,* or *misunderstanding.* The online thesaurus allows the writer to choose the best word or phrase. Other advanced features include an algorithm to calculate the reading level of the document, and logic to estimate the complexity level of individual paragraphs.

3. *Multiple page documents should be identified on every page.* Readers are frustrated when they discover that the important document under review is missing a page. Equally frustrating is realizing that the pages may be out of order. Slightly less upsetting is locating a page that is obviously part of another memo or document. Preventing such problems is simple: All pages of a multiple page document must have

identification such as a condensed title, date, page number, final page number (the page x of y format), and version number if applicable. Listing the author is beneficial.

Multiple page identification from a department or organization should be standardized. It is inefficient for each author to create his or her own style of multiple page identification, and it is inefficient to force readers to adjust their thinking to variable forms of identification.

Electronic mail documents—if the system does not provide such a feature—may need an author provided title on every screen. This may be difficult, but is still recommended. All electronic mail systems allow the reader to page backward with a single keystroke to obtain the title, author, and date. Other packages display the title and author for every screen in the document.

4. *Word processing and electronic mail should follow consistent formats.* One of the many advantages of a secretary is that every memo, letter, and document from a department tends to have relatively consistent formats. Readers become familiar with a specific format when components such as date, author, and recipient are always in the same place. Memos, especially, are significantly easier to read when all follow a consistent style.

With a do-it-yourself approach to documents, readers can be confused by a barrage of individual styles, formats, and approaches to written communication. The title in a memo from Tina Template may be on the right, but the title in a memo from Terry Transit may be on the left. Readers who regularly peruse stacks of written communication face small but annoying discrepancies. Each difference causes unnecessary effort and eventually interferes with communication. Effective written communication calls for standardized formats that readers will readily accept. A busy reader who must review 20 memos every day will appreciate seeing the title, date, and author in a consistent location.

Standards can be enforced by loading a common memo and document format on every personal computer, and insist that all users copy the model for their own work. This also eliminates the time individuals would waste creating their own formats.

5. *Electronic mail documents are especially vulnerable to unintended distribution to the wrong audience.* Certain documents and memos are not truly confidential but are clearly meant only for the recipient. Both hard copy and electronic mail information can be seen by the wrong person. Hardcopy documents—whether from a typewriter or word processing printer—can certainly be distributed to employees or staff members not on the distribution list. Organizations attack this problem by developing procedures for confidential and semiconfidential documents, such as requiring confidential papers to be transported in sealed envelopes, or limiting the employees who handle such envelopes. If

Terry Transit writes a memo to Tina Template criticizing the Accounting Department, Terry may not want the Accounting Department staff to see the memo. People in the business world, however, are familiar with the spoken and unspoken rules regarding distribution of paper memos that perhaps should be restricted.

Electronic mail complicates the confidentiality issue. A note designed for a specific reader could be forwarded by that reader with a single keystroke to everyone in the company, when the originator of the electronic note did not realize the implications of such an action. This possibility places a special responsibility on the author who must understand that a memo written for a single individual can be forwarded to another individual. Confidential, accusatory, or sensitive information should rarely be placed on electronic mail, despite vendor claims to the contrary.

Some systems do have security features that prevent the recipient from sending a restricted memo to others, but there is no guarantee that five others may not be looking at the CRT when the individual is opening his or her restricted electronic mail. Also, because security is generally controlled by password, and since individuals do occasionally exchange passwords, system confidentiality can be compromised. The only time that sensitive information can be passed relatively securely is when the two individuals involved have worked out their own procedures. Even then, however, the author has no guarantee that the information will be confidential. Paper in sealed envelopes may be old-fashioned, but until electronic mail systems develop proven security and restricted distribution procedures, the old fashioned method is still workable.

6. *Unless an application is on a network, PC operators are responsible for their own backups.* Mainframe and large minicomputer-based word processing systems provide professionally managed backup and recovery facilities. Mainframe disk files are often backed up every night, and a user who ruined a document can usually call for a restore. If the mainframe disk files are damaged by a hardware problem, the most recent nightly backup will bring back all information except those documents modified during that day. Users seldom worry about document recovery.

Personal computer-based word processing packages are only as good as the hardware and software. Disks in personal computers do occasionally fail, and unusual conditions in the software can destroy or erase a document. Without a protected power source, personal computers can damage documents or entire disks. Problems will happen, and user's who have not provided their own backups are at the mercy of the fates. Invariably, disk crashes happen only when the user is preparing the most important document of the month.

Good business practices dictate that users provide their own backups and learn the procedures for restoring files. The backups must be frequent enough so that restoring from a backup file is better than rekeying the entire document. However, users must not spend more time backing up their documents than they spends on word processing itself. Paranoia regarding personal computer failure is not justified. There is a happy medium, and it takes some thought and experience to reach that point. Daily backups of the entire fixed disk are seldom needed, because most word processing users change only a fraction of their documents during the day. Also, the capacity of the backup medium is a factor: If it takes five diskettes to backup a fixed hard disk, the process will take a considerable amount of time. One alternative is to back up the hard disk weekly, but copy any documents changed that day. Networked personal computers can take advantage of mainframe file storage for backups, shared disk units on the network, or another user's personal computer storage. Data processing professionals are familiar with backup criteria and can advise the personal computer user. Their advice should be carefully considered.

Word processing packages now have supplemental applications based on grammar and syntactical analysis. One such package is described as a "style replicator." A technical writer can load a well written sample document into the application, which analyzes the model for such factors as words per sentence and degree of word complexity. Other documents can be fed into the application and rated as to their degree of fit. The purpose is to achieve consistent memos, reports, or letters. This type of package is most useful for marketing and sales applications: Customers may respond better if all documents they receive from a company maintain approximately the same writing style. Consistency implies reliability in the minds of some customers!

WORD PROCESSING FEATURES

Since word processing is available on everything from a lap-sized microcomputer to the largest mainframe, MIS management may prefer stand-alone type word processors (e.g., a single user microcomputer approach) or a shared word processing system (e.g., a minicomputer or personal computer network) that allows many staff members to update, review, and share the same written material.

Selecting a word processing package involves comparing each package on a feature-by-feature basis. All WP systems have basic functions such as full screen text editors. Technical writers and analysts who write long or complex documents such as user manuals, need many of the functions in the following checklist:

- Selectively merge parts of other documents into a new one.

- Add bold face, underline, italics, or redline to text.

- Backup each document before the current version is saved on disk, and automatic backup of documents after a regular period of time.

- Archive documents to save at least one past version, and the capability to backout all changes made during the current session.

- Change tabs settings for each paragraph, allowing columns and straight text on the same page.

- Align text and divide words into syllables on different lines.

- Align margins by paragraph.

- Center titles.

- Call online help screens keyed to specific functions.

- Center pages top to bottom.

- Back out the previous command or action.

- Display documents according to even and odd pages.

- Search, search/replace, and list all lines and pages having the specified text.

- Access specific pages without paging through the entire document.

- Set variable line spacing.

- Print specific page numbers or a range of page numbers.

- Print multiple copies of the same document.

- Verify spelling using a programmable dictionary for technical words that can be updated by the author.

- Generate chapter and section headings (and footers) on each page, so readers know exactly where they are at all times.

- Provide "boilerplate" formats.

- Search all documents and locate ones having a specific keyword.

- Maintain a description for each document, and search documents by keywords in the description.

- Flag every line changed during an editing session, or since a previous version.

- Store internal notes that will not print, but serve as a reminder to the author.

- Maintain codes that reflect the status of the document (a 1 may mean production version while a 2 stands for a document in the editing stage).

- Copy screen formats or other graphics directly from an application into a document.

- Manipulate objects including graphics.

- Provide graphics capability for the common data processing symbols, such as squares, rectangles, and diamonds.

- Establish commonly used words, phrases, and paragraphs that can be inserted into a document with a single command.

- Index to allow automatic cross reference for author selected keywords.

- Provide 80 or 132 print positions, and a CRT that supports both formats without horizontal scrolling.

- Multiprocess so the author can edit one document while printing another.

- Allow different type fonts selected at each printing session.

- Call a readability index that gives a computed difficulty level for each paragraph in a document.

- View documents on the CRT exactly as they will be printed.

- Provide windows that allow the author to view more than one document at a time (helpful for comparing two or more user manuals).

- Allow password protection feature for sensitive documents.

- Maintain ownership of individual documents by category other than author (such as department or division).

PC GRAPHICS

Once professional quality graphics software was limited to mainframe computers and used primarily for scientific analysis. During the early 1980s, the first comprehensive and easy-to-use graphic packages appeared on personal computers. In the 1990s, literacy in graphic software will become as important as word processing skills. Most commercial graphic software packages are flexible, easy to use, and available for virtually every reasonably configured personal computer.

Yet the MIS professional or manager still has the responsibility to learn the best way to use graphics: The software may be flexible, but if it is used incorrectly it will produce charts and graphs that will hinder communication rather than enhance the information transfer process. Like desktop publishing, one can produce professional-looking but confusing results. Training must be tempered by common sense, and a desire to effectively communicate in spite of the glamour of a sophisticated software package.

Why are graphics a powerful tool to communicate ideas? Pictures are indeed worth a thousand words. Humans are visually oriented and are generally comfortable with well designed graphs, charts, diagrams, and drawings. For example, long columns of computer response times can be meaningless except to those who spend considerable time studying their relationships. But the central meaning can be obvious if converted to a simple line graph.

Graphics can emphasize key ideas without using any pictures. Word processing is excellent at communicating information, but does not readily allow the writer to emphasize the importance of one idea over another. The author of a systems design document may include the five critical user responsibilities on page 37 using bold print and carefully chosen words. But many readers will never reach page 37! And those readers who eventually finish page 36 and turn to page 37 may not grasp the significance of these five critical items. The author could mention user responsibilities on page 1, but the topic does not fit into the scheme of the first section. Graphics on page 37 can provide the solution. A simple chart—using enlarged text—defining the five key items will catch the reader's attention. The busy reader may not read the text, but he will remember the chart.

Graphics range from simple line graphs to carefully orchestrated slide show compositions to professional quality animation, simulation, and computer assisted design (CAD) packages. The problem is not a lack of software to accomplish a task, but rather selecting which of the many excellent products to use. Most MIS professionals and managers can perform their job responsibilities using only the simple graphics tools. They should consult experts if they need to progress into complex graphics capabilities.

The most common types of graphics are:

- Graphic text
- Bar and line graphs
- Organizational charts
- Pie charts

Graphic Text

Systems analyst Frank Forklift impressed staff and management with the design of the new warehouse inventory and shipping application, but failed to commnicate the need for extensive training in the very busy warehouse. Training, listeners realized, was seven months away. Frank is still worried. He knows the struggle to allocate training time for employees who are still expected to meet their daily work loads. His design document is 41 pages, contains extensive data flow diagrams, entity relationship models, and other tools to communicate the flow of data and how the data is processed. He spent many long days reviewing and validating the requirements. Yet the training issue—which will not become critical until the system test planning begins in five months—is important enough to raise the red flag of caution. Frank could bury his concern in the text, but needs to dramatically emphasize the issue before it becomes a problem. He first created the sample in Figure 12.2.

When Frank stepped back to admire his work, he realized that the graphic could offend the warehouse manager who has repeatedly promised that he understands the need for training. The warehouse manager does not want to hear or see any more about training! Even if a graphic communicates effectively, the author must still consider the psychological effects of emphasis: key points to one person may be a slap in the face to another. No one likes to see his or her failures, problems, or mistakes displayed prominently on a page or overhead.

Frank can still get his message across by using the technique of shared responsibility. He can modify the graphic so it contains items that pertain to other areas or groups. The information on training is still present, but the warehouse manager is no longer the only focus of attention. Figure 12.3 identifies training in items 1 and 4, but includes two other equally relevant project management aspects. No fingers are pointed. Instead, the reader has a balanced picture, and the warehouse manager does not feel that he is on display. The tone has changed from "I" to "we." If more detail is needed, Frank could follow with the original graphic in Figure 12.2.

Bar Charts and Line Charts

Numbers may be the basis for many business decisions, but understanding the implications of raw numerical values is difficult. Line charts and bar charts help uncover trends and point to conclusions.

Figure 12.2

> *Need for Training*
> *Before Implementation*
>
> ✔ Requires at least 30 hours per employee.
> ✔ Order filler must complete two hands-on sessions after initial training.
> ✔ Supervisors need 8 extra hours to learn code table maintenance procedures.
> ✔ Performance stats must be individually explained during hands-on sessions.

Figure 12.3

Critical Factors
For Implementation Success

✔ Training time before implementation:
30 hours per employee
38 hours per supervisor

✔ Control of project change requests

✔ Commitment of MIS programmers and analysts to development schedule

✔ MIS support during training sessions

Operations Manager Randy Rerun believes that average mainframe response times are getting worse. He wants to prepare management for an expensive hardware upgrade one year ahead of plan. But first he must convince a large number of people that response times are indeed increasing, and more importantly that the rate of increase is also climbing. Although Randy himself has studied the numbers intensively, he knows that even his direct superiors in MIS will not spend the same time laboriously analyzing raw numbers. By using a line or bar chart, he can graphically illustrate the problem. Graphics are especially useful with relatively small or relatively large numbers where the absolute differences do not accurately reflect the magnitude of the changes.

For the two-month period starting in January, the average daily response times during the peak load times of 2:00 P.M. to 3:00 P.M. were:

January	week 1	1.99
	week 2	2.01
	week 3	2.15
	week 4	2.23
February	week 1	2.32
	week 2	2.34
	week 3	2.56
	week 4	2.99

Figure 12.4 is a bar chart that shows the slow but progressive increase in response time.

Both bar charts and line graphs illustrate trends and relationships between one or more numeric variables over time. The time periods in a graph can range from nanoseconds to centuries. Such graphs are ideal for displaying patterns or suggested patterns, and can be used for such diverse purposes as comparing two approaches to solving a problem (clas-

Figure 12.4   Standard bar graph

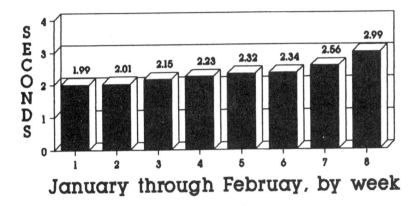

MAINFRAME RESPONSE TIMES
14:00 - 15:00 Average

January through Februay, by week

sical analysis versus structured analysis) to tracking maintenance costs across application systems by month.

Labels should be simple but clear. The time periods involved must be obvious. With flexible graphics packages, experimentation should be encouraged: A minor change in format can make the difference between a merely acceptable graphic or a masterpiece that truly impresses the viewers. Text should be added whenever needed to explain a variable or result. Experienced PC graphics designers often show samples to at least one person and watch closely for any indication that the graph is confusing. If there are questions, the designer can add text, rearrange the titles, or modify the graph itself. The viewer may not like the message on the graph, but he should always understand it.

Is it a good idea to place the conclusion on the diagram? The answer depends on the situation. If the message or conclusion is obvious and not subject to interpretation, one may legitimately add the conclusion to the graph. If, however, reasonable observers might reach different conclusions, one should be very cautious about trying to force a consensus. The type of audience is also a factor. Viewers who need to be led through the subject matter may appreciate the designer's conclusion, while another group who is intimately knowledgeable about the subject would rather draw their own conclusions.

Graphs can be manipulated to emphasize key points. By changing the minimum and maximum values, for example, one can project a conclusion that may not even be valid. Graphics can deceive better than words!

Figure 12.5 is a line graph using the same numerical data as the bar graph in Figure 12.4. Figure 12.6 is the same data, but the increase in response time is more pronounced. Only the y-axis minimum and maximum values have changed. Figure 12.7 is the same data, but with an even more restricted range on the axis. Identical data presented in different ways can lead to different conclusions.

Organizational Charts

An organizational chart is used to display a hierarchical or semi-hierarchical relationship. These include management structures, project teams, task force organizations, and data base structures. Hierarchies are common in both the business world and the data processing environment. Even matrix management and relational data bases will not completely eliminate the need for hierarchical structures.

Figure 12.8 is a typical organizational chart that defines lines of authority. The person on the right has a staff position, which is usually indicated by a dotted line. The functional areas of operations, analysis, programming, and database are identified by labels near the appropriate members of the team. Organizational charts always require an "as of" date, since reporting levels are often subject to change. One of the first documents issued at any project startup is an organizational chart.

Figure 12.5   Line graph with same data as Figure 12.4

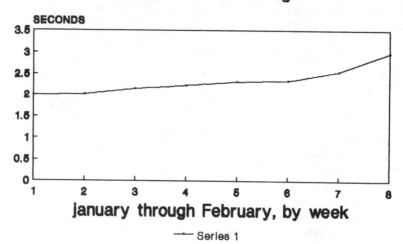

Figure 12.6   Same data, but lower range on y-axis

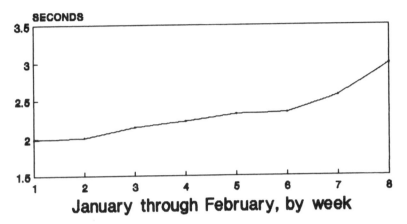

Figure 12.7   Same data, with even smaller y-axis

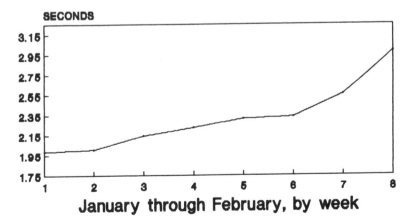

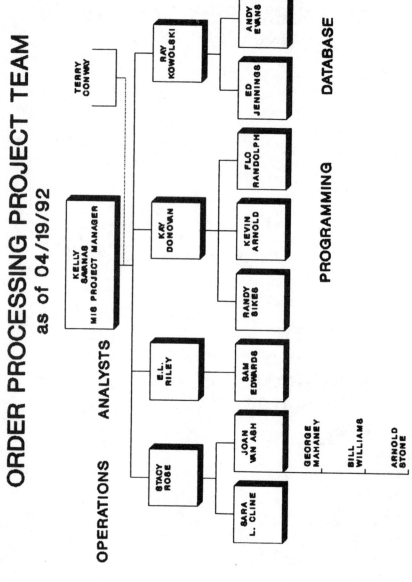

Figure 12.8 Organization chart

ORDER PROCESSING PROJECT TEAM
as of 04/19/92

Circle Graphs

Circle graphs are a common way to display numerical relationships. These so-called pie charts may be the most familiar graph to the average person. For example, newspapers generally use circle graphs to explain budgets. One often sees a pair of graphs, with one indicating sources of income and the other displaying the categories of expenditures.

Pie charts are often used to answer a question. Figure 12.9 is a graph that responds to the query, "Where do purchase orders originate?" The data could be summarized in the following list, but the graph instantly communicates that buyers are the largest single originator of these documents. Figure 12.10 is the same graph with a three-dimensional view. The raw data is:

buyers:	34
advertising:	13
warehouse:	7
other areas:	6

Circle graphs are flexible and most software packages allow dramatic touches that emphasize a particular idea. Figure 12.10 is the same data with the "other areas" slice separated from the rest of the pie. While Figure 12.9 leads to the conclusion that buyers are the main source of purchase orders, Figure 12.11 sends the message that the "other areas" is significant. The same data can lead to different conclusions by using selected presentation options for components of a graph.

SPREADSHEETS

Personal computers were first introduced to the corporate world through the power of the spreadsheet. These simple but elegant products amazed accountants by their flexibility, ease of use, and obvious advantages over the classic triad of pencil, eraser, and ledger. Accountants and their managers were finally able to play what-if games. Company management could then review financial alternatives and determine the effect on the bottom line. Spreadsheets were used in everything from household budgets to tracking project costs. Spreadsheets could provide much of the raw data for a profit and loss statement. Businesses soon learned to depend upon the results of spreadsheets, and accepted the theory that if it came from a computer, it had to be right. The corporate world quickly learned to love spreadsheets.

Later, electronic spreadsheets gained another reputation, as explained by the following complaint from a manager of accounting:

Bill's spreadsheet worked great until he left to open a bait shop on a South Sea Island. Then I asked Mary, who had written some of her own fancy spreadsheets, to make a few simple changes. Just modify the federal tax rate, and

Figure 12.9   Circle graph

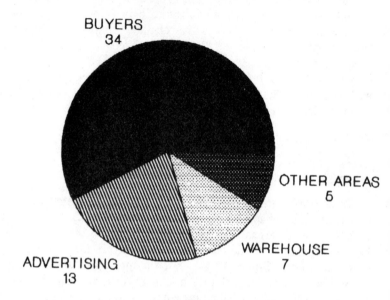

WHERE DO PURCHASE ORDERS COME FROM?

BUYERS
34

OTHER AREAS
5

WAREHOUSE
7

ADVERTISING
13

Figure 12.10   Circle graph with three-dimensional effect

WHERE DO PURCHASE ORDERS COME FROM?

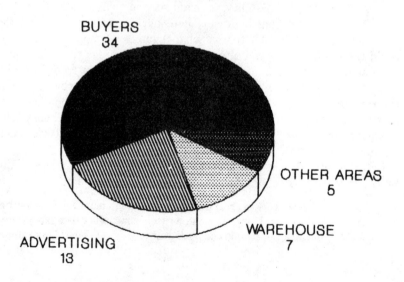

BUYERS
34

OTHER AREAS
5

WAREHOUSE
7

ADVERTISING
13

Figure 12.11   Circle graph with "out" slice

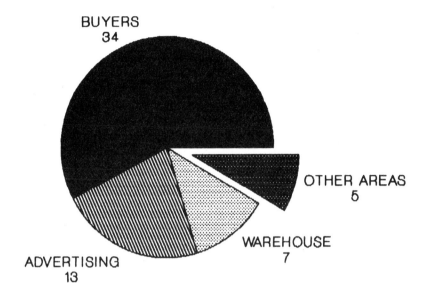

WHERE DO PURCHASE ORDERS COME FROM?

break down seven of the categories into parent and subsidiary company accounts. I thought it was simple. Mary spent one day and announced she might have to scrap the entire spreadsheet and start over. She says she doesn't understand it, and there are no notes for her to work with. Why, in the old days I could have made the change myself on ledger paper in an hour. This is progress?

Any computer-based application—from payroll system to inventory control system to electronic spreadsheet—is subject to maintenance. Business needs inevitably change. Companies are bought and sold. Tax rates go up and down. Change is constant, and virtually every computer application must keep pace with current events. Bill may have done an excellent job creating a working spreadsheet, but he failed to complete the project by documenting his product so that the next user could modify it. The design of a spreadsheet may be obvious to the author, but not to the unlucky outsider attempting to understand the logic. Spreadsheet languages display formulas easily, but they do not show the rationale, logic, and thinking behind the formulas, and it is often necessary to understand the rationale, logic, and thinking to modify the spreadsheet formulas.

Electronic spreadsheets critical to the business should have documentation provided by the author, and this documentation should be treated with the same respect as the spreadsheet itself. The documentation should be tested by reviewing a draft with another individual who is familiar with the particular spreadsheet language and style: If the second person can understand the spreadsheet construction from the documentation well enough to make significant logic changes, the documentation is satisfactory. If the reviewer cannot understand it, the documentation should be revised.

SUMMARY OF KEY POINTS

- Word processing software varies significantly in features, capabilities, and ease of use. Most are reliable and efficient. Selecting the "best" package requires careful study and actual hands-on experience.

- Word processing software is often integrated with graphics, statistical analysis routines, spreadsheet logic, and data base manipulation capability.

- Management should consider the potential problems when they replace secretarial support with do-it-yourself word processing and personal computers. Guidelines should be developed and issued before word processing is released to employees.

- Sensitive information on electronic mail can be seen by others. Special arrangements may help maintain security. Authors using electronic mail should always remember that the wrong person might be looking at the recipient's screen when the mail is opened.

- As with all personal computer applications, users are responsible for their own file backup and recovery. Most users need some advice from MIS.

- Complex spreadsheets that process data critical to the business should be documented, and the documentation should be tested.

- PC graphics include bar charts, line graphs, organizational charts, and circle graphs. More sophisticated software provides slide shows, animation, simulation, and computer-assisted design (CAD).

- Graphic text emphasizes key points.

- Bar charts and line graphs illustrate the relationships of variables to each other or to time

- Circle graphs or pie charts are often used to answer a question.

13

Presentations

MIS professionals and managers at all levels are criticized for their lack of presentation skills. Even managers who regularly stand before an audience are uncomfortable with their verbal presentation abilities. This chapter provides proven techniques for preparing, delivering, and evaluating project status reports, problem analysis speeches, and other forms of verbal presentations required in MIS. Professionals who develop above average presentation and speaking skills have an advantage over their peers in terms of management recognition, advancement, and increased responsibilities. This chapter is for every manager, project leader, systems analyst, programmer analyst, and programmer who makes presentations. Presentation skills can be improved dramatically!

Ask any group of experienced MIS professionals to list the aspects of their jobs they fear, and at least half will mention oral presentations. Even the most dedicated and knowledgeable systems analysts may feel a lump in their throat when asked to present a project status report to senior management. A skilled programmer may frown when asked to stand up before a group of peers and explain the performance considerations of a relational data base. Even managers who are expected to deliver formal presentations resist or even avoid as many requests as possible. MIS staff members are not generally known for their ability to perform in front of a group.

Those who reluctantly give oral presentations admit privately they could have done better, and in many cases they are correct. MIS presentations generally range from fair to barely tolerable. Those few professionals who have mastered the "black art" of public speaking are thought by the masses to have been "born with the gift." However, like technical writing, *presentation skills can be developed and improved.* By enhancing technical writing skills, an MIS professional is not expected to become a best selling novelist. Similarly, improving presentation skills will not always make the same MIS professional a lecturer on the public speaking circuit. But are presentation skills truly important for those in the technical or first level managerial arena? Is it justified to spend the time perfecting presentation skills, when such tasks may occupy only 1 or 2 percent of a professional's overall time on the job?

Absolutely! In the 1970s, data processing wizards kept to themselves and rarely ventured out of their sheltered cubicles. In the 1990s, MIS is an integral part of most organizations, and virtually every department has a stake in the computer software and hardware. MIS staff members are now *required* to communicate effectively with other employees. Critical business decisions may depend on such verbal information. As professionals in any business are judged by their writing skills, MIS staff members are also judged by the quality—or perhaps lack of quality—of their oral communication skills. Some MIS professionals excel at one-to-one communication, but perform poorly when faced with an audience of more than two people. Oral communication skills are just as visible as memos, design documents, and written status reports. MIS professionals who have mastered the techniques of effective oral communication have a definite advantage in recognition by both peers and management. Positive recognition generally leads to increased responsibilities, promotions, and higher merit increases.

The penalty for giving a poor or perhaps a minimally acceptable presentation is the unfortunate but understandably human perception that if the performance is poor, the person giving the performance is equally poor. The systems analyst who just finished a confusing speech explaining the advantages of artificial intelligence for warehouse replenishment may be respected for his or her knowledge, but emotionally the audience will react negatively toward the proposal and to the systems analyst as an individual. It may not be fair, but life is not required to be fair.

TYPES OF PRESENTATIONS

MIS professionals deliver a wide variety of presentations, and each has its own unique requirements. Understanding the characteristics of the more frequently requested presentations will help employees prepare their assignments.

The *project status report* is one of the most common stand-up presentations. It answers the inevitable management question, "Where are we on this project?" with all the unspoken concerns such as, "Are we on schedule?" and "Are we over budget?" It differs from other presentations in that the project leader, systems analyst, or first line manager may be asked to deliver the speech without adequate preparation time. This situation presents a challenging opportunity for the MIS professional to demonstrate presentation skills or the lack of them. Even the most cynical listener appreciates the difficulties inherent in delivering a project status report with only a few moments' warning. Experienced, successful project managers routinely prepare themselves for a sudden request to deliver a project status report. The requests for status reports increase when a project gets into schedule or budget difficulties. With or without time to adequately prepare, management appreciates professionals who can clearly describe the status of a project or major activity. The important factors in a project status report are balance, accuracy, and honesty. A balanced report covers all key areas of the project. An accurate presentation describes the true status of each area and projection for the future. An honest speech conveys disappointing or uncomfortable information in a form that shares the problems as well as a desire to remedy the situation.

Managers and senior staff members are often asked to give *problem analysis and resolution* presentations, where the speaker defines a situation, explains the options, and proposes at least one solution. Depending on the particular crisis of the day, some problem analysis and resolution speeches may concentrate only on the problem because the solutions have not been identified. Other presentations will spend little time on the difficulty and concentrate on alternatives. However, the presenter should always mention the problem, options, and solutions, even when the speech must obviously concentrate only on one or two of the three aspects. As in written communications, the audience needs a framework to fully compre-

Figure 13.1 Types of MIS presentations

	Project status	
Problem analysis and resolution		Information systems planning
	Education and training	

hend the information. Listeners need to be reminded of the overall situation.

MIS professionals at all levels perform *educational and training* presentations. The programmer may teach a group of trainees the procedures for using a test data base. The systems analyst could instruct the team of bank tellers on the logic in the new credit authorization system. The project leader may instruct a group on the correct time reporting procedures. The training specialist can give a lecture on the use of a new CASE tool. Educational and training presentations are often scheduled in advance, and the presenter usually has adequate time to prepare. There are a variety of training and educational instruction manuals available that define the unique requirements of instructional sessions. Instruction and education are specialized forms of presentation, and any professional who is not an experienced trainer should consult reference books on the educational process. Seminars on developing and conducting data processing training are worthwhile. "Training the trainer" is an important requirement that cannot be ignored.

Managers may lead a presentation on *long-range information system planning.* This is a complex session or more commonly a series of sessions that are part lecture, discussion, and learning experience. They are usually the culmination of a formal project to define application system and hardware needs for the next planning period. Often a group of managers will collaborate on this type of presentation.

DIFFERENCES BETWEEN WRITTEN AND VERBAL COMMUNICATION

Do verbal presentations follow the same principles as written communications? If one can create effective written documents, will one automatically deliver successful verbal presentations? After all, aren't the rules of communication the same, whether one is communicating in writing or on the stage?

The answer to all three questions is a uniform, "No, not exactly." Skill at written communication is not intrinsically transferable to oral presentations, and there are significant differences between communicating via the written word and through the mouth. The goals are the same, but the mechanics are different.

Written communication is designed for a single reader, even if the document is seen by everyone in the organization. Reading a document is essentially a private experience, with only the author and reader directly involved. Presentations are usually public experiences, and the interaction between members of the audience affects the experience for every individual. This interaction affects communication almost as much as the presenter and the material. The speaker must prepare for questions, challenges, and objections from the audience that could influence the direction of the presentation.

A document can be reread, while a presentation is performed once. The recipient of a document can study, review, and ponder the facts in the document. The information expressed in a presentation is heard and then must be remembered. The audience uses their auditory memory to retain information long enough for comprehension to take place, while the reader uses visual memory. Readers can ignore portions of a document if they already know the information, while the audience in a presentation must either listen, think of something else, or leave the room. The presenter must understand that individual members of the audience have differing awareness levels of the subject matter.

The written word is a visual medium. Readers interact with the printed page or CRT at a time and place of their selection. Effective communications depend more on the inherent quality of the material rather than on the quality of the medium. Of course, readers naturally prefer a typeset page rather than a document produced on a dot matrix printer with a worn-out ribbon. Content and effective writing skills are the primary concern. With presentations, content is only one critical factor that determines effective communication. Format, style, length, and speaking skills all affect the ultimate perception of quality. Even brilliant conclusions may be ignored, lost, or rejected if the speaker has poor presentation skills. Writing ability is very important in written communications, but speaking skills are even more critical to oral presentations.

Proficient public speakers recognize the three essential components of a successful presentation: *preparation, delivery, and evaluation.* All three aspects are equally important. The amateurs who stumble when giving a presentation generally fail to prepare adequately, and often ignore the final step of evaluation. The poor performers are so relieved when the ordeal is over that they refuse to reflect on their admittedly lackluster task. The experts, however, understand that detailed preparation is the first key to success. And they always evaluate their performance to identify ways to improve.

PREPARATION

The cardinal rule of presentations is to *know your purpose.* An astonishing number of MIS managers, systems analysts, project leaders, and programmers forced into a public speaking role fail to accurately define the purpose of their presentation and consequently fail the assignment. Successful communication demands that everyone in the room agree on the purpose of the presentation.

The purpose or goal of some presentations is not intuitively obvious. Even the most apparently straightforward meeting may have a complex, multifaceted purpose.

The presenter should attempt to define the purpose when the assignment or request is initially proposed. If MIS Director Sherman Super asks the new systems analyst Tina Template to report on her project to the MIS management committee, Tina may simply assume the purpose is simply to report the overall status. She could tell herself:

> The boss wants me to tell the Information Systems management group the status of my Order Processing Project. The purpose is to simply let them know how we are doing in the requirements definition phase.

Tina may have a simplistic, trusting, and slightly naive view of corporate life. What was behind the request for a project status report? Is it a routine matter to give a status report in this stage of the life cycle? Are there problems? Does management perceive there may be future problems? Is everything on schedule? *Why* did Sherman Super ask for such a presentation? The answers to those questions provide clues that eventually will define the purpose.

The requestor may indeed have a hidden or obscure purpose. Tina's boss may want to assure other managers that the Order Processing team is accurately addressing a set of very complex requirements. Perhaps Sherman called the meeting to investigate rumors of schedule slippage. Maybe the MIS director is concerned about the level of user cooperation. If Sherman does not make the effort to share his thoughts with Tina, she may assume the wrong purpose and thus prepare the wrong material. If Sherman is actually concerned about the level of user cooperation, and Tina spends only a few moments commenting on this aspect, Sherman will conclude that Tina has disappointed him and the audience. Sherman may sit quietly and shake his head at another example of a presentation that missed the mark. Tina and Sherman simply had different purposes for the same assignment. In a simple and perfect world, the requestor and presenter would automatically share their thoughts and ideas and come to an agreeable conclusion. MIS as a business is neither simple nor automatic.

Even if the requester and presenter agree on the purpose, the audience may have a different perception. If the group of MIS managers were led to believe they would hear about the intricacies of working with the slightly hard-to-handle Order Processing users, but Tina presents a balanced picture of all MIS activities, they will sit quietly and shake their heads in disappointment.

To prevent this common situation from becoming a problem, the presenter must acknowledge that the requester, presenter, and audience may have different purposes for the presentation. The MIS professional should interrogate the requester when the assignment is made: What do you want to accomplish with this presentation? If the requester is busy, the first answer may be very superficial. The presenter should repeat the question again at the next opportunity. Busy managers who ask for presentations usually have a purpose, but they may not have formed the purpose into words. Asking the question a second time gives the requestor a chance to compose his or her thoughts. Not all managers will be receptive to hearing the same question twice, so the presenter should phrase his questions with caution. A phone call or casual hallway conversation will often yield valuable information.

The presenter should also understand that many requests have multiple purposes. In politically sensitive or controversial situations, the requester may not even share the true reason for the meeting, but the MIS professional should make every effort to define as much as possible the true purpose or purposes behind the meeting. If Tina accepts the simplistic statement, "Just tell us how the Order Processing Project is coming along" without looking for a deeper meaning, she deserves whatever the fates give her. It is her responsibility to look for the truth.

After developing what they consider a reasonably accurate purpose, presenters should document their conclusions and ask the requester to review this brief but important statement. If the requester agrees with the wording, presenters should show the same document to at least one other person who will be in the audience and who may understand the background for the request. Although every member of the audience may have a slightly different purpose in mind, the audience perception will be shaped initially by the title of the meeting and the opening statements. Questioning a future attendee who may have "inside information" provides another viewpoint. Such an interview may take less than sixty seconds. Tina Template, knowing that the data base administrator will be invited to the presentation, can stop her in the hall and casually ask, "Please look at my objective for next week's meeting. Does this look OK to you?" The person may agree with the purpose, raise a warning that she expected something totally different, or not know enough to comment. Whatever the reaction, the effort of contacting at least one member of the audience is often justified.

The next step in preparing for a presentation is to identify the variables associated with the event. The presenter should ask the following questions:

Based on the purpose, who should be invited, other than the attendees suggested by the requester?

How many people will be present?

Where should the meeting be held?

What facilities such as projectors, lighting, sound equipment, erasable boards, etc. will be needed?

Is the scheduling of the meeting important?

How long should the presentation be?

The third step is to prepare the outline of the actual presentation. An outline is a logical sequence of key topics that will be discussed during the presentation. The list does not reflect the actual time spent in each subject: One topic may require only a minute, while another may cover ten minutes.

An outline consists of the following sections:

Introduction

- Self-introduction if needed
- Purpose of meeting
- Acknowledgment of people attending
- Probable length of meeting if different from typical schedules
- Policy regarding questions during the presentation
- Deliverables in terms of information at end of meeting (i.e., what will the audience get from this presentation)
- Starting and stopping times
- Availability of handouts or visual material
- Arrangement for meeting notes or minutes to be distributed later

Beginning

- Brief summary of the key points
- Identification of any important factors

Body of the presentation

- Words or phrases that mention each important element of the presentation, in sequence, and in a logical manner that the audience can understand.

Conclusion

- Phrases that summarize the important points and serve as an emotional balance

The conclusion depends primarily on the length of the presentation. A relatively short presentation needs a conclusion of only a few sentences, while a longer speech deserves a wrap of several minutes. Speakers often refer to the conclusion as the "tell 'em what you just told 'em." The conclusion should repeat the main ideas (always in a slightly different manner) and remind the audience of the purpose of the presentation.

Conclusions serve as an emotional balancer. When the arguments in a presentation are negative, the conclusion should provide an emotional balance by defining a positive reason for listening to negative arguments.

An audience who just heard 15 reasons for not using artificial intelligence at Wonderful Widgets needs to hear that listening to negative, slightly discomforting information will make them better decision makers. Mentally processing waves of negative comments is intrinsically depressing. The presenter should say something positive to counteract the continuous negative feelings. If everything the audience hears is negative, they may feel negative toward themselves and even the speaker.

If a presentation is overly optimistic, the conclusion can mention several cautions which help provide a more realistic picture. There are always cautions in MIS! Listeners should never be left on an emotional peak: If the presentation is excessively negative, the conclusion should end the speech with a positive statement, and if the presentation is overly positive, the conclusion should mention something slightly negative or at least neutral. The conclusion of the typical MIS presentation should leave the audience feeling "balanced" rather than drained.

An outline should have phrases rather than complete sentences. If the presentation is a formal speech, a separate outline is not needed since the presenter will be reading from a prepared text. However, the prepared speech should include the points listed in the introduction and conclusion. The outline should proceed from the macro to micro level, and start with a high-level overview in terms of key points. Generally, most outlines consist of no more than 10 to 20 important ideas. When the outline is later broken down into notes, further detail is appropriate. A natural tendency is to supply detail concurrently as one develops the key points.

For example, in giving a problem definition and resolution presentation for an accounts payable production problem, the first topic is to explain the problem. The phrase on the outline would be "incorrect checks produced on September 5 due to program error." The presenter, when listing the first key point, may immediately define the circumstances of the program error and explain why it slipped through quality assurance measures. This tendency is premature. Details should be developed only after the complete outline is prepared, because only a review of the outline can tell the presenters if they are satisfying the purpose. Creating details before the overall plan is generated may cause unnecessary work.

Using the key points in the outline, the presenter starts with the first idea and supplies details (from notes, backup documents, interview summaries, or memory). Inexperienced MIS professionals often provide too much detail in a presentation. There is a limit to the amount of information that can be absorbed in the typical 45- or 20-minute session. While developing detail for each idea, presenters should occasionally examine the outline of key points. This will remind them of the overall material that must be covered within the allotted time frame, and will reduce the tendency to overwhelm the audience with too many facts.

Index cards are still a useful tool for preparing presentations. The presenter can start with the first main topic, and write phrases or notes that explain the concept. Phrases should be used rather than long sentences. The print on the index cards should be large and easy to read. Small or hard to read handwriting requires more time to decipher while standing before a group.

VISUAL AIDS

Communication is enhanced when the speaker uses graphics or diagrams to emphasize points. Even the most informative 40-minute presentation will be considered slightly dull and perhaps even boring if the audience is forced to look only at the speaker. The availability of easy-to-use visual aids such as personal computer graphic software makes it relatively painless for a professional to quickly prepare a variety of sophisticated visual aids.

The original but still highly flexible visual aid was the blackboard or the erasable board. By tradition, MIS professionals are fond of using erasable boards to show logic, explain problems, and discuss ideas. These "on demand" visual aids are often created during the session while speakers are developing their concept. They have the advantage of allowing speakers' ideas to evolve on the board as they explain them. One disadvantage is that a speaker may spend so much time on the board that the audience pays more attention to the act of drawing than the material itself. Impromptu drawings are an excellent visual aid, if done only to help make a point. Portions of erasable board drawings can be prepared in advance. If used with restraint, colored erasable pens will help the audience understand. For example, blue could be used for input and green for output.

Typical visual aids are overhead transparencies, 35-mm slides, charts, diagrams, films, magazine and newspaper articles, videotapes, physical objects, and live demonstrations.

Overhead transparencies can be distracting. Some transparencies are so cluttered that the audience must decipher the message, while others contain so little information the audience wonders why the presenter went to the trouble of creating the overhead. Transparencies are categorized as *informational transparencies* which help the audience understand the main points of the presentation, or *positional transparencies* which help the listeners determine where they are in the schedule. The audience will follow a presentation better by locating the current topic in relation to other topics. In this case, a transparency serves the same purpose as a program in a theatre. The positional transparency (or equivalent) should be used in any presentation over 15 minutes.

A *positional transparency* is a single overhead with three to eight topics or checkpoints. Positional transparencies with more than eight stages are difficult to follow. The presenter can mark the completion of each stage as he shows the transparency. Or the presenter could prepare a series of positional transparencies with the appropriate stage marked by an underline, a box, a checkmark, or a different color. Having several positional transparencies is easier on presenters because they can have the positional transparencies mixed with the informational transparencies in the proper sequence. With a single positional transparency, the speaker must remember to reach for the transparency every time a topic changes.

Informational transparencies help the audience by displaying the key points mentioned by the speaker. Phrases rather than complete sentences should be used. Short, specific keywords communicate best. Speakers can use the overheads to trigger their own thought processes, but the informational transparencies should not be used as a script. Audiences remember the material on transparencies, so presenters should not simply use informational transparencies as an outline, but put the most important points on the transparencies. The speaker rather than the visual aid must control the presentation.

Colors make transparencies come alive, but some speakers avoid all colors due to a fear of color blindness among the male members of the audience. Blue is one of the rarest color deficiencies and can always be used. Red and green color blindness is more common, and some experienced presenters avoid using both of those colors in the same visual aid.

PRACTICE

Practice for MIS presentations does not include planning every word, gesture, movement, or intonation. Rather, the final result of the practice effort should be a confident presenter who knows what he will say, how he will deliver it, and how to answer probable questions and objections.

Using the outline, prepared visual aids, and notes on index cards, the presenter starts rehearsal. The goal of the first practice session is to organize the material and develop the sentences that will support each topic. This initial practice session should not be concerned with delivery: Practicing the delivery techniques should never begin until the presenter is confident he or she knows most of the sentences that will be spoken, although not with the exact words to be used.

The presenter should not worry about length in the initial practice session. Many first pass MIS presentations are either too long or too short, but later sessions will automatically adjust the length. The presenter should concentrate on the overall organization of the presentation, the format and style of the sentences used, and effective use of visual aids. *The first session should be silent*, with the presenter thinking out the sentences but using the visual aids. Not only is a silent run-through more efficient, but it avoids confusing the presenter with concerns about delivery. Professional public speakers often use silent practice as a simple and effective way to prepare their presentations. The goal of the first session is to develop the presentation in rough form. It is not necessary to take notes during the first session, because memory will recall enough of the important aspects of each sentence. Presenters who immediately rush to copy down every sentence after they have composed it may lose their own place and eventually confuse themselves. The first session should be a relaxed but slightly aggressive effort to compose the entire presentation. Changes to the outline and visual aids are to be expected, since the initial practice session is the first opportunity for the presenter to conceptualize the entire presentation. The silent run-through may be repeated several times.

After the outline, visual aids, notes, and topic lists have been modified, the presenter should have at least one final silent practice to verify that he or she has everything ready for the vocal sessions. Further adjustments can be made in the outline or visual aids. Note that much of the practice for a presentation can be done without uttering a single word!

Once confident that all the components flow together in a logical manner, the presenter can begin oral practice. Speaking without anyone in the room is uncomfortable for many people, but must be accepted as a necessary step in preparing quality presentations. Silent rehearsal is a good start, but once the presentation has been defined, the presenter must stand in a room and hear his or her own words. There is no substitute for this experience. One may object that speaking to a room full of people is qualitatively different from speaking to an empty room, but solitary practice is still highly beneficial. Some public speaking experts suggest that speakers try to imagine themselves talking to an audience, but it is hard for most adults to convince themselves they are facing a room filled with people when they are looking at a blank wall. Instead, most MIS professionals can avoid such mental gymnastics by accepting solitary practice as a solitary experience. Many adults feel a little silly talking to themselves, although they quickly lose this attitude once they have given several presentations and learn the value of solitary practice. Such private sessions are also flexible because presenters can simply stop, modify their speech, and continue without apologizing to a listener. Or, they can go back to the beginning when things seem out of control. Many of the world's most polished speakers regularly practice by themselves.

Having made at least one reasonably coherent rehearsal, the presenter should concentrate on the delivery. The first or second oral practice session can indeed be mumbled and hurried, but once the speaker has the presentation organized, defined, and formatted, he or she should begin preparing for the final delivery. Some speakers concentrate only on the words during rehearsal and ignore the fine points of delivery, assuming that when they finally do stand before an audience, the requisite delivery skills will magically appear. However, Murphy has proven that the public speaking fairy godmother does not visit MIS departments! Effective delivery is a skill that requires practice.

The final practice session should include at least one volunteer who is willing to sit through the entire presentation and provide constructive criticism. The lucky individual can be a colleague, a future member of the audience, or the requester. If a presentation is complex or unusually important, the requester is the ideal candidate. The reviewer should always take the seat farthest from the speaker and take specific notes on the material, delivery, and visual aids. Suggestions from the reviewer should be carefully considered, and a second final practice session may be needed.

The guidelines for effective delivery during the actual presentation are:

1. *Pause before starting the speech:* Never rush into speaking. Give the audience a chance to settle down and pay attention.

2. *Verify the position of projectors, erasable boards, slide projectors, and other devices before the session:* Arrange the visual aids before starting to speak if some manipulation must be done immediately. Listeners will understand the situation and appreciate not being distracted by a presenter trying to talk while fumbling with an overhead projector.

3. *Look at the audience before speaking:* Acknowledge their presence. Establish eye contact.

4. *Take a breath before speaking:* This simple physical act tells the body that the mind is still in control.

5. *Speak slowly and distinctly, recognizing that a common fault of poor speakers is talking too fast:* Pronounce words carefully, but do not exaggerate the lip and mouth movements. In adjusting volume, look at the person farthest away and speak loudly enough to carry on a conversation with him. During solitary practice, focus on the last row of seats in the room.

6. *Pause between major topics:* This allows the audience to assimilate the previous information and prepare for a change in subject matter.

7. *Occasionally vary the speaking rate:* Some topics or ideas are suitable for a slightly faster delivery. If the audience is familiar with the subject matter, talk faster. If the topic is new or very complicated, slow down.

8. *Acknowledge a raised hand from the audience with a smile and a hand movement if not taking questions:* Even if the speaker announced that questions should be saved for the end of the session, some listeners may still ask questions. These may be important queries and indicate that at least one listener did not understand or is lost. Experienced presenters—even if they ask the audience to save their questions for the end—still encourage listeners to stop them if they are confused. While the phrase "if you are lost" has different meanings,

most professional audiences will not interrupt unless they definitely need help.

9. *Occasionally frame the beginning of a new subject or key point with a question:*   In delivering a presentation on relational data bases, the speaker who is ready to introduce the topic of memory dumps and tracing data base calls could say, "And now let's talk about reading memory dumps to trace data base calls." An alternative is to ask, "Have you wondered how to trace data base calls when there is a problem?" The question is not only an interesting way to lead into another topic, but allows the audience to change their mental orientation from a passive observer to one who is actively participating. Yes, a programmer would need to trace data base calls through a memory dump, since solving problems is definitely a programmer's responsibility.

10. *Avoid choreographed body language:*   Body language is important, but not to the degree suggested by certain experts in the popular press. MIS presentations are generally information sharing exercises. The presenter is usually not selling or convincing a client in the marketing sense of the term. Body language should be natural, and most proficient speakers simply let their bodies create their own language. They still avoid such obvious distractions as hands that continually float about, or feet that move from side to side like a pendulum, or a face that regularly oscillates between the projector screen and the audience.

DELIVERY

To inexperienced presenters, the idea of a pause or interruption in the speech is abhorrent: It seems a sign of failure. Well placed pauses not only facilitate communication, but give the speaker a chance to plan ahead. A common but incorrect assumption is that presenters believe their mouth must be in constant motion. In the real world, even the best public speakers do not talk 100 percent of the time. They hesitate, pause, and intentionally create regular moments of silence. The MIS professionals should convince themselves that silence is to be welcomed in any presentation, and therefore allow themselves to pause without feeling guilty.

Eye contact with the audience is critical. Although it is clearly a simplistic generalization and seldom valid, human nature tells humans that a person who does not look directly at them must have something to hide. Conversely, the same simplistic human prejudice teaches the audience to have confidence in one who looks them directly in the eye. Obviously simplistic, obviously irrational, but still obviously important to an effective presentation.

At the start of the presentation, speakers should survey the audience and immediately make eye contact with one person. They should switch eye contact regularly and never concentrate on one individual, even if staring at one specific person is reassuring. Tina Template, when speaking to the MIS management committee, may know MIS Financial Manager Colleen Cashflow very well, but should not look at Colleen throughout the entire presentation. Even an unsophisticated audience will discern that Tina is focusing on one person, and resent the preferential treatment of one member of their group. Audiences demand fair treatment, in terms of understanding the visual material, having questions answered, and even maintaining eye contact with the speaker. The presenter can only look at one person at a time, but should alternate attention so that all areas of the audience (right, center, left, front, and back) feel they have experienced their share of direct eye contact.

Standing perfectly still during a presentation is not only difficult, but equally unnatural for both the presenter and the audience. Rather, the speaker should occasionally move about, or simply take a step forward, backward, and to the sides. The movements should not be choreographed, but the presenter can move when it seems appropriate. When answering questions, it is perfectly natural to step toward the person raising the question. When starting a new topic or idea, one can shift to another side. Speakers can move slightly, although they should never force themselves to pace between the sides of the stage area. Some presentations lend themselves more to movement than others. During training and instructional sessions, for example, the lecturer or discussion leader may frequently walk to the students, or even occasionally walk behind the group and talk from the rear of the room.

Successful speakers discover that presentations should be two directional rather than one directional. Presenters should be confident enough of their material that they can periodically survey the audience and determine if the audience comprehends the message. Facial expressions, body language, and overall movements will tell the presenter if the information is getting across. It is always important to read the audience. Are they following the material? Are they having trouble following the visual aids? Do they seem uncomfortable or ready to challenge the speaker? Upon perceiving a negative reaction, the presenter should stop and ask a question to define the apparent problem and solve it before continuing. Body language in an audience is hard to read but still gives clues as to the success or failure of the presentation. Observing several listeners leaning forward in their seats may indicate they are deeply absorbed by the fascinating information and superb speaker, or it may indicate they are having trouble hearing. Listeners squirming in their chairs may be bored, or it could mean that it has been two hours since the last break. Reading the audience is difficult, but it is a skill that can be developed with sufficient practice.

Sales professionals use a technique that is rarely appropriate for MIS presentations, even when the purpose of the presentation is to obtain agreement, gain approval, or win support for an idea. In the highly competitive world of sales and marketing, successful sales agents advise speakers to arrange their material so that the audience hears at least two statements they will support before they hear the controversial idea. They believe the audience, having said yes in their minds to the two previous ideas, will be more likely to say yes to the third. Perhaps the law of inertia does apply to psychology, where the listener is manipulated into the habit of saying yes. Nodding the head twice could make it easier to nod the head the third time. This sales tool may have an *occasional* use in MIS presentations, but the MIS professional should understand that such techniques are sophisticated tools that could infuriate an audience who expects a presentation based on facts rather than sales proficiency. Forget tricks!

Objections and questions should be regarded as an opportunity to reinforce the material and conclusions, rather than as a personal challenge to the speaker. It is essential to respond positively to questions. The audience will judge the presenter as much by the response to the questions as on the formal presentation. A good presentation can be downgraded if the speaker is unable to reasonably answer questions or comments.

Objections are more complex than questions. An audience member may simply say, "I don't agree," or may mention a fact, situation, or opinion that differs with the main points of the presentation. The objection must never be ignored or scorned. Even if the audience does not accept the objection, the lack of any response or a derogatory reply from the presenter will give it credibility. An objection should be treated with respect, and the speaker should phrase the answer carefully. A good response is, "I see your point, but let's consider..." or "I may not have made this clear, but...." The goal is to avoid a personal confrontation by directly challenging the objector. Never imply that one did not listen carefully or that one is asking a silly question. If necessary, rephrase the original idea mentioned in the presentation in simpler terms. In many situations the objection may not be clear, and the speaker can legitimately say, "I'm afraid I'm not following you. Could you say that again?"

Questions are easier to manage than objections, but it is difficult to decide how much of the presentation to repeat. If the questioner obviously did not understand a large portion of the material, the presenter could make a brief explanation, and then suggest a private session later. If the question can be answered by referring to the notes, or visual aids, the speaker should answer the question cheerfully. Presenters must never give the impression that they are uncomfortable answering questions or repeating material. In technical presentations, Murphy has proven that if one member of the audience is brave enough to ask a question, five others are equally confused.

EVALUATION

After the performance, MIS professionals have one more task. They must evaluate not only their own performance, but the total experience of the presentation. Evaluation is the key to improvement. No matter how many times MIS professionals give presentations, they will not improve significantly until they perform critical self-evaluation. This process is not meant to downgrade the speaker, but to locate areas for improvement and also point out those aspects of performance that deserve congratulations.

Evaluation has three aspects: First, presenters should ask themselves questions related to their own honest perception of the performance. Second, they should interview the requester to determine if the purpose has been satisfied, and to ask for general impressions. Third, they should question at least one member of the audience. The trilogy of responses should provide a realistic evaluation with the minimum amount of effort.

Presenters should ask themselves the following questions:

1. What was the general reaction of the audience, based on comments, feedback, and other clues? Did they seem to understand? Were there any indications of positive or negative responses?

2. Did the elapsed time of the presentation match the length of the final practice session? Did the presentation seem too long? Was it too short?

3. Was the overall tempo or rhythm of the presentation appropriate? Was the presentation delivered at the proper speed for understanding?

4. Were the visual aids a help or a hinderance? In a long presentation, one or more of the overhead transparencies, diagrams, or charts may have interfered with communication or simply failed to fill its function. Which ones seemed most effective, and which ones should have been designed better?

5. Was the level of detail appropriate for the subject? Were too many facts included in the presentation? Should there have been more or less information?

6. Were questions from the audience answered properly, with enough information to satisfy the questioner? Or did the questioners seem to give up rather than continue the search for facts? Were there enough questions? If not, was anything said or implied that questions would not be welcomed?

7. Did the speech pattern seem nervous or forced?

8. Were the right people in the audience? Should someone have been invited who was not present? Were there too many people?

9. If handouts were distributed, did the material match the information actually presented?

After the self-evaluation, the speaker should ask the requester for comments. This should not be an informal, impromptu hallway or coffee break conversation, but rather a serious person-to-person discussion. The requester should be asked:

1. What was the overall impression?
2. Did the presentation meet the purpose?
3. Are there any suggestions for improvements?

The final step in evaluation is to ask a key member of the audience the same three questions. This interview should also be considered a frank, honest discussion, where the presenter sincerely asks for constructive feedback.

By combining the answers from the self-evaluation, the requester, and a key member of the audience, MIS professionals should have enough information to improve the next performance. They should expect different answers from the self-evaluation, the requester, and the selected member of the audience. Those areas that match will need the most intensive work.

SUMMARY OF KEY POINTS

- Presentation skills can be mastered by learning the proper techniques and striving to continually improve.

- Examples of commonly heard presentations are project status reports, problem analysis and resolution speeches, educational and training sessions, and long-range planning discussions.

- Oral communication is similar to written communication, but there are differences. For example, presentations are public experiences where the reaction of the audience affects the quality of communication. Verbal sessions must consider the limitations of the human auditory learning mechanism.

- Three components to a successful presentation are preparation, delivery, and evaluation.

- In preparation, the first objective is to define a purpose understood by both the requester and presenter.

- Variables such as audience selection, length, and facilities should be defined early in the preparation cycle.

- The outline is a series of key phrases, one for each of the topics to be discussed, and consists of an introduction, beginning, main body, and conclusion.

- Use visual aids such as overhead transparencies, charts, diagrams, and erasable boards, and slides whenever possible.

- Long presentations need a positional transparency or chart that shows the agenda, and allows the audience to track their status in the schedule.

- First practice sessions should be silent so that the presenter can concentrate on the material.

- After the presentation is defined, the speaker should practice alone. The last practice session should include a volunteer who is willing to provide constructive criticism.

- Pauses during delivery are normal and actually serve many useful purposes.

- Proper eye contact with various members of the audience is critical.

- Presenters should periodically survey the audience and look for any positive or negative reactions. They should stop and investigate any serious negative impressions.

- Questions and objections from the audience deserve respectful and complete responses.

- After the presentation, presenters should do a detailed self-evaluation. They should also interview the requestor and at least one member of the audience to obtain suggestions.

Meetings

The daily life of managers and senior professionals is filled with meetings. Decisions are made during meetings. Careers are made and careers ruined during meetings. Policy is made, and policy is broken during these sessions. Some meetings resemble a battlefield, while others would cure the worst case of insomnia. Nothing would get done in MIS without meetings. Or perhaps as several cynics have observed, things get done in MIS despite meetings.

This chapter is for all managers and professionals who call, lead, and attend meetings.

MIS meetings are often criticized for their lack of professionalism. In fairness, meetings in the MIS world are not much worse than sessions in the overall business world. Surveys report that from 60 to 80 percent of business meetings are rated by at least one participant as "barely satisfactory." Meetings in modern corporate life are generally looked upon as an unpleasant necessity that must be endured. MIS meetings are no better or no worse than those held by areas such as accounting, engineering, manufacturing, or distribution. Unfortunately, MIS meetings tend to be more visible to the organization and therefore receive the most attention.

Why are most meetings less than satisfactory? The complaints vary, but some of the most common criticisms are:

- Participants who talk about everything but the original topic
- Unprepared discussion leaders
- Dominance of a single participant
- Boring and unnecessary statements
- Starting late
- Wrong participants
- Lack of any decision
- Ending late
- No agenda
- Lack of information to make a decision
- Vague or confusing purpose behind the meeting
- Personal antagonism between participants and discussion leader
- Overbearing and argumentative discussion leader
- Failure to summarize
- Lack of any rules or guidelines for the meeting

These problems are all symptoms of a fundamental lack of control. Inability to control events is usually blamed on the discussion leader, but the situation is more complex. Too often a discussion leader who officially calls a meeting and runs the session may have limited authority over events, personalities, and eventual outcomes. If someone must be blamed, perhaps the logical candidate is the organization itself. Most meeting failures can be traced to errors or omissions caused by some combination of the discussion leader, the participants, and management itself! If poor quality meetings are a common occurrence, managers should question their own attitudes toward the subject of meetings. Do they contribute to ineffectual meetings by their own attitudes and lack of knowledge of proper meeting management? Do they train their employees? Do they interfere rather than help?

MIS meetings are especially visible when other areas of the company are present. Since user departments are not always favorably disposed toward MIS, any problems in the meeting are often magnified when the non-MIS staffer reports back to his area.

MIS meetings may be difficult to control because they tend to have people of differing backgrounds. Meetings in the accounting or engineering areas generally have individuals of approximately the same training, education, and experiences. Virtually every accountant can agree on the procedures inherent in the double entry method of bookkeeping. Obviously, accountants in a retail organization look at financial reporting differently than accountants in a manufacturing organization. And accountants in different departments do have different reporting needs. In MIS, however, a meeting may have application programmers, data base analysts, telecommunication analysts, system software engineers, and hardware analysts, all of whom have differing training, vocabulary, and outlook. The opportunity for miscommunication is high with such a diverse group.

But MIS meetings can improve significantly. They are not absolutely required to be ineffective. They may never be considered the epitome of precise and well-defined business meetings, and some will always be better than others, but progress is always possible. The prerequisite for improvement is to understand that successful meetings depend on the discussion leader, participants, and management. As corporate citizens, the meeting attendees have just as much responsibility for the success of the meetings as the individual leading the session. As managers, those controlling the organization have a responsibility to educate their staffs and abide by the principles of effective meeting management.

Textbooks that emphasize only discussion leaders and performance ignore the other two-thirds of the equation. If discussion leaders must be trained, meeting participants must also be educated. And management must actively assert its responsibility to shape the environment so that successful meetings are encouraged.

ROLE OF MEETINGS IN MIS

A rose may be a rose by any other name, but a meeting can be a discussion, argument, exchange of ideas, or a waste of time. MIS meetings often fall into all four categories. Yet meetings are an indispensable link in the communication process. Like memos in written communication, meetings are often cursed but always needed.

Seldom do MIS meetings serve a single well-defined purpose, and most managers who encourage meetings as a way to solve problems may not consider the complex nature and human interaction that occurs during a session. Understanding both the importance and complexity of this group activity is the first step on the long road to productive meetings.

MIS meetings combine the following characteristics:

- *Information sharing:* The discussion leader and/or participants provide facts or opinions on a particular set of topics. Every meeting—even those with another stated purpose—have some degree of information exchange. In any discussion such informal education should be encouraged. Professional growth demands a consistent infusion of information. Those responsible for directing a meeting should fight the tendency to automatically stifle comments that seem purely educational and do not fit the official purpose of the meeting. Meetings should always focus on a goal, but education is a valuable byproduct. As long as the meeting progresses toward its goal, some information sharing statements should be allowed.

- *Problem definition and resolution:* Data processing is traditionally associated with problems, errors, questions, and periodic crises. When a problem occurs, management's first reaction is to call a meeting. This response may be triggered by a desire to help solve the problem, but also to an ingrained attitude that urges them to do something. Demanding an immediate problem resolution meeting is one way for a concerned manager to exert influence as well as feed his or her own ego. Problem resolution meetings should demand both extensive preparation and planning, but often have the least amount of preparation time. Attendees often find too many participants, or too few, or that no one has the facts, or that everyone has a preconceived notion of the truth. It is remarkable that most problems in MIS do eventually get solved.

- *Procedural discussions:* Large organizations display an appetite for policy questions or business decisions that fall into the general category of procedures. The development group might request a meeting to discuss a policy on implementing data base enhancements to the production systems. The accounts payable manager may discuss the procedures for correcting errors in the recently purchased software package. These meetings may be characterized by departmental rivalries and uncertainty over individual responsibilities. Managers as well as senior professional staff participate in or at least plan procedural meetings. Participants are often unsure if they have authority to approve tentative procedural agreements. Such meetings will produce a recommendation that must be reviewed by management. More often, a procedural meeting ends with an agreement to think about the issue and eventually call another meeting. Conflict avoidance is alive and well in many procedural type meetings.

- *Planning meetings:* Planning has always been an essential part of management. Meetings are a useful tool to develop, organize, and implement MIS plans involving hardware, software, applications, and staffing. Users may be invited to attend or even give short presentations on their needs. Planning meetings are often a matter of negotiation, where priorities are discussed, proposed, and argued until a decision is reached. The typical planning session is called by a senior manager to define priorities and budgets for the next planning cycle.

- *Consensus meetings:* The term *consensus meeting* is an umbrella for any session that requires an agreement from the assembled group. In a broad sense, every meeting is partially a consensus meeting. The subject matter could be hardware, software, user relations, performance tuning, training, documentation, or any of the multitude of activities associated with MIS. A true consensus meeting is not specifically to solve a problem, select a procedure, or plan staffing for the next year. Rather, the goal is to gain an agreement, indicate cooperation, or provide mutual support for a proposed direction. The method of agreement may be logic, coercion, or dictatorship, or some combination of all three, but the final result is the appearance of an agreement. Some meeting leaders honestly want the group to agree on an idea, even if the final outcome does not conform to their personal wishes. Less democratically oriented leaders seek only the appearance of an agreement, and use the meeting to announce the decision, request objections which never come from cowering employees, and close the meeting with a demand for action. The typical MIS manager of the 1990s may be too sophisticated to display obvious dictatorial tendencies, but the nature of the beast is still evident.

THE MYTHS AND REALITIES OF DECISION MAKING

Group decision making is a complex and fascinating subject. Business, psychological, behavioral, and popular journals proudly describe the latest study on the dynamics of decision making in group settings. The results are interesting. Many eminently successful organizations show qualitatively different styles of decision making than the unsuccessful companies. The difference is not so much good or bad, or even democratic or authoritarian, but rather effective and ineffective. Effective decisions accomplish goals that help the organization thrive, while the ineffective decisions fail to accomplish goals to help the organization, or accomplish goals which do not help the company. Doing the wrong thing well is a mistake triggered by an ineffective decision.

Figure 14.1 Myths of group decision making

Assumption	*Reality*
Groups make better decisions than individuals.	No!
Participants automatically take responsibility for decisions.	No!
Meetings are inherently democratic.	No!
Manager's presence will not influence results.	No!
Groups always override single dominant individual.	No!

Fully democratic decision making is not a prerequisite to success. A small company or department with a highly capable, knowledgeable manager may do quite well even if the person in charge uses a benevolent but slightly dictatorial style. Employees who lack the satisfaction of participating in management decisions may be compensated by other factors such as salary, working conditions, or genuine management appreciation. However, most studies have found that decisions are more effective when management encourages some degree of employee and staff participation.

There are many myths regarding decision making in organizational environments, and a manager who can separate the myth from reality is better prepared to control meetings.

Myth number 1. *A group will invariably make better decisions than individuals.* A group of employees can make a stupid decision just as easily as the boss. If the group is provided the wrong information, has incorrect perceptions about the solutions, or is dominated by one individual, the decision may be incorrect. Group thinking does not automatically trigger the logic and reasoning that evokes wise decisions.

Myth number 2. *Meetings will make participants feel responsibility for the ultimate direction.* Optimists believe that if ten representatives from various areas of MIS attend a meeting where a decision is reached, all ten will feel equally motivated to implement the decision. Wrong! The real world is not so simple. If a decision is later proven incorrect, nine of the ten participants may remember the tenth attendee who argued forcibly for the decision. That unfortunate individual may have only proposed the idea or merely nodded when the chairperson asked if anyone agreed. Failure to object or even simply shrugging the shoulders does not guarantee that all meeting participants will assume personal responsibility.

Myth number 3. *Meetings are an inherently democratic institution.* Even the most sincere appeal for participation may not produce a truly democratic session. Rarely will each individual have an equal opportunity to present his or her side of the argument or even pose all his or her questions. Studies have consistently shown that one or two individuals often dominate a discussion and influence the direction more than all the other participants combined. Subjective reports from attendees often reflect the attitude, "Why did I bother to show up?" Decisions may be reached by consensus, but the consensus may be only one or two people.

Myth number 4. *The presence of managers will not unduly influence the meeting.* Managers or directors who attend an MIS meeting often have their own expectations of the outcome. It is unrealistic to expect employees to ignore their presence. Even if the managers carefully trys to appear neutral, their facial expressions, body language, and occasional comments will generally reflect their own preferences. Employees may mold the discussion toward those ideas that make the manager feel positive. One can often explain the typical meeting that ended in a bland or neutral decision by observing that the staff was trying not to upset the boss.

Myth number 5. *A group setting will usually negate the effects of a single dominate individual.* If a meeting will be dominated or led by a key individual who typically forces his or her own ideas, the meeting will have little value. Information will not be shared. Logical analysis and honest differences of opinion will not emerge. Everyone knows the final result before the meeting begins. Morale is low or nonexistent during such a session. Participants willing to give an honest evaluation will generally use the phrase "it was a waste of time."

PREPARATION

Do MIS employees prepare well for meetings, or do they prepare at all? Although impromptu, hastily called meetings do not allow time to prepare, the majority of MIS meetings are scheduled, and allow both the discussion leader and the participants advance notice. Of course, smaller meetings with a single, well understood focal point and individuals acquainted with the details may not need extensive preparation. If the hardware analyst Charley Channel and the operations supervisor Rita Rerun meet to discuss the I/O constraints on second shift production jobs, little preparation is needed when both know the subject intimately, have discussed it several times, and understand the nature of the session.

The degree of preparation needed varies with the nature and complexity of the meeting, but the typical meeting requires at least as much preparation time as the length of the meeting. A leader who spends five minutes preparing for a one-hour meeting is cheating himself and his colleagues. MIS participants also need to increase the time they typically spend preparing for meetings.

As with informative presentations, the first step to a successful meeting is to define the purpose. If specifying the purpose for a presentation is difficult, determining the purpose of a meeting can seem impossible! Although many meetings have a seemingly obvious purpose, others are called for multiple, or even conflicting, reasons. Unless the purpose is clearly defined, five employees attending the same meeting may perceive five different purposes. Much depends on the style, personality, and position of the person requesting the meeting. It is the requestor's responsibility to define an acceptable purpose, specify deliverables, communicate the information, and set the tone for the entire meeting. Such analysis and decision making must take place before the meeting rather than three minutes before the session begins.

A common organizational error is that a manager says to a subordinate, "Call a meeting on the situation" and turns away to deal with another problem. The subordinate who is given only a brief statement for direction will make assumptions about the meeting and hope for the best. Managers who criticize employees who were asked to call a meeting and bungle the assignment often have only themselves to blame. If the requester is not conducting the meeting, he or she should work with the discussion leader to plan for the event.

Either the person requesting the meeting or the discussion leader has the responsibility to:

1. State the purpose in understandable terms.

2. Define the deliverables.

3. Plan an agenda that is feasible under the time and staffing constraints.

4. Communicate the information to attendees.

5. Work with participants who will have a key role in sharing information and ideas, and verify they are ready for their part in the effort.

6. Prepare materials for the meeting.

Requesters may delegate, but they are ultimately responsible.

1. *Stating the purpose* tells the "why" of the meeting, which also justifies the expense of taking employees away from their jobs for an hour to sit in a room. An unacceptable purpose is, "The boss told me to call a meeting on the Accounts Receivable situation." A slightly better version is, "The meeting is to talk about the weekend problem in the Accounts Receivable system." A very clear and informative version is, "The meeting is to explain the problem and rerun this weekend of the Accounts Receivable system, evaluate the MIS response, and decide if there is anything that could have been done better." The latter sentence communicates the purpose with little room for misunderstanding.

The purpose should be listed in a concise memo or standard meeting announcement form sent to all participants. Simply notifying attendees of date, time, and location without specifying the purpose causes confusion and misunderstanding. If an attendee must ask, "What is this all about?" the requester has failed the first task.

2. *Defining the deliverables* insures that the meeting will produce something of value. Is the deliverable a greater awareness of how the incorrect parameter got into the last Accounts Receivable production job? Is the deliverable a document recommending procedures to prevent such an occurrence? Requesters should define what they expect to accomplish from the effort. If a meeting will not accomplish a goal that can be put into words, why have it? A deliverable is not always a formal report. It could be a set of notes taken by a designated individual and sent to all participants.

A deliverable could be a five-line memo acknowledging when the meeting was held, listing the subjects discussed, and noting any conclusions or open items. Defining the deliverable is an analysis step that helps the meeting requester or discussion leader plan the agenda.

3. *Planning an agenda* is more complicated than the traditional format of opening, discussion, and conclusion. Developing a useful agenda forces the discussion leader to visualize the meeting from start to finish, define the deliverables, and create the steps needed to reach the final goal. An agenda is a design for a meeting, much as a systems design is the proposed view of a new payroll system. As system designs are seldom accurate on the first attempt, the first draft of an agenda is seldom perfect. Experienced discussion leaders review their initial attempt and adjust the contents several times before the meeting. But successful meeting leaders recognize that the deliverables and goals are more important than the agenda, and if circumstances change during the meeting, they will deviate from the agenda.

4. *Communicating information* such as time, place, and subject to all attendees is critical. Leaders should also appoint a backup for themselves if they are ill or unexpectedly called away. Frequently, meetings will be cancelled and rescheduled at great effort if the requester or discussion leader is unavailable the day of the meeting. If the requester is essential to the success of the meeting, the cancellation is justified. If, however, another person could serve as moderator if they were even minimally prepared, the meeting should go on as scheduled. Cancelled meetings affect every attendee, as well as the clerical support staff who must reschedule another meeting. The substitute leader may not do a complete job, but the meeting can still accomplish its goal.

5. *Preparing the final agenda* is the last step. An agenda has three sections: introductory remarks, discussion, and closing. The introductory remarks have four topics:

- Introduction
- Purpose
- Deliverables
- Ground rules for discussions

The introduction is required if one or more attendees is not acquainted with any other individual in the room. Even if informal introductions have taken place before the meeting, formal introductions officially recognize every member of the group. Introductions during MIS meetings should include something more than the person's name. Perhaps the attendee's position, title, area of knowledge, and reason for attending are appropriate. Attendees should be identified for their potential contribution. Such effort takes only a few seconds, but starts the meeting on a positive tone.

The purpose should explain why the requester called the meeting. The deliverables should be stated in clear terms: Everyone must understand the desired outcome. Ground rules for discussion prevent misunderstanding. Perhaps the leader will call on one participant to summarize a problem or idea, and then ask for discussion. Or the leader may go around the table and ask for opinions on the written proposal of May 15. The attendees should understand how the meeting will be conducted and how they can participate.

The middle of the agenda should be a listing of specific topics or items that will be reviewed. Key words or phrases should be used rather than sentences—participants should focus on the verbal comments and not on lengthy written agendas. Some agendas may have only one or two main points, while others will list 10 or 15. It is the discussion leader's responsibility to use the agenda as a guide. Comments should be initially limited to the points listed, although the group can agree to change the agenda if new topics are more important to meet the purpose and create final deliverables.

The last major item on the agenda is the closing. While discussion leaders are often expected to summarize, in complex meetings they may be the poorest choice to deliver an effective summary. Their primary and often full-time role is to control the discussion. An alternative is to ask one attendee to deliver the summary at the end. Participants assigned this role will act differently than the other participants. They may not talk as much, and they may listen more carefully. They may interrupt to clarify specific points. Gathering information for a summary is a continual listening process.

5. The leader must *work with key participating individuals to verify they understand their roles*. A discussion leader who expects the operations supervisor to spend a few minutes summarizing the weekend production problem must let the supervisor know exactly what is expected. The term "a few minutes" can mean 30 minutes reciting a blow-by-blow description of the abend to the operations supervisor or a 40-second explanation to the discussion leader. Sharing expectations with those who have assignments is critical but often overlooked.

6. The leader *must prepare materials* such as overheads, transparencies, visual aids, and sample documents and review them for relevance. A sophisticated visual aid may be impressive, but considering it in relation to the agenda, deliverable, and time constraints, the discussion leader may reluctantly decide not to use one or more of the visual aids. However, at least one visual aid (even if it is a simple diagram on the erasable board) should be used for most technically oriented meetings. While meetings are not presentations, visual aids, even a simple diagram of the four steps in the accounts receivable jobstream with an arrow pointing to the culprit, gives participants a focus point. Also, some attendees are reluctant to be

the first to use a visual aid such as a scribbled diagram on the board. The discussion leader should legitimize graphics through his own attempt and thereby give the OK for the participants to use visual aids themselves.

GUIDELINES FOR DISCUSSION LEADERS

Effective discussion leaders are skillful people managers as well as strong managers of ideas. As good people managers, they must accept a neutral rather than a directive role. Discussion leaders who are primarily interested in swinging the sentiment toward their own ideas will invariably do a poor job of managing the discussion. The best discussion leaders are those who are willing and capable of acting in a neutral and objective manner. They are more interested in an effective and productive meeting than forcing their preferences on the group. If the requester is so committed to an idea or approach that he cannot be objective, he should let another individual run the session. The rules for effective meeting management are based on objectivity, professionalism, and productivity. Guidelines do make the difference!

1. Start and End on Time

The most glaring problem with many MIS meetings is that they do not start on time or end on schedule. This difficulty can be traced to the lack of management commitment to the old-fashioned but still viable value of punctuality. Indeed, some managers typically arrive late to meetings and force everyone else to wait for them. Perhaps this is an ego problem rather than a lack of business sense. Or possibly they have never calculated the cost of wasted staff effort. Whatever the reason, a middle or senior manager who habitually arrives late is a liability to the organization in terms of productivity. A scheduled start time for a meeting should be viewed as a personal commitment.

Even if one or more attendees is late, discussion leaders should start the meeting on time or as close to the starting time as practical. By closing the door to the room, they gain the attention of those in the area and prevent late arrivals from continuing their hallway conversations and delaying the meeting even further. Closed doors signal a formal start of a meeting or presentation. This may not be feasible when a senior manager is the culprit, but the discussion leader should make it clear to everyone that the group is waiting for the late arrival and will begin as soon as he or she arrives.

The discussion leader should monitor the clock. When the scheduled end time approaches, the leader should remind the group of the deadline by announcing that the meeting will end on schedule. The leader who routinely allows meetings to drag on quickly develops a reputation for tardiness.

Employees respect an individual who keeps a commitment to end a meeting on time.

The ability to end a meeting on time is aided by the *50-percent rule*. Thirty minutes into a one-hour meeting, the discussion leader should examine the agenda and announce to the group if they are falling behind schedule. The statement should not be made if the group is ahead of plan. Attendees who have covered more than half of the material and are ahead of schedule should not be interrupted. Participants should know at the half way mark if they have an obligation to speed up the proceedings.

Controlling meetings by moving things along is a skill related to people management. Body language, intonation, and general attitude all convey messages. A worried frown and a quick look at the wristwatch can be a meaningful signal if the right people are looking at the discussion leader.

What should the leader do if all the agenda items will obviously not be completed? What if the allowed time is not enough to accomplish all the objectives? The leader should follow the *75-percent rule*, where he evaluates the progress made at the three-fourths mark and decides if another meeting is necessary, or if private discussions will suffice to finish the objectives. By that point most of the attendees will have recognized that the session will not meet the objectives. It is the discussion leader's responsibility to suggest the next step. The group is free to agree or offer another approach.

2. Maintain a Schedule

It is difficult to cover all the topics in the agenda within the allotted length of time. Not every item should get an equal amount of time: Some points will naturally take longer than others. Yet the discussion leader must still verify that each topic is covered enough to meet the deliverable, and then move quickly to the next one. Deciding when to stop conversation on an item is a difficult analytical decision. The discussion leader should periodically ask, "Even if the subject is interesting, and we are still sharing useful information, is more conversation or comment justified in terms of the deliverable?" If the answer is no, it is time to close the issue and move on. How can a discussion leader recognize that a subject has been sufficiently covered? Look for:

■ Participants repeating what others have already mentioned.

■ Increasing episodes of silence.

■ Obvious general agreement or obvious general disagreement that will not be immediately resolved.

■ Increasing number of participants talking about irrelevant matters.

■ Circular arguments.

■ Lack of information to close a topic or answer a question.

In the transition from one completed topic to another, the leader should say more than, "And the next topic is. . . ." A more positive statement that acknowledges completion of a topic serves as a reward to the group. It also provides the attendees a mental break and allows them to prepare for a change in subject. Progress, which in the world of meetings is defined as completing an item on the agenda, should be rewarded as a definite achievement.

The phrases used in the transition should appear smooth rather than abrupt. The new systems analyst Tina Template might say, "Next is online resources. John, you start." Her brevity would be admirable, but the speed and shock of transition will stun John and surprise the rest of the group. In the same situation, the more experienced MIS Manager Sherman Super would explain, "We've reviewed the subject of disk space needed for testing, and now let's move on to the next item of online resources." Smooth transitions allow the participants to shift their mental gears and concentrate on the next subject. Human minds do have their own law of inertia.

3. Take Notes—the Role of the Secretary!

Except for small, informal, or single topic discussions, all meetings should have a written summary of results. A formal memo is not necessary in many situations, but one person should take the official notes. Discussion leaders are not always the best choice to take notes—in fact, they may be the worst person in the room to take accurate notes! Properly moderating a vigorous discussion is a full-time job that requires full-time mental effort. Taking accurate notes in active meetings is a part-time job that often requires full-time mental effort. Attempting two jobs at the same time always causes a lack of quality in one or both assignments.

Instead of relying on the discussion leader, one attendee should take notes and serve as the official recorder. Important agreements, ideas, suggestions, assignments, conclusions, and open issues should be listed. Memories will eventually fail, but written notes will survive.

4. Keep the Discussion on Target

The perpetual struggle during a meeting is to bring participants back to the subject. This ability is often synonymous with "controlling the meeting," and is a people management skill that can be developed.

For example, if the purpose of a meeting is to discuss the weekend production problem with the Accounts Receivable System, one participant may insist on reviewing a disaster with the General Ledger system last month that particularly affected him. Another participant may wonder if operational errors have increased during the past month. A third participant may complain that the Accounts Receivable system is so old that it will always have problems. Why do people change the subject? Some simply like to hear themselves talk. Others feel their opinions are always valuable, even if they have nothing to do with the subject under consideration. Still others mistakenly feel an obligation to say something during a meeting. And still others erroneously think their subject is indeed relevant. Whatever the reason for the interruption, the discussion leader must respond in a manner that brings the conversation back to the agenda items. How can one do that without offending the speaker?

The new systems analyst Tina Template, while leading a discussion on a proposed hardware change that may impact first shift testing schedules, could respond to the concern raised by computer operator Connie Cartridge:

> I really don't care about your problems printing the production warehouse reports. We're here to talk about the new disk drives and if they will impact our test turnaround.

Connie will obviously never vote for Tina in a popularity contest. More importantly, Connie will probably keep quiet and her potentially valuable contributions will never be heard. If an attendee perceives that his statement has been ridiculed, he may either stop contributing or become angry and cause further interruptions. While few discussion leaders would use such offensive language, the effects of more subtle ridicule are equally damaging. Even if Tina used a seemingly more tactful response but followed the same attitude, her words would trigger the same net effect:

> I'm sure that's important, Connie, but let's get back to the subject.

Connie would be less embarrassed but still feel rejected. There are considerate ways to bring an out-of-scope attendee back to the subject and discourage others from following the same path. The more experienced Frank Flowchart could have answered:

> Yes, I've heard about the problem with those long print jobs. Connie, will the hardware change we are discussing be affected by those monstrous print jobs?

Frank has deftly acknowledged her contribution as worthy of intelligent response. He knows disk drive changes have little impact on test job printer backlogs, and that most other people in the room share this opinion. He has defused the situation by allowing Connie to decide if her objection is relevant to the discussion. Connie will respond with, "No, I guess it's not." Frank will smile and say, "Good, that's one problem we don't have to worry about," and return to the agenda. Frank learned that after making a statement, most MIS professionals are capable of determining if their statements are truly relevant.

Another solution when faced with an irrelevant statement is for the discussion leader to ask the entire group, "Should we consider that question right now?" and then shake his head in answer to his own rhetorical question. Or he could scan the audience and agree with the first nodding head. The leader could then add, "Let's get back to that at a later time," knowing that in all probability the topic will never be discussed.

Some stubborn participants will repeatedly change the subject and ignore the considerate but subtle approach. A less desirable but sometimes necessary alternative is to ignore the irrelevant statement by asking a question that relates directly to the main point. The question should be directed to an individual who must respond. This trick will change direction, although the out-of-scope participant will still feel ignored. He is correct—he has been ignored.

Some attendees admit to the group, "This isn't relevant to our meeting, but..." and launch into a long explanation or discourse on a totally extraneous subject. How can this be handled politely?

Discussion leaders have two choices: They can either accept the delay and wait for it to dissipate, or they can interrupt. The patient approach will waste everyone's time, but may be necessary if the person has the status or authority of one who is generally not interrupted. If discussion leaders decide to intervene, they can use several approaches that will stop the interruption:

> I see the point, and I think it should be discussed after we finish these other topics. Would you mind waiting until then?
>
> That seems like a complex subject, and probably deserves a separate meeting. Can I arrange one for next week?
>
> I'm sorry to interrupt, but I don't think Melinda finished her statement about the last topic on the agenda. Melinda, what were you saying about referential integrity?

GUIDELINES FOR PARTICIPANTS

Attendees have just as much responsibility for the success of the meeting as the discussion leader, yet few professionals accept their obligation and even fewer are told how to participate. Their attitude is critical: The attendee must sincerely feel a commitment.

Figure 14.2   Meeting attendees' responsibilities

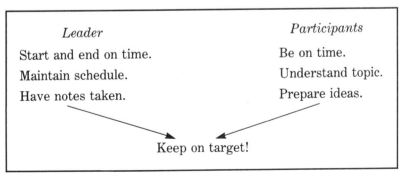

Leader	*Participants*
Start and end on time.	Be on time.
Maintain schedule.	Understand topic.
Have notes taken.	Prepare ideas.

Keep on target!

In some situations, professionals are passive participants when they simply observe and answer an occasional question. Their responsibility is therefore less than an active participant who must provide detailed information to the group. If professionals are active participants, they should follow these rules:

1. *Be on time.* Punctuality is a virtue in the business world. Help the organization develop a style and consistency that encourages meetings to start and end on time.

2. *Understand the topic before the meeting.* With the increasing use of office automation systems to maintain personal schedules, titles of meetings are forced to fit fixed length descriptions. The original title of a session might be "Investigate the effects of the proposed data base reorganization on the nightly batch processing in Accounts Payable and General Ledger." The secretary who is trying to fit the title into an electronic calendaring system might condense it to "Discuss proposed file reorganization" or "Discuss effects on General Ledger and Accounts Payable."

   Even the original title may not always convey the full meaning. A systems analyst may call a meeting to discuss the suspected MIS overcharges to the Engineering department for online computer time. She might use the title "Engineering chargebacks," but the attendees, unless they knew the specific problem, would be confused. Which chargebacks? Online, batch, hardware rental, or employee? Short titles often raise more questions than they answer. Longer, more specific titles often prevent confusion.

3. *Consider the topic and your contribution before the session.* For the typical MIS meeting, an attendee may need only several minutes of preparation time. But even a few moments will make a significant difference in the success of the meeting. If every MIS professional spent even this minimal effort reviewing the topic and perusing background material, the quality of information shared would rise dramatically. Each attendee who plans to contribute during a meeting should prepare his or her ideas and statements: A meeting is the place to make a statement, not to formulate one.

SUMMARY OF KEY POINTS

- Meetings are not only the responsibility of the discussion leader: Attendees and management are equally responsible for the success or failure of a meeting.

- MIS meetings, like those in other areas of the organization, are often ineffective.

- MIS will hold improved meetings when both discussion leaders and participants are trained, and when management understands its own obligation to properly shape the environment.

- There are at least five types of MIS meetings, but most meetings have a combination of purposes: information sharing, problem definition and resolution, procedural discussions, planning, and consensus development.

- Group decision making is a complex process. The goal is to make effective decisions rather than "correct" choices. Effective decisions are those that help the organization meet its business goals. Ineffective decisions fail to meet those objectives or satisfy the wrong objectives.

- Meetings will not always generate better decisions than a single individual working alone. Meetings are not inherently a democratic process, and even truly democratic proceedings do not always produce more effective decisions.

- Good preparation requires defining the purpose, selecting the deliverables, planning the agenda in detail, communicating with attendees before the session, working with participants who will play a key role, and preparing materials for the session.

- An agenda has three sections. The first is the introductory remarks, which consist of the introduction, purpose, deliverables, and ground rules for discussion. The middle section is the agenda items. The last section is the closing.

- The discussion leader is generally too busy to take notes or deliver the final summation. A participant should serve as the official recorder, and another attendee should summarize.

- Every meeting requires some written notes or documents that record the event, date, participants, and key points or decisions reached.

- Discussion leaders should start and end on time, maintain progress on the agenda, keep the discussion on target, and verify that notes are taken.

- Participants should be on time, understand the subject before attending, and plan their contribution before the meeting starts.

15

Desktop Publishing

*Desktop publishing is a powerful tool to produce impressive
newsletters, sales documents, price catalogs, customer
announcements, and a host of written materials. Inexpensive
desktop publishing software and laser printers can even
handle some jobs formerly given to outside printers. The cost
in money may be relatively low, but the effort needed to
establish procedures, resolve issues, and train personnel can
be high. Desktop publishing can introduce problems or produce
disappointing results if not carefully managed. This chapter is
for anyone who is using or considering purchasing a desktop
publishing system.*

Professionally designed and produced documents impress any reader. A
newsletter created on a lowly typewriter may have the same wisdom as a
newsletter with four-color glossy pictures produced by a commercial print
shop, but the more appealing product always receives the attention.
However, the value of professional printing goes beyond visual aesthetics.
Professional quality printing—usually with graphics, charts, and easy-to-
read text—communicates effectively. Better communication can translate
into greater productivity and increased sales.

Then why aren't more documents sent to professional designers and
printers? There are three major drawbacks: the cost of professional printing, the time delay inherent in sending information between author and

printer, and the difficulty in changing a professionally printed document. Every change costs time and money. Managers, systems analysts, and forms designers have often tried to justify professionally prepared documents, but the disadvantages of cost, time, and change difficulty have outweighed the advantages.

The power of desktop publishing changed that scenario. Personal computer-based desktop publishing can handle some publishing jobs that were customarily assigned to printers. The speed and relatively low cost of desktop publishing allow professional quality printing of documents that were formerly relegated to the word processor. With an outlay of less than $10,000, near professional quality black and white documents can be produced in the office environment by the internal staff, without going to outside services. Color will eventually come to desktop publishing.

Desktop publishing can lower costs and reduce turnaround time for complex assignments that still require professional printing. Using the personal computer-based package can eliminate the laborious rekeying of text by feeding text directly into the computer controlling typesetting machine. Or it can feed the completely formatted document directly into the typesetting machine. Some quite successful desktop publishing operations never print a page!

APPLICATIONS FOR DESKTOP PUBLISHING

Forms, user manuals, price lists, customer proposals, newsletters, annual reports, and small inhouse magazines can be transferred from a print shop or internal printing department to an inhouse desktop publishing system. After the initial cost outlay for the personal computer, laser printer, software, and accessories, the recurring cost savings will be significant. The overall time needed to produce such documents will be reduced. Jobs that once required weeks of elapsed time can be done in days or even hours. Figure 15.1 lists only a few of the many documents that are candidates for desktop publishing.

Customer price lists are one example of a document typically produced on a word processor that would look better if professionally typeset with photographs for each item or major category of items. In some organizations, marketing managers dream of typeset quality catalogs showing their products in use, but reject the idea because of the time and expense. Project proposals and budget analyses are more convincing when companies employ a desktop publishing system. Many personnel managers are eager to create a monthly internal newsletter to improve communication and boost productivity. The range of applications is limited only by the user's imagination, although it is certainly possible to select a document for desktop publishing that is simply not worth the effort.

Figure 15.1 Applications for desktop publishing

Internal	External
MIS forms	Annual reports
User forms	Customer mailings
Employee bulletins	Catalogs
Employee awards	Contracts
Promotion notices	Price lists
Schedules	Marketing brochures
Status reports	Apologies
Budgets	Invitations
Inhouse magazines	Announcements

WHAT IS DESKTOP PUBLISHING?

In physical terms, desktop publishing is a combination of a computer, peripheral devices such as printers, and multiple software packages.

Desktop publishing software consists of:

- Word processing for text entry and editing.

- Graphics or drawing package that lets the author manipulate pictures and designs.

- Chart or statistical analysis package for graphs.

- Page composition software that arranges the text and graphics in final output form.

- Page description language (PDL) that controls the laser printer.

In organizational terms, desktop publishing requires at least one individual trained to utilize the physical components and a realistic determination by management to invest the time and personnel resources needed to utilize desktop publishing appropriately. Desktop publishing is an approach rather than a collection of tools.

Publishing systems reside on minicomputers, personal computers, and stand-alone workstations, and the minicomputer variety is generally reserved for high volume, complex applications. Workstations are generally minicomputer-level processors with extremely high resolution display screens, and are more expensive than personal computers. Some workstations have multitasking operating systems which allow multiple applications to run concurrently. Many workstations were originally designed as engineering or CAD (computer-assisted design) units, but can run desktop publishing applications if the operating system is compatible with the software. Several publishing packages are designed for workstations rather than personal computers. Personal computer-based systems, however, can easily produce professional quality or near professional quality forms, newsletters, proposals, and documents. Desktop publishing cannot handle every publishing need of every organization: Many companies with successful desktop publishing departments still utilize outside printers for some complex documents. Large circulation magazines, for example, are not suitable for desktop publishing, although a networked desktop publishing system can be used for initial page composition.

Typical desktop publishing systems include a personal computer with at least 1 meg memory, 60 megabyte hard disk, monitor with enhanced or extended graphics, keyboard with 12 function keys, and a "mouse" input device to simulate keyboard cursor directional commands. The personal computer usually has a floppy disk or removable hard disk (cartridge) to allow exchange of information with other computers. A modem to allow communications to other computers is often useful. Figure 15.2 shows the typical input and output devices used in desktop publishing systems.

Various input devices including keyboards, mouses, graphic input pads for original drawings, and digitizers are used in desktop publishing systems. The better keyboards have been designed for operator comfort as well as flexibility. A mouse can replace the cursor movement keys. Original drawings can be entered into memory with a graphic pad, where the movement of the stylus activates impulses based on the location of the movement within the matrix. Both text and graphics can be entered into the computer memory by a device known as a *scanner* or more correctly as a *digitizer*. Video patterns are converted into digital impulses and are enhanced by electronic circuitry augmented by computer control. Rather than laboriously retyping text from an existing hard copy document into a new desktop publishing electronic document, a digitizer can convert a page of text into digital representations of symbols (based on varying shades of light and dark). The computer program converts the representations into

Figure 15.2 Desktop publishing hardware

Input	COMPUTER	Output
CRT		Laser printer
Digitizer		Typesetter
Graphic pad		Fax
Keyboard		Copier
Mouse		Modem

recognizable characters by a "best guess" matching program. Digitizers are highly accurate if the software operating parameters are adjusted carefully.

Graphics and photographs can also be converted by a digitizer. The device and associated software converts each specific point in the object to a value that represents a level of gray. This process is more complicated than converting text, and low-cost digitizers may lose details when converting complex graphics. Digitizers allow an author to copy a graphic image such as a drawing, art work, or photograph into a document for page manipulation and eventual printing.

Desktop publishing sends output to a laser printer copier equipped to receive from a personal computer, FAX machine for transmission to other FAX machines, or directly to a phototypesetter, which is a computer-controlled typesetting machine. Some typesetting machines can be driven directly by a personal computer, while others require an intermediate disk file and processing by their own software.

The terms *professional quality* and *near professional quality* are often defined by the resolution of the text and graphics, although other factors are also important. Resolution is measured in terms of dots per square inch, with a printer producing more dots per square inch having higher resolution and therefore the most professional look. Books and magazines are printed by typesetting machines at more than 1,000 dots per inch, with some up to 2,540 dots per inch. A standard laser printer produces output at 300 dots per square inch, although enhancement boards will increase their effective resolution to 600 dots per square inch or even more. Some lasers now print at 1,000 dots per inch.

The development of low-cost laser printers in the middle 1980s made desktop publishing practical. Laser technology is an outgrowth of the office copier, but uses a three-step process. First, the laser beam loads a series of positive electrical images on a drum. Second, the image on the drum is transferred to paper. Finally, the image on the paper is fused permanently on the surface by pressure, heat, or other means. Laser printers display both text and graphics, but some print graphics at lower resolution than text. Lasers vary significantly in terms of printing options and software control: The capabilities of a given laser printer must match the programs that drive the printer. The most expensive, full-featured laser will perform like a low cost model if the software does not provide adequate flexibility. Software and hardware either complement or limit each other.

PAGE DESCRIPTION LANGUAGES

For simple desktop publishing applications such as flyers or newsletters, an author will be satisfied with the type fonts loaded by the desktop publishing software to the computer. A font is a specific size and style of type that is available from the software and acceptable to the printer. But after the publications reach a certain level of sophistication and require specialized fonts and complex graphics, the desktop publisher will graduate to a Page Description Language (PDL).

The purpose of a PDL is confusing to those without a background in personal computer graphics. They assume that the picture appearing on a terminal is automatically and easily transferred to a printing device. The terms *automatic* and *easily* are misleading. Many terminals with sophisticated graphic capabilities use the "what you see is what you get" feature, which is often abbreviated as WYSIWYG. But displaying the output on a screen is qualitatively different from transferring the image to a printer. The display is directly under the control of the software package producing the document. The printer is not under such direct connection. There is no magic command that tells the printer to print what is on the screen.

The problem is relatively simple if the designer is satisfied with the fonts that come with the desktop publishing software. The printer will simply utilize that series of characters and create an image on paper. If, however, the designer specifies a more complex document, an interface is required from the desktop publishing system to the printer. This interface is a translator that generates a series of detailed instructions to the printing device. In this situation, the printer functions like a microcomputer.

Why is a PDL better than the fonts that come with most desktop publishing software? The advantages are:

- More fonts.

- Scalable fonts, where the size of the font can be adjusted in smooth, user-controlled increments.

- Full-page graphics (in contrast to one-quarter or one-half page graphics in some laser printers without a PDL).

- Rotated type and text manipulation.

- Graphic manipulation.

- Printer independence (allowing a computer to output drafts to a laser or dot matrix and final copy to a computerized typesetter).

The disadvantages are:

- PDL printers require a microprocessor, which increases the cost of the printer.

- The personal computer may require extra processing cycles to create the PDL output.

- The printer may require extra time to translate the PDL into its hardware level instructions.

If the publication calls for advanced printing features—or if the final output of the desktop publishing effort is a computerized typesetter or computer—a PDL is better than the fonts that come with the desktop publishing software.

There are several excellent page description languages on the market, and a company or organization often standardizes on one. The PDL used by many vendors allows the user to send a print file to several models of printers. For example, one may print drafts on a laser printer and send the final output to a phototypesetter. This is practical only if both devices use a common page description language. A PDL supported by multiple printing devices provides device independence. A PDL used only by one manufacturer locks the user into that brand or type of printer. The choice of PDL is as important as the selection of a desktop publishing package.

Some PDLs are interpreted rather than compiled languages. An interpreted language must be translated by the printing device one command at a time before execution. Interpretive languages typically run slower than other products, but the speed inherent in many printers makes this problem less noticeable.

TYPOGRAPHY

Desktop publishing thrusts the MIS professional in the role of editor, writer, typist, proofreader, designer, and typographer. Selecting the best typeface for a document is only one piece of the design puzzle, but definitely more complicated than novices expect. The desktop publishing package comes with multiple styles and sizes of types, and other vendors have a seemingly inexhaustible supply of additional specialized type styles. Indeed, the problem with typography in desktop publishing is not the lack of variety, but the overabundance. Most desktop publishing projects need only the basic styles and sizes of types, and look atrocious if the designer demonstrates his creative powers by using type faces interesting to look at but distracting to the reader. Too much variety in typography will hinder communication rather than enhance it.

A *font* is a collection of letters, numbers, and special characters that have a specific width, height, and type style. An almost infinite variety of type styles is available.

Type is classified horizontally by a measure called *picas* to the printing world, and *characters per inch* by many of those outside the print shop. The two measures are not truly equivalent, but close enough for most desktop publishing projects printed internally. A desktop publishing package can create type based on picas or on characters per inch. There are six picas per inch. Figure 15.3 illustrates the same style of type at different horizontal measures.

Figure 15.3   Horizontally, type is sized by characters per inch (cpi) or picas (6 picas per inch).

```
This is type at 17 CPI.


This is type at 12 CPI.


This is type at 10 CPI.


This is  type  at  6  CPI.


This   is   type   at   5   CPI.
```

Type is measured vertically in units called *points*. Figure 15.4 shows the same style of type at several vertical sizes. Note that horizontal dimensions (picas or characters per inch) and vertical spacing (points) are somewhat related. The greater the vertical measurement, the greater the horizontal measurement. Type at 24 points would look ridiculous printed at 20 characters per inch.

There are numerous families of type faces, each of which may have its own role in professional printing. Figure 15.5 illustrates five common styles. This book is printed in serif type, which is commonly used in book and magazines. Helvetica is a very popular style for headings. New York style is another option of heading, but is more formal and slightly harder to read. Beginners in desktop publishing can always select New York for text and Helvetica for titles and headlines. A banner or newsletter title could be in New York style. More than three styles in the same document can be visually overwhelming.

WORKING WITH PRINTING HOUSES AND TYPOGRAPHERS

For small volume or lower-quality publications, one would normally use a copy machine rather than a print shop. The term *lower quality* as used in desktop publishing, is a term for publications that do not need a professional typeset look to accomplish their purpose. The annual report to the

Figure 15.4 Vertically, the size of type is measured in points.

This is New York style at 12 points.

This is New York style at 14 points.

This is New York style at 18 points.

This is New York style at 24 points

Figure 15.5a   Many styles of type are available.

> This is ELITE type.
>
> This is GENEVA type.
>
> ## This is HELVETICA type.
>
> ## This is NEW YORK type.
>
> This is PICA type.

stockholders is clearly a job for printing professionals while the monthly MIS newsletter could be printed on a laser and simply duplicated with the office copier. There are also many situations where the author creates the publication on desktop publishing but must send it to a printer for printing and duplication.

In order to communicate with the experts in the printing world, the MIS professional must appreciate the complexities of the printing business. A little knowledge could even save money! The hours a printer or the sales representative spends with a client may not be reflected as a specific billable item on the final invoice, but one can be sure this cost is included in the total amount. MIS professionals who minimize this time will find better terms for their organizations than the staffer who leaves everything to the printer. Also, desktop publishers who can clearly explain their wishes to the printer will usually see a final product that matches their expectations.

Even specifying the paper requires planning. Size varies according to the type of paper. Printing paper has a standard sheet size of 25 × 38 inches while other types of paper are found in different sheet sizes. Printers can supply nonstandard sizes at a premium, but most business applications should use only standard sizes to reduce cost and eliminate

Figure 15.5b   There are many variations within each style.

> This is ELITE type in bold.
>
> This is GENEVA type in bold.

unnecessary steps. Typical business papers include bond, duplicator, copier, and onion skin. There are various grades within each major type. Bond paper, for example, is often graded from 1 to 5, with 1 as the premium grade. Book paper is used for larger volume documents such as technical manuals. Coated book paper provides significantly better quality than uncoated book paper.

The color and finish of the paper are important. Glossy red paper for the MIS business plan is not acceptable. Soft white is a better choice because it is neutral in tone and is more readable. High gloss paper is hard to read, while smooth paper tends to provide sharper graphics.

Usually, the print shop representative will select the printing and duplicating method, but the client who understands the mechanics of large-scale printing can provide intelligent feedback. Too often a desktop publisher will quietly accept the decision of a print shop manager without understanding the alternatives. Several different methods are available in the modern, well equipped print shop, and each has its own advantages and disadvantages for a particular job. A print shop may not have the best alternative for a given project, although the print shop manager may not volunteer such information. Knowledge is indeed power.

There are four common methods of printing:

Photocopy

Letterpress

Offset lithography

Offset duplicating

Photocopying was once dismissed as a fast way to make barely acceptable quality reproductions. The copiers of the 1990s are vastly superior to even the advanced copiers available in the late 1980s. Sophisticated computerized copiers will duplicate on both sides of a paper, collate, and bind the finished product. The results will never equal a professional print job, but the quality is impressive. However, cost per page for large volume copying jobs may be higher than printing presses. Photocopying is always the first alternative considered.

The letterpress is used for special applications such as envelopes and business cards, and is probably the easiest to understand. The image to be printed is raised above the surrounding areas. A series of mechanical rollers wipes the raised edges with ink. The paper to be printed is held firmly on a planten, and the relief plate is pressed against the paper.

Offset lithography is a rather complicated but common method for high quality reproduction. The printer follows several steps.

1. The components of the document are separated into text, photographs, and graphics.

2. Each piece is transferred to a lithographic negative. Text is converted to a *line negative*, while photographic images are converted to a *halftone*

negative which preserves the shades of grey inherent in black and white photographs. The process of creating negatives varies according to the type of material and the desired output.

3. In a procedure called *stripping*, the negatives for text and graphics are arranged in a pattern corresponding to the actual position on the page.

4. The printer creates plates from the stripped negatives. This procedure involves a metallic plate (usually aluminum coated with a light sensitive material) and a metal frame which insures a tight contact between the metal plate and the negative. A light shines through the frame, and the image of the negatives is burned into the plate.

5. The plates are loaded into the offset press. Ink is applied to those areas of the plate that have an image, while water is sprayed on the plate to remove ink from those areas that do not have an image. The image on the plate is then transferred to a rubber cylinder, and the paper is forced into contact with the cylinder.

Another method of professional printing is offset duplication, which is a variation of offset lithography. Offset duplication is simpler but provides the quality and speed acceptable for general purpose printing assignments. This method uses a plate, which can be prepared from the original document in much the same manner as offset lithography. Some offset duplicator plates even allow the printer to type directly onto the master.

Establishing electronic communications over telephone lines with printers requires experience with basic telecommunications procedures and data transmission. But even if another individual sets up the hardware, software, and procedures, the desktop publisher should understand the overall process.

The device that allows transmission from the personal computer to the printer's computer (or computer-controlled typesetter) is called a *modem*. Many lower priced modems send data *asynchronously*. A more sophisticated form of data transmission is called *synchronous*, which requires both computers to participate fully in the exchange. Modems are manufactured by different vendors but traditionally follow the so-called Bell standards. Modems are rated in terms of speed, from 300 bits per second (bps) to 4,800 bps or 9,600 bps. Faster modems are available but more expensive. The device chosen by the desktop publisher must be compatible with the modem installed by the print shop, in terms of speed, transmission type (asynchronous or synchronous), and line protocol. The protocol is simply a series of rules related to the transmission of individual pieces of information.

Since the modem is simply a hardware device that translates information into a form acceptable to telephone lines, the personal computer must have telecommunications software. This product is sometimes included with the modem.

After the document is printed, the author will receive *galley proofs*. These are sample pages of the document on large paper. The printer expects the originator to carefully check the galley proofs. Even if the designed and formatted document is transmitted electronically, there still may be errors! If the text was rekeyed into a typesetting machine, the chance for mistakes increases.

In the printing business there is a distinction between errors caused by the printer's staff and changes requested by the originator. Human or mechanical mistakes caused by the printing department (*printer's error* or *PEs*) are corrected free of charge. The printer is certainly willing to make other changes if the author desires, but there may be a fee for such changes. Some contracts do allow a certain number of *author's alterations* (AAs).

Checking galley proofs is tedious, boring, and frustrating. While a few individuals actually view proofreading as a challenging and rewarding profession, most of us cringe when handed a set of galley proofs.

A quality job of proofreading requires a positive mental outlook:

1. Expect to proofread the materials several times. Good proofreading takes more than one pass through a document.

2. Contrary to popular belief, authors of a document can accurately proofread their own work. A fresh set of eyes is nice to have, but not absolutely required.

3. Select a style manual for reference, such as *The Chicago Manual of Style* (Prentice-Hall). Scan the chapters for content. The style manual will serve as the authority for language questions that may arise.

4. Locate the original style guide used to create the document. A style guide is a set of rules that pertain directly to a specific document, and contain notes on spacing, abbreviation, definitions, and formats. Consistency within a document is absolutely vital. Desktop publishing managers should create a master style guide for a class of documents, such as training manuals or newsletters.

How does one proofread? The approach varies with the individual and nature of the document under review. Many authors follow a "high to low to high" philosophy, where the person reviews those components such as titles and headings (high level), examines the text in detail (low level), and ends with a final look at the overall product (high level). Other authors simply start at page one and look at every line. The results are the same, but some people do review better when considering all titles or headings in one pass, and the detail text in another. Whatever the approach, the proofreader should locate at least the following types of overall errors:

- Titles off center
- Titles in the wrong style or size
- Titles in the wrong location
- Captions for illustrations or pictures that are incorrect
- Uniform paragraph indentations
- Uniform right and left margins, and uniform top and bottom margins
- Incorrect page numbers
- Missing sections of text or missing graphics

When reviewing the text, one should first read a sentence word by word, and again as a logical whole. Possible errors follow:

- Characters out of alignment
- Words that don't belong
- Misspellings (which still happen in spite of word processing dictionaries)
- Letters not spaced correctly
- Sentences that are clearly redundant
- Hyphens in the wrong place
- Last line of a paragraph on a new page (called a "widow")
- A single line at the end of a page (called an "orphan")

Corrections are made on the galley proof using a standardized set of proofreading marks. Print shops often supply a copy with the proofs, or they can be found in English and journalism texts.

After the document is printed, the shop will bind the materials. Technical and training manuals often use mechanical binding, in which spirals of wire, plastic, or other material are punched through the edge of the copies.

CAUTIONS AND CONCERNS

Desktop publishing is not the solution to every written communications problem. Companies who rushed into desktop publishing without understanding the limitations and requirements realized only marginal benefits, and in some unfortunate cases, simply abandoned the whole idea.

Four critical problems surfaced.

First, managers underestimated the time needed to learn the basics of the complex but powerful software.

Second, and more common, the document eventually made it to a laser printer, but the material looked bizarre, unorganized, and confusing. The design was poor. Desktop publishing guarantees nothing—it is only a tool that performs well under suitable conditions. Design is more complex than most people realize, until they actually create something more than a simple memo. Newsletters are often the first attempt at using the marvels of desktop publishing, and therefore the first to show the results of poor design. Desktop publishing tools allow an operator to efficiently create a horrible looking newsletter that scares away the reader rather than communicates effectively. Common symptoms of poorly designed documents are the overuse of graphics, unneeded lines, arrows, pointers, and conflicting type styles that look like a demonstration of printing options.

If an inhouse person is assigned design responsibility, management should encourage him or her to fight the natural tendency to try every feature and option. Complexity is not the goal. Rather, the objective is to use the minimum combination of features to achieve a harmonious final product. Another approach is to hire a professional designer familiar with the particular hardware and software who can set up models or templates. Such a consultant may charge as much or more than the computer software, but the cost is well justified. A qualified graphics designer is not overwhelmed by the variety of options and will choose those graphic ideas that enhance rather than detract from communication. If a professional does not set up the models, authors or operators should be given time to experiment so they can develop a sense of practicality. The first attempt by an inexperienced author on desktop publishing should not be regarded as the best.

Even if an outside consultant develops the templates, the inhouse operator will require significant training time just to operate the software. Desktop publishing is significantly more complex than word processing. While most professionals can learn basic word processing with an online tutorial or a short demonstration, effective use of desktop publishing requires more sophisticated computer skills. A vendor who sells desktop publishing as a turnkey system can often provide technical support and thereby reduce the need for hardware expertise. A consultant can serve as an advisor on the software and design questions, and reduce the need for inhouse software expertise. Whatever the source, some person or persons must supply hardware, software, and design expertise. If outside support services are not available, the organization must allow one of their employees an opportunity to develop such skills. Managers should consider sending that employee to a seminar or training program in desktop publishing. The time and expense are well justified.

A third problem is selecting the best combination of software to meet both current and future editorial needs. The most expensive software is not necessarily the best for a given company, and different departments within an organization may need different software packages. As desktop publishing software matures, products will inevitably perform some tasks better than others. Like word processing, desktop publishing software varies by price, ease of use, features, and flexibility. An experienced consultant who is willing to listen and not automatically promote his favorite brand of software is a valuable ally.

A fourth problem with desktop publishing is the question of departmental responsibility: As a highly visible application, desktop publishing can be either an honor or a punishment. Rivalries between MIS and user areas can make a desktop installation project a corporate battleground. Even after desktop publishing has been successfully installed, territorial disputes may arise. A department with a successful desktop publishing operation quickly develops a reputation for efficient, professional print jobs, and other people ask the inevitable question, "Can you do me a little favor?" If the sales management area has a desktop publishing system originally justified for creating sales and marketing brochures, the purchasing manager, traffic coordinator, and credit specialist may ask for assistance. Should the Sales Management area do work for other departments? At what point can they legitimately refuse?

One solution is to create a separate desktop publishing department to serve all areas of the organization. This avoids departmental jealousy if the new group serves all users in an equitable manner. The manager will need approved guidelines to judge the value of user requests: Success in desktop publishing often triggers a flood of demands that have dubious justification. Another approach is to fold the desktop publishing operation into the MIS division. MIS is familiar with evaluating and prioritizing requests, and usually accepts new technology faster than nontechnical areas. Desktop publishing, however, does not fit neatly into the typical MIS organization, and some realignment of responsibilities may be needed. Whatever solution is chosen, management must prepare the organization for a potential avalanche of desktop publishing system requests.

SUMMARY OF KEY POINTS

- Desktop publishing is more than a visual impression: It communicates better and more efficiently.

- Desktop publishing can send documents to devices such as laser printers, FAXs, copiers, other computers through a modem, or directly to a phototypesetter.

- Some complex design and printing projects should still be handled by a professional printing shop.

- Selecting the most appropriate combination of hardware and software may require a consultant.

- Problems can arise with desktop publishing, such as lack of design experience and organizational disputes.

- Poor design can make a desktop publishing document look ridiculous.

- Overuse of type styles and sizes will create a confusing visual impression.

- Working intelligently with professional printers requires a basic understanding of their terms, procedures, and needs.

- There is no substitute for slow, careful proofreading. It is the responsibility of the submitter to correct all errors before returning the galley proof to the printer for the production run.

Index

A-B-C requirements, 38-39
Active data dictionary, 155
Answer book, 160-161
Appendix, 174
Application system documentation, 184-186
Application software maintenance, 180-183
Asynchronous data transmission, 256
Audience, 9-10
Automated operational documentation,
132-133

Bar charts, 197-199
Benefits, 168
Business plan, 33-36

Change control page, 44
Chrono file, 53-54
Circle graphs, 203
Clarity, 16-17
Communication, importance of, 3
Concept document, 26-29
Conciseness, 16
Consultants, 179-180
Cost/benefit analysis, 48-51

Data center statistics, 134-135
Data dictionary, 154-156
    active, 155
    passive, 155-156

Decision making myths, 231-233
Desktop publishing management, 260
Digitizer, 248-249
Documentation standards, 103-104
Double ratings method, 148

Electronic mail, 188-193
Electronic mail security, 191-192
Errors, 47-48
Estimates, 30
Examples, 14-15
Experience evaluation forms, 74-86

Feasibility statement, 29-33
Field testing, 112-113
Filing subject heading, 91
Flow charts, 42, 159-160
Font, 251
Formal conversation, 12-13

Galley proofs, 257
Graphic input pad, 248
Graphics, 195-203
Graphic text, 196-197
Guidelines for word processing, 189-193

Hierarchical approach, 108
HIPO, 42

Honesty, 13-14

Index, 112
Informal conversation, 13
IPO, 42, 52

Laser printer, 249
Laws of MIS documentation, 5-6
Letter of reference, 143-145
Letterpress, 255-256
Line charts, 200-201
Logic, 8-9

Maintenance program documentation, 156-157
Management by objectives, 72
Management policy and communication, 4
Master system documentation, 133-134
Meetings:
  consensus, 230
  information sharing, 229-230
  planning sessions, 230
  procedural discussions, 230
  problem definition and resolution, 230
  problems with, 228
Memos, 89-91
Microcomputer backup, 192-193
Microcomputer graphics, 195-203
Modem, 256
Module-to-module (MTM) approach, 52
Monthly reports, 86-89
Mouse, 248

Natural approach to style, 12-15
Negative recommendations, 32

Offset duplication, 256
Online manuals, 113-114
Organizational charts, 200, 202
Overviews, 106

Page description language, 247, 249-251
Passive data dictionary, 155-156
Photocopy, 255
Picas, 251
Points, 252
Presentation:
  outline, 214
  types, 208-210
  visual aids, 216-217
Problem reporting logs, 124-129
Program documentation justification, 152, 154

Programming specifications, 51-53
Project reporting, 64-70
Proofreading, 257-258
Proposal, 26-29
  justification, 26

Quarterly reports, 86-89

Redundancy, 18-20
Request for proposal (RFP), 143
Requirements categories, 38-39, 147-148
Requirements document, 36-39
Restart and rerun instructions, 118
Run sheets, 116-124

Scanner, 248-249
Sentence structure, 15
Service requests, 58-64
Special procedures documentation, 129-132
Spellcheck, 190
Spreadsheets, 203, 205
Standalone sections, 40
Strategic project:
  detail, 174
  evolution, 167-168
  questionnaire, 172
  sponsor, 167, 171
Style guide, 257
Synchronous data transmission, 256
System log, 161-162
System design documents, 39-48

Task control, 68-70
Technical subjects, learning, 95-97
Tenses, 20-21
Transparencies, 216-217

Unethical behavior, 145
Unpleasant news, 91-92
User manual:
  control, 102-103
  types, 94-95
User/Computer Timing Chart, 45-46
User cooperation, 100-102

Vendor evaluation form, 138-143

Weekly status reports, 70-76
Word processing:
  features, 193-195
  guidelines, 189-193
Words to avoid, 17-18

ABOUT THE AUTHOR

Currently employed by Ross Laboratories, a division of Abbott
Laboratories, Larry Singer has over twenty years' experience
in MIS. He is the author of articles on MIS management topics
and manufacturing automation and two books on data
processing.